THE AMERICAN PRESIDENT LINES AND ITS FOREBEARS 1848-1984

THE
AMERICAN
PRESIDENT LINES
AND ITS FOREBEARS
1848-1984

From Paddlewheelers to Containerships

JOHN NIVEN

DELAWARE

Newark: University of Delaware Press
London and Toronto: Associated University Press

Associated University Presses
440 Forsgate Drive
Cranbury, NJ 08512

Associated University Presses
25 Sicilian Avenue
London WC1A 2QH, England

Associated University Presses
2133 Royal Windsor Drive
Unit 1
Mississauga, Ontario
Canada L5J 1K5

The paper used in this publication meets the
requirements of the American National
Standard for Permanence of Paper for Printed
Library Materials Z39.48-1984.

Library of Congress Cataloging-in-Publication Data

Niven, John.
   The American President Lines and its forebears,
1848–1984.

   Bibliography: p.
   Includes index.
   1. American President Lines, Ltd.—History.   I. Title.
HE753.A465N58   1986   387.5'06573   85-40660
ISBN 0-87413-299-1 (cloth) (alk. paper)
ISBN 0-87413-321-1 (paperback) (alk. paper)

Printed in the United States of America

CONTENTS

To the memory of Allan Nevins
Pioneer in Entrepreneurial
and Oral History

PREFACE

American President Lines, Ltd. (APL) is one of the largest and perhaps the most efficiently operated shipping company in the United States, if not the world. Its modern container and breakbulk fleet of twenty-three vessels handles a significant amount of the nation's import-export trade between the West Coast of the United States and the Far East. An elaborate and sophisticated electronic data-processing system controls its traffic not just in transit from or to its market areas but within those market areas themselves. An intermodal transportation company, APL takes responsibility for the shipment of freight from its point of origin, whether in the United States or abroad, to its point of delivery. As such it is in fact not merely a shipping line but the controlling agency in a worldwide transportation system that involves ships, trains, and trucks.

This company has evolved to its present status over a century and a half of dramatic development, beginning with its predecessor the Pacific Mail Steamship Company, which ran the first shipping line between Panama and California in 1849. It has seen profits and losses; mergers and acquisitions; and leaders who were merchants, railroad tycoons, speculators, lumber magnates, oilmen, and management experts. Fortunes have been made and lost in its varied history, which began with coal-burning paddlewheel steamers of 2,500 gross tons and now features modern diesel-powered containerships of 40,600 gross tons.

Much of APL's history, as with most human endeavors, has been the product of accident or chance. William H. Aspinwall, the New York merchant who founded Pacific Mail, could never have known that his risky venture of establishing a Panama-to-California shipping line would become immensely profitable due to the discovery of gold. Nor could Robert Dollar's tramping operations at the turn of the century have been considered anything more than an adjunct to his prosperous lumber business. A strand of entrepreneurial action and achievement threads its way through APL's history as venture capitalists risked their careers and fortunes in the economic potential of the West Coast and its vital shipping component. It was an open, highly individualized business.

Until 1915, the various shipping lines of the West—coastal and transoceanic—were relatively free of government influence. Of course such indirect public policies as tariffs, safety-at-sea regulations, and modest mail subsidies affected both coastal and ocean commerce. But shipowners were free to hire crews at the lowest wages possible, which generally meant the employment of Orientals, especially Chinese nationals. Even officers were frequently of foreign nationality.

Pacific Mail flew the American flag, but its deck and engine-room gang were aliens, as were its stewards. The Dollar Line was proud of its Chinese crew. Its trans-Pacific vessels sailed under British registry and under British officers, and most of its freighters were British-built. Then, as now, wages for American merchant mariners were prohibitively high, considering the international competition American vessels faced. And ships built in American yards were from one-third to one-half more costly than those built abroad.

But American shipping lines, among them the predecessors of APL, were fiercely competitive in coastal and ocean trade, and nowhere was this more evident than on the West Coast. Eventually most of the competing lines disappeared. Some went bankrupt and others were purchased or merged into larger, better-financed, or better-managed companies. This trend was increasingly apparent when the government became more directly involved with the American merchant marine.

The La Follette Seamen's Act of 1915 was the first step in effecting necessary reforms that required better working conditions for merchant sailors on ships sailing under the American flag. In addition it placed a quota on foreign crews by requiring that a majority of them be able to understand any lawful order in English. Although the La Follette Act was hard to enforce and of course did not apply to ships sailing under foreign registry, it did improve wages and working conditions for American merchant mariners. Moreover, it gave a considerable stimulus to the unionization of unlicensed crews.

While subsequent legislation improved the lot of the average American crewman, it also raised operating costs and hastened the end of small, highly competitive lines. But the impact of regulation on West Coast shipping was minor compared to the shock of American participation in World War I. Most of the vessels in the fleet that plied between West Coast ports were taken over by the government. A seller's market for ocean vessels transferred much of the tonnage from the West Coast to the East Coast and from the Pacific trade to the Atlantic.

What had been scarcity for West Coast shippers during the war became a glut afterwards as millions of tons of government-built ships were thrown on the market. True, the Shipping Acts of 1916, 1920, and 1928 placed further restrictions on what had been largely an unregulated industry. Astute businessmen like "Captain" Robert Dollar and his son R. Stanley Dollar, however, were able not only to adapt themselves to the new order but to flourish in the postwar period. The Dollar Line, which acquired a modern fleet from the government at bargain prices, absorbed Pacific Mail and its competitor in the Northwest, the Admiral Oriental Line. For a brief period the Dollar Steamship Company was one of the most profitable shipping companies in the nation. But the Dollar enterprises became overextended, and management practices hurt the financial well-being of their companies. When the Depression struck in 1929, the Dollar Line was seriously weakened. The maritime strikes of 1934 and 1936 drove it closer to bankruptcy.

In 1936 Congress passed the comprehensive Maritime Act, which put the entire American merchant marine on a new footing. The domestic condition of the industry and the rise of hostile, totalitarian states in Europe and in the Far East prompted the Roosevelt administration to establish a subsidy policy and a large shipbuilding program to strengthen the merchant navy. A new government agency, the Maritime Commission, took over all the powers of the previous maritime agencies and was assigned additional powers to regulate the industry. Joseph P. Kennedy, as first chairman of the agency, began a thorough investigation of the by-now crippled Dollar Line. The result was that the commission forced the Dollars to transfer most of their stock to the government, relieving them of liability for the huge mortgage debt the company owed. The new concern was renamed American President Lines, Ltd.

From 1938 until 1952 American President Lines was operated by the government, but from 1946 and for the next six years the Dollars sought to recover the line in one of the longest law suits in American maritime history. A compromise was finally reached whereby the line would be put up for bid and the proceeds divided between the

Dollars and the government. In 1952 a group of venture capitalists headed by Ralph Davies formed APL Associates and acquired the government-owned stock. From that date until his death in 1971, Davies was the principal management force behind the line. In 1954 he acquired a controlling interest in American Mail Line, a major shipper in the Northwest that had been a Dollar subsidiary and had gone bankrupt in the late thirties. The reorganized American Mail, like American President Lines, had operated profitably since 1940. In 1959 Davies added to his shipping interests by purchasing control of Pacific Far East Line, a World War II-born competitor of American President Lines on its Pacific trade routes.

Meanwhile Davies had merged APL Associates, the holding company that controlled the shipping lines, into a gold-dredging firm called Natomas Company. In the early sixties, Natomas became increasingly involved in the exploration and production of oil and gas, particularly in Indonesia. Its interest in Pacific Far East Line was sold in 1967. But until Natomas was acquired in 1983 by Diamond-Shamrock, a large Texas-based oil company, it maintained its control of American President Lines. In 1974 American Mail was merged into American President Lines.

After Davies's death, Chandler Ide, who had been president of Natomas, became chief executive officer as well. He brought in a new management team at Natomas and at American President Lines. Dorman Commons, an oilman who had specialized in financial management, was elected president and chief executive officer of Natomas in 1974. Ide became chairman. In 1976 Bruce Seaton, senior vice president of finance at Natomas, was induced to become president and chief operating officer of American President Lines, with Dorman Commons becoming chairman and chief executive officer. Under their leadership the company's operations were decentralized along intermodal lines.

Seaton recognized that if management were to utilize fully the new container technology it must extend its control from the ocean-shipment link in the transportation process to the domestic or land-bridge link within the United States. Accordingly he assembled and coordinated a management team of transportation specialists in all aspects of railroad, trucking, and shipping operations that understood the dynamics of containerization and electronic tracking systems. In 1983 the line regained independent status under the newly created American President Companies, Ltd. APL's former parent organization, Natomas, had been acquired by Diamond Shamrock and American President Lines was spun off. Thus the line had come full circle, becoming again the separate corporate entity it had once been. With its new container terminals, its modern fleet, and its capable management, American President Lines has positioned itself to share in the profitability of Asian markets that now constitute a significant segment of the world's trade.

This book could not have been written without the assistance of the executives of American President Lines. During research fifty oral histories were recorded, amounting to over 1,500 typescript pages. These invaluable recollections constitute a unique historical archive of the shipping industry on the West Coast during a period of dramatic change. My thanks go to all the participants in that program.

Pamela Petersen of APL's marketing department and Colette Carey of APL's archives, freely gave their time and knowledge of the company's history. In addition, I would like to acknowledge my grateful appreciation to the Bancroft Library of the University of California, Berkeley for the use of the Robert Dollar Papers; to the California Historical Society for the Dollar v. Land litigation papers; to Alan Yost, who generously lent his collection of American Mail papers; to Chandler Ide, who initiated the project and gave it his never-failing interest and support; and to Austen Hemion, whose knowledge of maritime history of the Pacific Northwest was invaluable.

A special acknowledgment goes to my colleague Professor John H. Kemble of Pomona College, who brought his vast knowledge of Pacific maritime history to the project by editing various drafts and writing sections of the final version. Two other colleagues, Alfred Louch and John B. Rae, read the entire manuscript. I would like also to thank James M. Merrill and Lisa Reynolds of the University of Delaware Press and Katharine Turok, Verna Groo, and Julien Yoseloff of Associated University Presses. Lelah Mullican and Patrick Delana typed all the drafts.

THE
AMERICAN
PRESIDENT LINES
AND ITS FOREBEARS
1848-1984

1
ORIGINS

THE evening of 8 November 1982 was a very special one for employees and guests of American President Lines, Ltd. It was an event that would, they felt, affect significantly the future of shipping on the West Coast of the United States for many years to come. To the management of APL and especially to its president, Bruce Seaton, it was also the culmination of a building program begun six years before in which the line had committed the greater part of six hundred million dollars of the company's funds. The occasion was the maiden voyage of the company's newest vessel, the M.V. *President Lincoln*, first of the three container vessels that represented a large part of APL's investment in the future.

The *President Lincoln* displaced about 55,000 tons and was 860 feet long. Her lofty bridge stood well over a hundred feet above the waters of San Pedro Harbor, Port of Los Angeles, where she was moored. She towered over APL's terminal and over the hundreds of containers emblazoned with APL's distinctive red eagle that were even then being craned aboard her. Since the *President Lincoln* would sail as soon as loading was completed, the ceremonies were brief. There were some remarks from Seaton and from the *President Lincoln*'s captain, Pieter Boele, a commemorative poem written and read by Gerry Commons, whose husband, Dorman, was chairman and chief executive of Natomas Company, then APL's parent organization. But for those whose interests ran to maritime history, and especially since it occurred on the West Coast, the imminent departure of the *President Lincoln* for Japan recalled an occasion in 1867 when APL's predecessor company, the Pacific Mail Steamship Company, dispatched its steamship *Colorado* on the first regular trans-Pacific run between San Francisco and the Orient.

The *Colorado* was at the time one of the largest commercial vessels ever built in the United States. She and her sisterships represented a heavy capital investment of five million dollars, which today would be not less than fifty million dollars.

Maritime historians would have noted certain comparisons between the *Colorado* and the *President Lincoln*. Both vessels were built to withstand boisterous seas while heavily laden. The *President Lincoln*'s double bottoms, and independent longitudinal and transverse box structures were designed for container storage; the *Colorado*'s transverse bulkheads supported three decks. A latticework of heavy iron bars strengthened her wooden hull, yet at the same time allowed maximum passenger space, cargo storage, and coal bunkers.

And the Pacific Mail, like APL well over a century later, celebrated the sailing with a gala occasion. In this instance, the festivities were more elaborate than the simple ceremony for the *President Lincoln* at San Pedro. Billed as a "Grand China Mail Dinner," the banquet room of the Occidental Hotel in San Francisco was overflowing with state and local dignitaries, shipping officials, religious leaders, and commercial agents. Governor Frederick Ferdinand Low presided at the head table, where a sugar model of the *Colorado* formed the centerpiece. Eighteen toasts punctuated the drone of conversation while magnums of champagne accompanied the elaborate cuisine that was standard at such affairs. Symbolizing what was hoped would be the rich prospects of trade for the Far East, three Chinese merchants, well known in the community, sat at both sides of Governor Low and proposed a toast to a profitable future.[1] But with these similarities all other comparisons end.

In mere size and cargo capacity, the *President Lincoln* and her sisterships the *President Washington* and *President Monroe* dwarfed the *Colorado*. If the *Colorado* had been taken apart and packed into APL's new forty-five-foot aluminum containers, any one of these ships could have stowed a half dozen vessels of her tonnage with cargo space to spare. The *President Lincoln*'s class, the C9s as they are designated, are the most advanced in hull design and propulsion plant of any cargo ship in the world. On the other hand, the *Colorado* and her companion ships the *America*, the *Great Republic*, the *China*, and the *Japan*—all of them built between 1864 and 1867—were obsolete before they were launched at William H. Webb's and Henry Steers' shipyards in New York.

At a time when new steamers were being built with iron hulls, these vessels were constructed of wood. Nor did their propulsion units reflect advances in marine engineering that were becoming standard in European freight and passenger vessels. Instead of screw propellers that had proven their superiority as the most efficient means of marine propulsion, the Pacific Mail steamers were equipped with paddlewheels. Their power plants also recalled designs of the 1830s: walking-beam, low-pressure single-cylinder engines with piston strokes of twelve feet turned the wheels. Intended to operate on the Pacific, far from sophisticated repair facilities, it seemed wiser to equip these ships with the simple, time-tested walking-beam engines. Compound engines were only then just coming into use, and the state of metallurgy was such that propeller shafts sheared away all too often from metal fatigue, leaving the single-screw steamers of the day helpless except for their sails.

On the inauguration of this trans-Pacific service, the Pacific Mail was a venerable enterprise in California terms. Since its inception in 1848 the line had been a most profitable venture for its owners, a syndicate headed by William H. Aspinwall. This lean, bewhiskered New York merchant had founded the line in 1848, just at the conclusion of the Mexican War. By the terms of the peace treaty with Mexico, the United States was ceded California and the territories that now make up the states of Arizona, New Mexico, Nevada, Utah, and Colorado west of the Rockies.

Considered a conservative merchant, Aspinwall startled the business community when it learned that he had secured a charter from the New York legislature to incorporate a steamship line to operate from Panama to the Oregon territory. But in fact the firm of Howland and Aspinwall had three steamers under construction for the Pacific trade in New York shipyards before it announced the new enterprise. Opinion in the city's maritime circles changed from surprise to skepticism that the venture would succeed. True, the federal government had awarded a ten-year mail contract to the new firm. But, asked tough-minded merchants, what was a subsidy of $199,000 a year when one considered the initial investment, not counting the costs of operations and the risks involved?[2] Surely, the scant population of the new territories on the West Coast, a mere twenty thousand inhabitants scattered over two thousand miles of coastline, could not provide much trade. No one knew, least of all Aspinwall and his associates, what resources were available in that far-distant country or whether any profit could be made from their carriage over immense distances to market. Chances were heavily weighted against the venture.

The scoffing comments of fellow merchants did not deter Aspinwall, whose three ships, the *California, Oregon,* and *Panama,* were all completed in the fall of 1848. According to the terms of the mail contract, the steamers had to meet navy specifications so that they could be converted to warships in times of national emergency. The new vessels met all requirements and sailed from New York at intervals during October and December of 1848.[3]

Whether or not Aspinwall's initial judgment was sound, the Pacific Mail proved to be one of the luckier speculations in a century that was to witness monumental treasure troves like the Comstock Lode, Colonel Drake's oil strike in Pennsylvania, and the discovery of the fabulous Mesabi iron range in Minnesota. Indeed, the Pacific Mail's good fortune was the direct result of yet another mineral-rich Golconda, the California gold strike on the American River. The discovery that was to lead to the California gold rush took place in January 1848, but first news of it did not reach the United States until summer, and popular excitement only followed President Polk's announcement of its richness in his message to Congress in December. Meanwhile, in October the first of the new line's steamers cleared New York Harbor for the long and what would prove to be the difficult voyage to the West Coast.

Before the *California* touched at Rio de Janeiro her captain, Cleveland Forbes, became seriously ill with a tubercular infection. Although he was able to pilot the ship through the treacherous passages of the Straits of Magellan, he was so ill when the ship reached Valparaiso, Chile, that the local agents of Howland and Aspinwall replaced him with John T. Marshall, an experienced captain. Forbes continued on the voyage as a passenger, however.

News of the gold strike at Sutter's Mill had reached the West Coast of South America. Under considerable pressure Howland and Aspinwall's agent at Callao bowed to public excitement and allotted the *California*'s passenger space to Peruvians. He booked fifty-two passengers at the exorbitant fare of $300 for cabin class and $150 for steerage.[4] He also took at what amounted to monopoly rates considerable cargo that speculators had shipped from Lima. Captain Forbes estimated that the leg of the voyage from Callao to San Francisco would net $15,000 profit for Howland and Aspinwall in cargo alone.[5]

When the *California* arrived at Panama on 17 January 1849, she was greeted by a mob of gold-seekers, mostly Americans, demanding passage north. The *California* and her sisterships had been designed

California. The first Pacific Mail steamer; inaugurated the line between Panama and San Francisco in 1849. (Courtesy The Peabody Museum, Salem, Massachusetts.)

primarily as cargo carriers. Passenger accommodations were therefore limited to about 60 berths in cabins and steerage. Captain Marshall was faced with a serious problem that he had not anticipated. He honored the tickets of those few individuals at Panama who had purchased them in the United States. But when it was learned that there were Peruvians on board, disappointed Americans loudly claiming the rights and privileges of citizenship insisted that they deserved priority. The Peruvians must be put ashore. To Captain Marshall's credit he refused to accede to the clamor, although the Peruvians were equally as stubborn, insisting that their tickets had been purchased in good faith. They did agree to temporary bunks that Marshall installed in all open spaces. He then devised a system that permitted embarkation of some 300 additional passengers, almost double the ship's usual capacity. One of the passengers described conditions aboard the *California:*

Everywhere the ship is crowded; the passengers on each side of the machinery, the upper and lower forward decks, the long steerage extending from the bows far aft on both sides of the engine—all are full, and many of the berths are occupied by two passengers each. . . . The staterooms and cabins are all crowded to their utmost capacity, and of course the passengers are deprived of many of the conveniences to which they are accustomed. The writer of this article obtained his ticket very early in New York, and yet has had no berth on this ship, and neither sheet nor pillow since he left Panama, and had he not fortunately kept his camp blanket within reach, would have been under the necessity of sleeping in his clothes during the whole voyage.[6]

Some of the passengers taken on at Panama were well behaved and put up with the discomfort and the poor food on the over-crowded vessel. But in Captain Forbes's words, many more were "the scum of creation, Black legs, gamblers, thieves, runners and drunkards." While the *California* sailed northwest along the coast of Mexico at a steady nine knots, fighting over food and drink became a commonplace occurrence. Careless passengers started at least four fires on board. Theft, especially for food, was rife. On one occasion there was a mutiny of the stokers in the ship's crew.[7] Callous behavior was not confined to unruly passengers. "Even the Rev. Devines [*sic*] are very apt in the great profession," observed Captain Forbes. "In one instance one of these worthy gentlemen while saying grace was hauling a dish of green peas toward his plate and in conclusion emptied the whole on his plate & sought for other requisitions with a most hungry & wild countenance and devoured his meal as if his life depended upon it." Another passenger, naval purser Rodman M. Price, charged that Captain Marshall was incompetent and that "the entire want of discipline of the crew, made our situation unsafe, dangerous and sometimes critical."[8]

The *California* ran out of coal as she approached Monterey. Marshall dispatched a work party ashore to cut wood. In a scene that might have been taken from Jules Verne's *Around the World in Eighty Days*, the crew began dismantling the ship for fuel to keep the furnaces going. Before much damage had been done additional sacks of coal, enough fuel to make San Francisco, were found in some unused cargo space under the cabins. When the *California* finally reached San Francisco on 28 February 1849, she discharged not only her passengers but all her officers and crew, who deserted for the gold fields, leaving only a convalescent Captain Forbes and one engineer aboard the vessel.

Had it not been for the U.S. Navy commodore present in San Francisco Bay, Thomas ap Catesby Jones, the *California* might have swung on to the rocks and been wrecked. Jones put a navy crew aboard her while Captain Forbes, who had by now recovered his health, went through the lengthy and laborious process of signing on a crew. Everything was in short supply, especially coal, which the company had ordered from England but which did not arrive for several months. Fortunately for Howland and Aspinwall, the navy looked after its $200,000 investment. The one man who remained aboard with Forbes kept the machinery oiled and in operating condition.[9]

Surely this first voyage of the Pacific Mail Steamship Company was an inauspicious one. But the fledging line could not be faulted for failing to anticipate the gold rush, nor could its management be blamed for the illness of Captain Forbes. The experience of the *Oregon*, which followed the *California* to San Francisco, bears out this point. Captain Richard H. Pearson maintained strict discipline over his crew and his passengers. When he reached San Francisco he anchored near the navy squadron and sought information on local conditions before he permitted the landing of passengers and cargo. He requested and received a detachment of U.S. Marines to patrol his ship with orders to prevent any of his officers and men from going ashore. Since he had been fortunate enough to find a collier in the Mexican port of San Blas, he had sufficient coal to make the return trip to Panama on schedule.[10]

Both Captains Pearson and Forbes had to raise the pay of officers and men to reflect the extreme manpower shortage in the San Francisco area. On their own responsibility they increased wages across the board by a factor of ten from the normal wage of $12 a month for a seaman to $120 a month.[11] Even at this rate of pay, incredible by any contemporary standard, it took Captain Forbes almost two months to recruit a ship's company.[12]

When company headquarters in New York was finally able to form a reasonably coherent picture of chaotic conditions on the West Coast, it moved rapidly to develop policies that met local conditions and market expectations. Always hampered by a time lag of two to three months in transcontinental communications, Aspinwall and his colleagues proved themselves capable and imaginative businessmen.

Fearful that their ships might be unable to operate because of insufficient crews and mindful of the risks to their valuable property, they readily conceded the need for the exorbitant rates of pay for seamen on the West Coast. In addition, Aspinwall promptly sought assistance from the Navy Department to protect the company's investment and to maintain scheduled operations. Citing a broad provision of the company's mail contract, he argued that the public interest and credit required a row guard in port and the loan of men from the navy for the trip to Panama and back when not obtainable otherwise. Secretary of the Navy Preston replied that he would urge Commodore Jones to render whatever assistance he could, but would not order him to act in effect as an auxiliary to the Pacific Mail.

Besides making every effort to ensure efficient and profitable operation, the Pacific Mail moved promptly to protect and capitalize on the surging market. It purchased additional steamers in order to increase sailings between Panama and San Francisco from the monthly frequency originally envisioned to fortnightly and then to every ten days. However, the company was not permitted to enjoy the California boom without competition.

For the next quarter century there was continual actual or potential competition for the Pacific Mail. There were three ways in which this threat could be handled. One was to reduce rates to such an extent that the competitor would be ruined or at least forced to withdraw. Ordinarily cabin rates from New York to California were between $200 and $300 and steerage from $50 to $100. In periods of competition, however, they went much lower: cabins were $75 or $100 and steerage was $35, including a rail ticket across the isthmus, which cost $25. A second means of dealing with a competing line was to buy its ships whether the Pacific Mail needed them or not, thus removing them from the run. The third method was to compromise with the competitor, either dividing traffic, arranging sailings at staggered intervals, or paying the competitor a subsidy for withdrawing from the business.

The first rival faced by the Pacific Mail was the Empire City Line, which dispatched three small steamers to the Pacific in 1850. Their route from Panama to San Francisco directly paralleled that of the Pacific Mail. Aspinwall met this threat by purchasing two of the Empire City Line's steamers, thereby effectively maintaining his monopoly.[13]

A far more serious competitor, the United States Mail Steamship Company, began business on the West Coast the same year. This line had been established about the same time as the Pacific Mail and also enjoyed a government mail contract. Until 1850 United States Mail was exclusively an Atlantic carrier between East Coast ports and Panama. In that year, however, it extended its operations to the West Coast with four ships, the *Isthmus, Columbus, Republic,* and *Antelope.* None of these vessels could match the Pacific Mail's ships in size, speed, or capacity, but they immediately began a potentially disastrous rate war.

The owners of the United States Mail were not only rough and rather unprincipled speculators, but they had important political connections in the new Whig administration of Zachary Taylor. George Law and Marshall O. Roberts were the principal powers of the line. Law had made a fortune in New York City street railroad contracts. Roberts had been equally adept at exploiting public works for profit through his party connections. Both men had plenty of money behind them from a New York business community eager to cash in on the expected California bonanza. But in tackling the Pacific Mail in what it now regarded as its own preserve, Law and Roberts were taking on Howland and Aspinwall, who were well prepared to divert some of their Atlantic steamers from European routes and build additional ones that would challenge United States Mail's own monopoly on the Atlantic side of the isthmus.

The rate war now on the East as well as the West Coast was of short duration. Law and Roberts agreed to sell their small Pacific fleet to Pacific Mail, while Aspinwall sold his four competing vessels on the Atlantic route to United States Mail. The contesting forces then agreed that they would remain in their established spheres and would cooperate in arranging for through passenger tickets and freight moving from the East Coast to the West.[14] This arrangement continued for the next eight years.

A more stubborn and even more dangerous rival surfaced just as the threat from United States Mail was being contained. Cornelius Vanderbilt sent three steamers to the Pacific and at the same time challenged Pacific Mail's route across the isthmus.

Six years earlier the United States had concluded a treaty with New Granada, now Colombia, which gave American companies the right of transit across its province of Panama. At Aspinwall's insistence, agents for his firm concluded an agreement with New Granada that gave it special rights of transit across the isthmus from Chagres on the Atlantic side to Panama City on the Pacific. Ratified by the New Granada Congress in 1850, the contract gave the Panama Railroad Company exclusive rights for a line across the isthmus and 250,000 acres of land wherever it chose to build terminal facilities. In due course Howland and Aspinwall constructed wharves and warehouses at Navy Bay on the Caribbean side of the isthmus, and this site, better protected from the seas than the mouth of the Chagres River, became the port of Aspinwall (later known as Colon). Tidal conditions at Panama City never permitted the construction of adequate wharves, and goods and passengers always had to be lightered from the beach to the ships.

Vanderbilt, a shrewd and remorseless competitor, had realized that if he were to break the Pacific Mail's monopoly he must find another route across the isthmus. Nicaragua to the north offered the best possibility. Though the transit was longer, almost all of it was by river and lake. Accordingly, Vanderbilt secured the necessary agreement from one of the transient Nicaraguan governments and began building port facilities. For the next fifteen years, a period punctuated by rate wars and compromises, Pacific Mail had to contend with the tenacious and grasping Vanderbilt. The only other competitor was the hastily organized New York and San Francisco Steamship Line. In 1852 it placed two large steamers, the *Cortes* and the *Winfield Scott*, on the West Coast. But Pacific Mail purchased them a year later and added them to its expanding fleet.

Not relying on the purchase of competitor's ships alone to ensure its preeminence in the West Coast trade, Pacific Mail also engaged in a large-scale shipbuilding program. From 1850 through 1854, New York shipyards and engine works produced a vessel a year for the line. With the exception of the *Columbia*, designed for the San Francisco–Oregon run, all of them were wooden paddlewheel steamers ranging from 1,600 to 2,300 tons. Having gained experience in the market potential for passenger traffic, Pacific Mail had designed these ships to carry in considerable comfort as many as nine hundred passengers each.[15] The *Golden Gate*, which entered service in 1851, began the succession of ships designed for the needs of the

Golden Gate. Hailed as a "steam clipper" when she entered service in 1851, she could carry 750 passengers. (Courtesy The Mariners Museum, Newport News, Virginia.)

expanding California trade. A steamer of over 2,000 tons, she was 269 feet long and had a 40-foot beam. Her two oscillating engines drove side paddlewheels 40 feet in diameter, and her initial passage of eleven days four hours between Panama and San Francisco stood as a record for four years. Two years later the 2,183-ton *John L. Stephens* went into the Panama–San Francisco trade. She had accommodations for 350 cabin passengers and 550 in steerage. An amenity was a suite of bathrooms with instant hot and cold water for cabin passengers.

By now the line had established coal depots along its route where fuel was available, as well as water, provisions, and spare parts that were not carried aboard. Only infrequently did the ships resort to their auxiliary sails and then only because the captains took advantage of favorable wind conditions to reduce fuel cost. In 1850 Pacific Mail established its own commercial agency on the West Coast, separate from the firm of Howland and Aspinwall.

The ebb in the gold excitement that began in 1851 eased the manpower problem. Company officers in New York were thus able to improve service and plan schedules and operating budgets with greater accuracy. Under the careful though aggressive management of Aspinwall, Pacific Mail began paying dividends that ranged as high as 50 percent in 1850 despite heavy capital expenditures for new ships and the purchase of competitors' vessels. Because of adverse business conditions profits declined during the next three years, and the company omitted dividends. It lost $40,000 in 1854. But from 1857 until 1867 the company paid annual dividends from 10 percent to 30 percent on a capitalization that had been increased eightfold.[16]

These were piping years for the Pacific Mail, which had tied itself in to the dramatically expanding economy of California. While the new state was exporting over $40 million in gold each year, it was also experiencing an almost continuous boom from its unprecedented population growth. Year after year the Pacific Mail's fleet, which by 1865 consisted of twenty steamers, sailed with very nearly every berth full. As the only bulk carrier from Panama to the West Coast and utilizing the fastest, most comfortable, and least dangerous route for westward-bound emigrants, Pacific Mail became the largest and most profitable American shipping concern.

Through the foresight of Aspinwall, Pacific Mail had a secure accommodation with the Panama Railroad that had been completed across the isthmus in 1855. With the railroad in operation, the trip from ocean to ocean at Panama was reduced to four hours, in contrast to the previous requirement of three to four days of travel in dugout canoes on the Chagres River and by muleback from the head of navigation to Panama. Coordination of rail and steamship schedules resulted in travel time of about twenty-one days between New York and San Francisco and secured for the Panama route the premier place in intercoastal transportation until the advent of the transcontinental railroad in 1869. Although the Panama Railroad was a common carrier and took passengers from Pacific Mail and competing lines alike, the Pacific Mail enjoyed the principal benefit of its service.[17]

In 1856 William Aspinwall retired from the presidency, although he remained the principal stockholder and a member of the board of directors. William Davidge, secretary of the company and an Aspinwall protégé, succeeded him. The Davidge regime was one of consolidation rather than expansion. It was also a period when the line was relatively free from competition, though Vanderbilt was kept at bay only through the payment of an annual subsidy. No new steamers were built, nor were any acquired from other shipping lines.

Near the end of Davidge's stewardship, the restive Vanderbilt made a final try at breaking Pacific Mail's monopoly. He sent four steamers to the Pacific, each over 1,000 tons: the *Cortes*, which Pacific Mail had sold to Vanderbilt earlier, the *Orizaba, Sierra Nevada,* and *Uncle Sam.* All these steamers were relatively new and designed for passenger service, although they had substantial cargo capacity.

Vanderbilt immediately engaged in a rate war that soon proved too costly for him. Pacific Mail agreed to buy his ships at a sizable profit to him, and he agreed to withdraw from competition. Never again did Vanderbilt try to challenge Pacific Mail. A costly nuisance for Pacific Mail was finally abated, but not before it had yielded over $2 million in profits to Vanderbilt. Exhausted by the Vanderbilt episode and pleading illness, Davidge was glad to turn over the management of the company to Allan McLane, a young aggressive ex-naval officer. The son of Andrew Jackson's secretary of treasury and state, McLane had important political connections that had come to be a necessity for anyone aspiring to the management of Pacific Mail. McLane combined family influence in Washington with a thorough knowledge of ships and shipping. Like his father, Louis McLane, he was a dynamic, intelligent person who sized up the future prospects of the company and renewed a policy of expansion. He also had powerful backing from a Baltimore and New York banking and investment group, Brown Brothers and Company, who were moving to control the line. It was most useful to McLane that his brother Louis was president of Wells Fargo, the largest express and banking firm on the West Coast. Another brother, Charles, was its San Francisco agent.

McLane had been president for only a few months when the Confederate forces around Charleston Harbor forced the surrender of Fort Sumter and began the Civil War. But the line had more difficulties with rival banking groups and speculators who sought to manipulate its stock than with Confederate seagoing raiders. In 1863 Aspinwall resigned from the board and the following year a pool organized by Brown Brothers assumed control of the line. By the war's end, this financial group was ready for a dramatic expansion of Pacific Mail's operations and an even more dramatic increase in its capitalization from $4 million to $10 million in 1865, which was further increased to $20 million a year later. With these new funds McLane and his banker associates purchased Vanderbilt's Atlantic Mail Steamship Company, thus giving a through route under one management from New York by way of New Orleans, Aspinwall, and the Panama Railroad to San Francisco.[18]

The Brown Brothers group promoted the new arrangement skillfully, driving up the stock on Wall Street. Insiders netted $12 million in less than a month. Despite these speculative transactions Pacific Mail for a brief period enjoyed the economies of scale from the consolidation of the Atlantic and Pacific lines. It was able to provide better service and even passed on some of its savings to its customers in the form of reduced rates.[19] In all, Pacific Mail now employed ten steamers on the Atlantic-to-Panama run and another ten on the route from Panama to San Francisco. A profitable future seemed to be indicated for the nation's largest shipping line.

NOTES

1. *San Francisco Alta California*, 10 January 1867.

2. The three ships cost $609,942. See John H. Kemble, *The Panama Route: 1848–1869* (Berkeley and Los Angeles: University of California Press, 1943), 218, 239, 242.

3. I. McKeever, W. L. Hudson, and T. Hartt to John Y. Mason, Navy Yard, New York, 28 September 1848 in "Commandants of Navy Yards," New York, 1848, National Archives, Record Group 45. *New York Herald*, 30 November; 1, 2, 27 December 1848; 6 January; 18 February 1849.

4. John M. Pomfret, ed., *California Gold Rush Voyages, 1848–1849* (San Marino, Calif.: Huntington Library Publications, 1954), 192–219.

5. Ibid., 219.

6. *Littell's Living Age* (Boston) 21 (April–June 1849): 164–65.

7. Letter of Stephen Branch in (New York) *Journal of Commerce*, 15 February 1849, quoted in Victor M. Berthold, *The Pioneer Steamer California, 1848–1849* (Boston and New York: Houghton Mifflin Co., 1932), 55; Edward E. Dunbar, *The Romance of the Age* (New York, 1867), 83–84.

8. Pomfret, *Voyages*, 226; Editing Committee, *The First Steamship Pioneers* (San Francisco: H. S. Crocker, 1874), 352.

9. Kemble, *Panama Route*, 128.

10. Pomfret, *Voyages*, 230.

11. Ibid., 242.

12. Ibid., 233.

13. Kemble, *Panama Route*, 129.

14. William Heilman v. Marshall O. Roberts, New York Superior Court (1861), 22–23; *New York Herald*, 14 March, 1 April 1851.

15. Kemble, *Panama Route*, 228–33.

16. Pacific Mail Steamship Company, *Proceedings at a Meeting of Stockholders*, 1855, 5–7; *New York Herald*, 11 July 1850, 6 January 1853, 26 June 1862, 13 August 1863, 20 November 1866.

17. *New York Herald*, 11 November 1859; *Panama Star and Herald*, 18 February 1860.

18. John A. Munroe, *Louis McLane, Federalist and Jacksonian* (New Brunswick, N.J.: Rutgers University Press, 1974), 44, 92, 99, 438, 467.

19. *Panama Star and Herald*, 11 January 1866.

2

PACIFIC MAIL: THE LATER YEARS

EXCEPT for the brief depression of 1866, prosperous times and mounting revenues during the later 1860s justified the placing of additional ships into service. Management was aware, however, of competition more enduring than rival shipping groups. The transcontinental railroad lines that had been under construction since 1863 now posed a new threat. Well before the westward-bound Union Pacific and the Central Pacific going east neared a juncture at Promontory, Utah, the Pacific Mail had secured a government subsidy for a scheduled trans-Pacific service. Meanwhile, on 1 January 1867, the *Colorado* inaugurated the trans-Pacific line when she sailed from San Francisco for Yokohama and Hong Kong.[1]

Along with the service to Yokohama and Hong Kong, Pacific Mail established feeder lines to Kobe, Nagasaki, Shanghai, and to the Japanese port of Hakodate, capital of Hokkaido, the northernmost of the main Japanese Islands.[2] To carry out the service, the Pacific Mail ordered the construction of four steamers, the *Great Republic, China, Japan,* and *America.* The largest wooden side-wheelers ever built for oceanic service, their tonnage ranged from 3,800 to 4,400 tons, their length was about 360 feet, and their beam about 47 feet. The vessels were driven by enormous walking-beam engines with cylinders 105 inches in diameter and strokes of 12 feet. The latest in comfort and spaciousness for passengers in first class, cabins were paneled with black walnut, flooring in the interior was light spruce and black walnut in a zebra pattern, and silken drapes were fastened to each port. As befitted the taste of the Gilded Age, furnishings were upholstered in colors ranging from peach and pea green to lavender and purple. Besides accommodations for 250 passengers in first class, there was steerage capacity for 1,000 to 1,200 passengers.

An increasingly important share of Pacific Mail's business until the first decade of the twentieth century was the carriage of Oriental

Colorado. The steamer that inaugurated the trans-Pacific service of the Pacific Mail in 1867. Here she is shown in the dry dock at Hunter's Point, San Francisco. (APL Archives.)

Chinese steerage passengers aboard the Pacific Mail steamer *Alaska* bound for San Francisco. (*Illustrated London News, Extra Supplement,* 29 April 1876.)

passengers, primarily those from China, but after 1900, Filipinos and Japanese as well. Until 1916, cooks and stewards were always Chinese, as were most of the crew. Chinese stewards were always an object of interest and curiosity to cabin-class passengers. Though few spoke more than a smattering of Pidgin English, there were always interpreters at hand. Menus, room service directions, and other useful passenger information were printed in English with its Chinese equivalent. Pacific Mail stewards were all dressed in wide black trousers, dark blue tunics, black silk pillbox hats, and white-soled slippers of black felt. With pigtails swinging down their backs, these "blue-gowned boys," as the press called them, were attentive to passenger needs.[3]

The Pacific Mail enjoyed highly profitable operations until the panic and depression of 1873, despite the gradual loss of its passenger traffic to the railroads. It achieved this prosperity through the growth of its trans-Pacific service, its wise policy of expanding its coastal fleet on the West Coast, and its ability to compete with the railroads for freight, especially bulk freight of low unit cost.

In 1872, the government doubled its subsidy for the trans-Pacific service to a million dollars a year, but insisted that the company increase its sailings to the Far East and that it modernize its fleet. Five iron-hulled, screw-propelled steamers were delivered to the Pacific Mail in 1873, three in 1874, and three more in 1875. The most notable of these were the *City of Peking* and *City of Tokio*, vessels of 5,079 tons, the largest ships flying the American flag at the time of their construction. The *City of Tokio* came to a tragic end on a reef off Yokohama Harbor in 1885, but her sistership served the company well for some thirty-five years. The last of the wooden side-wheelers was phased out of service in the early 1880s. New schedules required a departure from San Francisco every two weeks. This meant that Pacific Mail had to accelerate a construction program already under-way of iron-hulled, screw-propeller steamers. Of course, the new program sharply increased both the amount and the rate of capital expenditures. But the strong earning potential of the company argued against any serious problem, even though its stock plummeted in the market during 1870 and 1871. Unfortunately, two events occurred that tarnished the reputation of Pacific Mail and eventually threw it into the hands of speculative railroad interests.

McLane resigned the presidency in 1871 and the board elected Alden B. Stockwell to be his successor. McLane had some faults as

City of Peking. She and her sistership, the *City of Tokio,* were iron screw-propelled steamers built for Pacific Mail in 1874. (Private collection.)

the guiding spirit of Pacific Mail, but at least he was highly experienced in the shipping business. Stockwell, though an intelligent, energetic person, was completely without experience in transportation either by rail or by ship. He was a speculative stockbroker who immediately began a construction program that he hoped with proper publicity would enable him and insiders to make a killing on the stock market. Thus he lobbied extensively for an increase in the government subsidy, citing the benefits to the military of having a modern merchant fleet in the Pacific.

Stockwell's plans foundered with the depression of 1873, which found Pacific Mail's financial resources overextended, not just because of its ambitious building program, but because its liquidity had been seriously impaired through Stockwell's mismanagement as well as fraudulent and reckless use of its resources. In addition the company was weakened by a series of maritime disasters that claimed six of its steamers in fifteen months between August 1872 and October 1873. Stockwell resigned under a cloud and was replaced briefly by George H. Bradbury, a member of the board and one of the line's senior captains.

Though Pacific Mail was near bankruptcy, its stock trading at a fraction of its former price, it still had valuable assets, not the least of which were new iron-hulled, screw-propelled steamers. Pacific Mail's coastal fleet, its revenue reduced by the depression, still enjoyed a strong position whose enhanced profitability merely waited the return of good times. Its other routes and vessels and its close association with the Panama Railroad all remained intact. Though burdened with debt, it was a property that had all the requisite qualities to attract Jay Gould, the master speculator.

Apart from the stock-trading prospects offered in Pacific Mail, Gould was planning to gain control of the Union Pacific Railroad, also reeling from mismanagement and overcapitalization. He may have had his eye on the Central Pacific Railroad, too. Control of that line would have brought the nation's entire transcontinental rail system into his hands. Pacific Mail was the only serious competition to the railroad lines and its acquisition would thus be an essential prime bargaining counter in his strategy. Should his plans succeed it would become valuable property that would enhance his railroad investments. Several obstacles stood in his way, the greatest being the indomitable figure of Collis P. Huntington, driving force behind the Central Pacific and a person not likely to be fooled, cajoled, or intimidated by Gould.[4]

In any event, shortly after Stockwell became president of Pacific Mail and began speculating with the company's funds, Gould quietly began buying its stock. In May 1873, just before the panic, Gould had enough shares to place two of his henchmen on the board, Russell Sage and C. J. Osborne.

In the jungle warfare that characterized Wall Street during the Gilded Age, partnerships among speculators were fragile as each sought his own advantage. Sage had parlayed his savings gained as a grocer in Troy, New York, to a fortune in stocks and bonds. Gould with good reason regarded him as unreliable and marked him for early retirement—preferably shorn of his wealth. But Gould bided his time until he was ready for the next phase in his strategy, the takeover of Union Pacific. Meanwhile, the panic of 1873 interposed, requiring readjustments in his timetable.[5]

About the same time, Pacific Mail canceled an informal cartel it had with the railroads. Under this arrangement the railroads had guaranteed almost full freight capacity for the Pacific Mail coastal steamers, although they retained the right to allocate cargo and set rates. Its effect had been to ensure that most of the bulky, low unit-value freight moving from east to west would be shipped by Pacific Mail. Profitable for the shipping line, the agreement injured the Panama Railroad, especially after Pacific Mail established its trans-Pacific service. Not only was lucrative passenger traffic drastically curtailed, but high unit-value goods from the Orient destined for markets in the eastern United States were now shipped overland.

At this point Sage became president of Pacific Mail. Consulting his own interest and under some pressure from the Panama Railroad, he had no compunction about derailing Gould, and Huntington as well, for that matter. Thus Pacific Mail denounced its cartel with the railroads and launched a full-scale rate war. Coming as it did at the height of the 1873 depression, this action cut sharply into the already diminished earnings of the Union Pacific and Central Pacific. Gould, who had finally secured control of the Union Pacific, threatened to organize a competing line but was unable to bring the Central Pacific behind it or to frighten Sage and his allies into submission. When Huntington, acting for the Central Pacific, was no more successful than Gould had been with the Pacific Mail, he became receptive to organizing a competing line that would be backed by both railroads.

Huntington and Gould incorporated the Occidental and Oriental Steamship Company with a capitalization of $10 million, although a mere fraction of this sum was paid in. Taking advantage of the worldwide shipping slump, the Occidental and Oriental chartered vessels from the British White Star Line to threaten the Pacific Mail's trade. The new shipping line was profitable from the beginning. But neither Gould nor Huntington wanted a lengthy rate war. Pacific Mail was sufficiently chastened to break its ties with the Panama Railroad, and its management signed a contract with the two railroads that restored essentially the old cartel.[6]

Huntington seemed satisfied with the agreement; Gould was not. He would not feel secure in his plans while Pacific Mail remained independent, and he did not trust Sage. Accordingly, Gould resorted to his familiar tactics. He floated disparaging rumors about the prospects of the shipping line, and he directly accused its president and board of directors of selling its stock short. Gould himself contributed to the run on Pacific Mail's stock by selling all of his shares in the company and by also taking a short position. Though Sage denied the allegations, he and his fellow directors were forced to resign. The stock of Pacific Mail was now trading at such a low price that it was ripe for a Gould takeover. He did not hesitate and by the end of 1874, Gould and a new group of associates who would do his bidding had a controlling interest in the line.

Another blow fell in 1875 when the three-year-old addition to the trans-Pacific mail contract was canceled by Congress after an investigation into Pacific Mail's lobbying activities for the contract. Thus the million dollars a year that had been received for the service from San Francisco to the Orient was halved.

Gould was also consolidating his position in Union Pacific stock. A supporter, Sidney Dillon, had been installed as president, and by carefully concealed purchases Gould and his associates owned a majority of Pacific Mail's shares by March 1875. They now promoted both companies, insisting that there be no more rate wars and that future operations complement each other. Dillon became president of Pacific Mail as well, and Gould personally guaranteed the financial future of the line. The days of uncertainty and of near insolvency that had prevailed for the past three years seemed over. The stock of Union Pacific and Pacific Mail soared and insiders, including of course Gould, made huge gains. But the period of euphoria was short-lived. As it had been earlier, the Panama Railroad Company was the culprit and its president, Trenor Park, a sometime Gould associate, was the prime mover.

Park, a diminutive Vermonter who had lived and prospered in California, was tenacious, shrewd, and as calculating as Gould himself. He had early sensed the importance and value of the Panama Railroad in any dealings between the Pacific Mail and the transcontinental railroads. Park had put together a Wall Street group that over a period of time gained a majority interest in the Panama Railroad. Assuming its presidency and mindful of Gould's intentions, he stood ready to extract maximum advantage from any combination of the Union Pacific and the Pacific Mail.

When Dillon announced that Pacific Mail would henceforth carry only bulk freight, Park, whose railroad would lose revenues by such an arrangement, objected. He backed up his objection by organizing the Panama Transit Steamship Company to compete with Pacific

Mail. A rate war quickly followed during which the Pacific Mail was
again driven close to bankruptcy. Gould's resources, encumbered as
they were with other investments, were not equal to a protracted
fight over the freight concession, so he began unloading his Pacific
Mail stock and made no effort to stop the Park forces from gaining
control of Pacific Mail in the summer of 1876.[7]

Temporarily rebuffed, Gould had not lost interest in the line. He
simply waited for a more favorable opportunity to perfect his long-
range plans. During the next two years under the Park management
the line slowly regained some of its former prosperity while the
long, severe depression began to lift. Unfortunately its growth was
stunted considerably when Park unloaded the steamer fleet of his
Panama Transit Company on the hapless Pacific Mail at exorbitant
prices.[8] Having extracted maximum gains from the railroad and
shipping line, Park retired from the scene to his native Vermont.

From 1878 through 1884 Pacific Mail was relatively free of outside
influences, but its earnings were not sufficient to provide dividends.
What profits were made went to lighten its debt load, though the
line did strengthen its coastal fleet with five steamers, ranging from
the 2,000-ton *San Jose* to the 3,550-ton *City of Rio de Janeiro*. Despite
these heavy capital expenditures, operations were now profitable
enough for the directors to declare a dividend of 3⅓ percent on the
par value of its capital stock, the first payout since 1869. In 1885 it
declared a 5 percent dividend, but by then the line again had come
under the control of the Union Pacific, which was acting in harmony
with the Central Pacific to its disadvantage. In 1887, George Gould,
the playboy son of Jay Gould, became president.[9]

Despite weak management, Pacific Mail made some prudent capital investments. In 1889 the elegant steamer *China* joined the Pacific
Mail fleet. A two-stacked steel vessel of 5,061 tons, she was built at
Govan, Scotland, by the Fairfield Yard. *China* was the only
ship built expressly for the trans-Pacific run between 1875 and 1902,
and was the only vessel the Pacific Mail ever ordered from a foreign
yard. The *China* initially flew the British flag, then after a brief
period under the Hawaiian flag she came under American registry
with the annexation of the Hawaiian Republic in 1898.

After six years of George Gould's feeble leadership, Collis P. Huntington took over the line. Huntington had his faults as a businessman, but lack of vigor was not one of them. Although the Central

Pacific and Southern Pacific railroads always claimed first priority, neither he nor his associates could be faulted for merely serving time in the management of any of their properties.

One of Huntington's first moves was to hire a competent executive for the shipping line. He installed Rennie Pierre Schwerin as vice president and general manager. A graduate of the U.S. Naval Academy in the class of 1879, Schwerin had met Huntington in Alaska. The trim, bearded young officer (he was thirty-three years old at the time) impressed the railroad titan, who persuaded him to give up a career in the navy and became one of his assistants in the Southern Pacific Railroad.[10]

When Pacific Mail came under the railroad's control in 1893, Schwerin seemed the ideal manager for the line. His naval background, industry, habit of command, and direct, forceful manner soon made themselves felt. For the next twenty-two years Schwerin ran an efficient, profitable enterprise. Though directly responsible first to Huntington and then to his successors, he was permitted almost complete autonomy. Pacific Mail, for so much of its stormy life a victim of speculators, now enjoyed a lengthy period where a distinct policy formulated and directed by a knowledgeable shipping man governed its operations.

During Schwerin's tenure the line gradually increased its coastal business, pioneering in the fruit and coffee trade from Central America. However, for the second time in its history it was faced with serious competition from other lines that could not be bought up or driven out of business. The Occidental and Oriental, which had shared a part of its Pacific trade in a mutually beneficial arrangement, ceased operations in 1906. Pacific Mail took over two of its steamers, the *Coptic* and the *Doric*, which it renamed the *Persia* and the *Asia*. But in order to maintain its service against the aggressive Japanese line Toyo Kisen Kaisha (or TKK) and the Canadian Pacific, both of which had entered the Pacific trade, Pacific Mail had to expand and modernize its fleet.

Schwerin had anticipated tightened competition as early as 1898, when he induced Huntington to commit large capital sums for new construction.[11] Huntington died suddenly in 1900, and the directors of the Southern Pacific purchased enough of the stock of the Pacific Mail from his estate to bring the company under the direct control of the railroad. Two years later Edward H. Harriman gained control of the Southern Pacific and with it control of the Pacific Mail. He

Korea. A steel-hulled steamer of 11,300 tons, she entered Pacific Mail's trans-Pacific service in 1902. Her sistership was the *Siberia*. (APL Archives.)

Manchuria. With her sistership, the *Mongolia*, she began service to the Orient for Pacific Mail in 1904. Later in her career she became the *President Johnson* [I] of the Dollar Line and APL. (APL Archives.)

became president of the steamship company in 1902 and remained in that office until his death in 1909.

The line and its parent railroad company responded to general prosperity in the wake of the Spanish-American War and a renewed popular and government interest in the Far East. By 1902 Pacific Mail had the largest and fastest combination passenger-freight ships in the trans-Pacific run. Its *Korea* and *Siberia*, 11,300 tons each, easily outclassed in speed, comfort, and capacity any competing ships. And in 1904, two new 13,638-ton steamers, the *Manchuria* and the *Mongolia*, joined them on the Pacific route.

Despite a series of maritime disasters during the next ten years, the line's trans-Pacific trade continued to be profitable. Six steamers were lost in wrecks between 1898 and 1911, the most costly in lives and cargo being the sinking of the *City of Rio de Janeiro* on the rocks just off Fort Point at the entrance to San Francisco Bay. One of Pacific Mail's iron-hulled single-screw steamers, the *Rio de Janeiro* had been built at the John Roach Yard, Chester, Pennsylvania, in 1878. She registered 3,548 tons gross. The *Rio de Janeiro* had made an uneventful trip from ports in the Far East, called at Honolulu, and reached San Francisco Bay on 21 February 1901, where she took on a pilot. On board were 201 passengers, officers, and crew and a cargo valued at $200,000, worth at least $2 million on today's market.

As Captain William Ward and Frederick Jordan, the pilot, made preparations for entering the harbor, a heavy fog set in. Ward anchored the ship. When the fog lifted early in the morning of 22 February he weighed anchor and set a course for the Golden Gate. Within fifteen minutes a heavy fog bank again suddenly enveloped the ship. But instead of anchoring, the captain felt sure enough of his bearings to continue on his course and speed. At 5:20 A.M. the ship struck the rocks head-on just below the fort. Thirteen minutes later she sank and with her were lost 122 passengers and crew. Seventy-nine lives were saved.

The circumstances of the sinking, so close to her destination and so clearly the fault of her captain, resulted in serious public criticism of Pacific Mail. Rennie Schwerin did not try to excuse Captain Ward:

> Time and again we have warned our captains never to leave or enter a port during a fog. Not only have we given our captains verbal instructions, but letters have been written to them to the same end. From what I can learn I think that it would have been

wiser for Captain Ward to have waited outside until the fog cleared off. He was the only man who had authority to bring the vessel in. It is erroneous to think that when a pilot boards a vessel the Captain has no more responsibility. A pilot is simply a guide for a Captain.[12]

Pacific Mail's reputation for safety and reliability suffered briefly from this particular loss but its earning potential soon recovered.

After 1904 Schwerin's policy favored the bigger ships on the Pacific route over coastal business. Vessels that were lost were not replaced; nor was there any capital invested for modernization. In 1912, the Panama Canal Act forbade the use of the canal to any shipping line controlled by railroads that were engaged in interstate commerce. Schwerin had planned to build new, large liners and place them on the run between New York and Manila by way of the Panama Canal, San Francisco, Japan, and Hong Kong, but this now became impossible. And Pacific Mail was losing money to the newer, faster ships of three competing coastal lines, American–Hawaiian, Grace, and Luckenbach. As a result Southern Pacific decided to abandon its Central and South American routes and to concentrate on local passenger and freight business, along with its profitable trans-Pacific service.

But in 1915, the future of this trade seemed in grave jeopardy because of the La Follette Seamen's Act, which required a large proportion of the crews of American flag vessels to be able to understand orders given by officers. This meant, of course, orders in the English language. Pacific Mail had employed Chinese crews ever since it began its trans-Pacific Service. Compliance with the La Follette Act meant sharply increased operating costs in the higher wages that had to be paid white seamen. Since profit margins, even with the five large steamers on the Pacific run, had declined because of increased competition, particularly from subsidized Japanese lines, Southern Pacific decided to cease all operations and sell its vessels. At the same time capitalization of the Pacific Mail was reduced from $20 million to $12 million.

The decision proved to be unfortunate. Although the five trans-Pacific steamers, *China, Korea, Manchuria, Mongolia,* and *Siberia,* were sold for high prices on the rising shipping market of World War I, demand for trans-Pacific tonnage under the then neutral American flag increased dramatically before the year 1915 ended. As a result, W. R. Grace and the American International Corporation purchased the Southern Pacific's block of Pacific Mail stock in December. Early in 1916 a meeting of Pacific Mail stockholders rescinded the offers to sell the remaining ships and authorized the increase of the capital stock of the company to $4 million. The seven vessels remaining to the company were suitable only for coastal trade, however, and strenuous efforts were initiated to purchase ships for the trans-Pacific service. Eventually Pacific Mail was able to purchase three new Dutch vessels, the *Colombia, Ecuador,* and *Venezuela,* although they were only about 5,600 tons each and the seller's market made the price for them high.[13]

By August 1916 Pacific Mail ships were again plying their traditional trade routes across the Pacific. The familiar red, white, and blue swallowtail house flag was again seen flying from the main-masts of vessels working alongside the busy quays of Yokohama, Shanghai, Hong Kong, and Manila, although hulls were now painted green and stacks were buff, white, and black instead of the proverbial black that had been their color for over sixty-five years.

A major and significant change in Pacific Mail affairs was the retirement of Schwerin. John H. Rosseter, West Coast manager for W. R. Grace, succeeded him. There followed five years of renewed activity and significant growth under the spur of wartime and immediate postwar demands.

The entry of the United States into World War I stimulated the American economy and especially enhanced the demand for shipping. Though the United States Shipping Board requisitioned all of Pacific Mail's vessels for war service, the line operated all but two of its ships on its established routes. And in 1917, it started another service between San Francisco, Manila, Calcutta, and Colombo with two chartered vessels.

Besides the ships sailing on these routes, Pacific Mail operated another twenty-three for the Shipping Board. Since the restriction on trade through the Panama Canal no longer applied after the Southern Pacific sold its interest in the line, Pacific Mail opened a service to the East Coast through the Panama Canal with the purchase of four freighters. In 1920 it pioneered the first round-the-world service when it began to send Shipping Board freighters west from San Francisco. That year marked the apogee of Pacific Mail's fleet. Forty-six steamers under its house flag carried over one million tons of cargo between American, European, and Asian ports. The following year, however, traffic began to slacken as a postwar depression set in.

In the past American shipping had weathered these downturns and had experienced a surge of renewed confidence with the return of prosperity. Pacific Mail management expected such a pattern to repeat itself. With a surplus of Shipping Board vessels now available, it increased its trans-Pacific operations as managing operator of five large steamers. These were twin-screw vessels of 14,000-plus tons and 535 feet in length, a dimension that gave them, as a class, the designation 535s. These ships had been laid down as transports but were completed as passenger-cargo liners with remarkably fine accommodations. At first they received the designations of state nicknames: *Golden State, Empire State,* and so on, but they were soon renamed for American presidents. The Pacific Mail operated *President Cleveland, President Lincoln, President Pierce, President Taft,* and *President Wilson,* names that were to be carried on by the successors of the Pacific Mail down to the present day. The first of these ships sailed from San Francisco in March 1921, and now the Pacific Mail could offer fortnightly service between San Francisco and the Orient in ships admirably suited to the trade. The addition of these ships made it possible for the Pacific Mail to place the *Colombia, Ecuador,* and *Venezuela* in trans-Canal service between San Francisco and Baltimore.[14]

Between 1922 and 1925 the company was forced to cut back. It continued to make reasonable profits on its curtailed service, but the management and board of directors seemed to have lost the aggressive leadership that had characterized its past policies, even when it was the victim of Wall Street speculators.

In particular the Pacific Mail neglected its Washington connections, so its influence with the Shipping Board declined. When the Board offered for sale the five "President" ships that the Pacific Mail had been operating on the trans-Pacific run, both the Dollar Steamship Lines and the Pacific Mail bid for them. The Dollar bid was $5,625,000 cash, whereas the Pacific Mail offered $6,750,000 partly in cash and partly in preferred stock in a new company to which the ships would be transferred. The Shipping Board decided that the Pacific Mail's higher bid did not meet the terms set in its advertisement for the ships and therefore awarded the ships to Dollar. In April 1925 they were sold to the Dollar Steamship Lines, which continued to operate them in the trans-Pacific trade.

With its trans-Pacific fleet gone and no other comparable ships available on the market at acceptable prices, W. R. Grace and Company, the owner of a controlling interest in the Pacific Mail, decided to withdraw from the Oriental trade. The remaining coastal and intercoastal ships under its house flag were brought under Grace ownership and continued operation under the trade name of the Panama Mail Steamship Company.

Herbert Fleishhacker of the Anglo-California Bank and a close associate of the Dollars headed a San Francisco syndicate that purchased the Pacific Mail name, house flag, and good will. The following year the corporate shell was sold to the Dollar Company, which had in the meantime carried on the trans-Pacific service with the "President" ships. A long period of colorful maritime history in the West had come to an end, a time when paddlewheel, wooden-hulled steamers had given way to iron-hulled, then steel-hulled, screw-propelled liners.[15]

NOTES

1. *San Francisco Alta California,* 2 January 1867.

2. Henry G. Langley, *Langley's San Francisco Business Directory and Metropolitan Guide* (San Francisco, 1869), (1871), xxxi; (1872), vi; (1874); iv; (1875), iv.

3. Kathryn C. Hulme, *Annie's Captain* (London: F. Muller, 1961), 153, 155, 174.

4. David Lavender, *The Great Persuader* (Garden City, N.Y.: Doubleday, 1970), 6.

5. Julius Grodinsky, *Jay Gould, His Business Career, 1867–1892* (Philadelphia: University of Pennsylvania Press, 1957), 124–26; Edwin P. Hoyt, *The Goulds, a Social History* (New York: Weybright and Talley, 1969), 59, 60.

6. Hoyt, *The Goulds,* 59, 60, Lavender, *Persuader,* 297–98; John H. Kemble, "The Big Four at Sea: The History of the Occidental and Oriental Steamship Companies," *Huntington Library Quarterly* 3 (April 1940): 341–46.

7. Grodinsky, *Gould,* 145–48.

8. Ibid.; D. S. Babcock, *To the Stockholders of the Pacific Mail Steamship Company* (New York, 1878).

9. Lavender, *Persuader,* 337.

10. *San Francisco Chronicle,* 12 January 1936, p. 3.

11. Pacific Mail Steamship Company, Annual Report 1899, p. 10, Huntington Library.

12. *San Francisco Call,* 23 February 1901.

13. Pacific Mail Steamship Company, Annual Report 1916, p. 4, Huntington Library.

14. Ibid., Annual Report 1922, pp. 3–4, Huntington Library.

15. N. E. Harrison, "Dollar Steamship Company," *The Guide,* 29 August 1969; *Shipping Register,* 4 April 1925.

3
RISE OF THE DOLLAR STEAMSHIP COMPANY

ON a bright day in early July 1902, the 5,000-ton Pacific Mail steamer *China* headed out through the Golden Gate bound for Honolulu, Yokohama, Kobe, Nagasaki, Shanghai, and Hong Kong. She carried a cargo of general merchandise consigned not only to her ports of call but also for transshipment to Korea, the Philippines, Java, Singapore, Penang, and India. In her strong room was $280,572 in treasure. Although it was summer and the peak of the travel season, her cabin accommodations were only a little over half-filled—fifty-eight passengers. Of these, half were destined for Honolulu, fifteen for Japan, and twelve for Chinese ports. In a pinch she could accommodate 1,150 people—primarily Orientals—in steerage, but she had only about half that number aboard.[1]

The most notable of her cabin passengers was former Queen Liliuokalani of Hawaii, who traveled with a party of three. Among other passengers however, was a spare, vigorous man of fifty-eight who soon made himself known to the ship's officers and to many of the passengers. Whether he came to know the former queen and whether he and his wife sat at Captain Freile's table is not a matter of record. He was certainly intensely curious about the ship, her engines, her Chinese crew, her ports of call, cargo, and other aspects of her operation. His fellow passengers also found him to be curious about their own interests and lives, especially if they had lived in the Orient. They in turn would have noted that he was a deeply religious man whose conversation was punctuated with biblical expressions, that he did not drink or smoke, and that he was a Scot by birth.

He was Robert Dollar, a resident of San Rafael, California, a lumberman and ship owner himself, as he proudly explained. In fact, he was president of the Dollar Steamship Company, which had just been organized, and which operated the largest fleet of steam schooners on the West Coast. These ships carried lumber from Dollar's and other mills in the forests of northern California, Oregon, and Washington to the cities and railheads of central and southern California. One of them, the *Arab*, built at Hunter's Point, California, 375 feet in length and with a timber capacity of 3,150,000 board feet, was chartered by Dollar from her owners for a test voyage to the Orient.[2]

A canny, cautious man, Dollar would not have made this experiment had he not first secured a government cargo for the Philippines, which covered the costs of a round trip. Satisfied with her performance in an ocean voyage with a cargo other than lumber, Dollar purchased the *Arab* and then chartered her to the Sperry Flour Company. She carried a full load of flour to the Orient without incident, and returned with a mixed cargo of fragile merchandise from China and Japan. Her consignee in San Francisco reported that not one piece of her cargo had been damaged in transit. Reassured that the *Arab* could be put to profitable use in the trans-Pacific trade and anxious to exploit the Chinese and Japanese demand for lumber, Dollar decided to ship a cargo to the Orient at his own risk. He would pick up whatever freight he could for the return voyage.[3]

Through San Francisco agents, Dollar had managed to sell a shipload of his lumber to Chinese merchants. Leaving the details of loading and arrangements for the departure of the *Arab* to his sons, R. Stanley and J. Harold, and his office assistant Hugo Lorber, Robert Dollar preceded her in the *China* with the intentions of meeting her in Shanghai. By then he was hopeful that he would have arranged a full cargo for her return voyage. He had, of course, written all of the established agents and export houses in China and Japan but had received no specific replies when he sailed in July 1902. Nor did he have any connections in the Far East other than the American consuls and ministers, none of whom he knew personally. For a shrewd Scotsman who had already made a fortune in the lumber business and who had capitalized on the sudden demand for shipping on the West Coast following the Klondike gold rush between 1896 and 1900, Dollar was speculating on the Far Eastern trade without any thorough preparation. Indeed, Dollar's involvement in shipping was purely accidental and was still in 1902 incidental to his lumber interests.

Just five years earlier, Robert Dollar had purchased his first vessel, the *Newsboy*, a 120-foot steam schooner of 185 tons. The *Newsboy*, which had been built in San Francisco in 1888, was especially designed for the northern California lumber trade. Except for Humboldt Bay, there were no harbors of any consequence adjoining the prime lumber lands. Harsh winter storms played such havoc with piers that lumbermen resorted to light-draft, powerfully built "lumber schooners" that could moor close to shore even in rough seas and swing logs or roughly sawn lumber aboard with either their booms or have them winched in by cable from high ground above the loading areas. Dollar himself has described these schooners:

> They are a peculiar type of vessel and can be found nowhere else in the world except on this coast. They are strongly built, with a low hull, and when loaded their decks are down to the water's edge and sometimes under. Ordinarily this would be considered dangerous, but the records on this coast for the last twenty years show that not a life has ever been lost by carrying this kind of load.[4]

For some years, Dollar, like other lumbermen in northern California, arranged with shipowners to pick up and deliver his lumber and to ferry supplies for his camps. But in the spring of 1895, the *Newsboy* failed to meet her schedule for a large shipment of Dollar lumber. Exasperated because he could not make delivery on time and thus had to find another customer, Dollar went to a ship broker and offered whatever amount was necessary to purchase a controlling interest in the *Newsboy*. When this was concluded, Dollar found himself in the shipping business because the savings in charter costs for the *Newsboy* pointed to the acquisition of other lumber schooners. By 1902, his newly formed shipping company owned ten steamers or steam schooners ranging from the tiny *Newsboy* to the *Arab*, which was twenty times larger and capable of trans-Pacific navigation.[5]

When Dollar arrived in Yokohama, he sought and received information on the markets of the Far East from two American shipping firms. Still fact-finding, he made several visits in Hong Kong before he felt prepared to approach any of the big trading firms. In the midst of a downpour he journeyed to Kowloon and had an interview with one of the partners of the rich and powerful trading company Jardine, Matheson. Polite but distant, company principals would be willing to act as Dollar agents but were distinctly unenthusiastic about future business prospects for what they made plain was a carrier unknown to their clientele. To the astute, aggressive Dollar, such an attitude was clearly not in the interest of a new enterprise. He would search elsewhere. But he met several rebuffs until he realized that he would not only have to sell himself and his company to a reputable agent, but communicate his own enthusiasm so that his ships would be well represented in the freight market.[6]

Dollar knew that he could sell his lumber in Japan, China, and the Philippines. What he desperately needed were return cargoes that would provide a decent margin of profit. And this meant an energetic and imaginative sales effort, not just in the Far East, but also among American import traders. In particular it meant building up a network of agents and personal contacts with merchants, manufacturers, and government personnel in the Far East and potential customers for their exports in the United States. Before he left Hong Kong, Dollar did manage to secure a satisfactory agent in Arnold Karberg and Company. But then and for the remainder of his active career, Dollar was his own best agent. With his white goatee, his habit of cocking his head to the right when he talked, his direct speech, and his unerring instinct to seek out and flatter just the right person for swinging a deal, Dollar became a well-known and highly successful figure in the shipping world.[7]

Meanwhile, through his own efforts, Dollar managed to secure a large cargo of sulphur for the *Arab,* which he met as arranged in the Yangtze River off Woosung. He then sailed in the *Arab* for Japan, where he was able to load 400 tons of general cargo for the United States. But he was still very much the lumberman. Though it was now fall and the stormy Japanese winter was near at hand, Dollar journeyed to northern Japan, where he had been told large stands of prime oak timber were available. He satisfied himself that this was so and departed for home in the *Arab* during a fierce, icy gale.

Besides her cargo, the *Arab* carried twenty-six Chinese sailors Dollar had recruited for manning a new acquisition that he had named the *Stanley Dollar* after his second son and office manager. When the *Arab* arrived in San Francisco, the immigration service refused permission to land her Chinese passengers, citing provisions of the Chinese Exclusion Act. After a month's delay which tied up the *Arab* as well as the *Stanley Dollar* and thus cost the company a considerable sum, Dollar managed to get a Treasury Department ruling that released the Chinese to the *Stanley Dollar.*[8]

The fledgling shipping line could not afford such costly delays in the future. Competition in the Pacific trade was intense. Not only the mighty, long-established Pacific Mail, but Japanese and British carriers were bidding for the market. Dollar placed the vessels he intended to use in the trans-Pacific trade under British registry, thus avoiding any foreseeable problem in using exclusively Oriental crews. He also employed foreign officers, usually of British nationality.[9]

Dollar would have been happy to have his ships flying the American flag, provided they were subsidized for all outward-bound voyages so that operating costs, including of course wages for officers and men, were in line with those of foreign carriers. He also insisted there be no requirement that his ships be built in American shipyards, where construction costs were from one-third to one-half more than those abroad. One of the factors in cost differentials for American-built ships was the high price of domestic steel because of the tariff. Like all American shipbuilders and merchants from colonial days, Dollar found that free trade coincided with his interests. Testifying before the House Merchant Marine Committee, Dollar pointed out that the new 7,000-ton steamer *Hazel Dollar,* which was being built for his company in Port Glasgow, Scotland, would cost $195,456, while the lowest bid he had received from an American yard was $450,000.[10]

By now Dollar had committed himself to the Pacific trade. Westbound cargoes were primarily lumber, and his newest ship, the *Hazel Dollar,* was designed as a lumber carrier. The problem of return cargoes now claimed all his energies.

Never a man to miss an opportunity, Dollar took advantage of the war between Russia and Japan to charter the *M. S. Dollar* to the Russian government, which was anxious to supply Port Arthur, its outpost in Manchuria, then under Japanese siege and blockade. She was, however, seized by the Japanese navy and condemned as a contraband carrier. Fully covered by war-risk insurance, Dollar stood to make a substantial profit whether she succeeded in running the blockade or not. As it turned out, Dollar was able to repurchase the *M. S. Dollar* from a Japanese prize court for $60,000 after Lloyd's had paid him $180,000 for the loss.

Even when the converted army transport *Stanley Dollar,* his other ship in the Pacific trade, ran aground off Japan and was adjudged a total loss, Dollar in effect got rid of an old, inefficient steamer and received an insurance settlement that was more than he had paid for her. These were typical of the shrewd business practices Dollar engaged in during the early years of his Pacific shipping venture.

Dollar was, of course, taking some risks, but luck was running with him as he slowly and cautiously expanded his commitment and scurried about the Orient, making contacts and digging up business. His most successful venture in these early years was in the purchase and carriage of Japanese oak railroad ties to China and, incredible as it seems, to the U.S. West Coast, where there was an abundance of wood. Despite the efforts of Pacific Mail to drive Dollar Steamship out of the Pacific market, Dollar succeeded in selling its parent company, the Southern Pacific Railroad, large quantities of Japanese oak railroad ties. From 1906 until the advent of World War I, Japanese oak logs formed an important return cargo for Dollar ships. And in 1911, Dollar ships brought the first cargo of Philippine mahogany to the West Coast.[11]

The business of the line during these formative years was largely a tramping operation. Lumber cargoes, many of them the product of Dollar mills, were shipped out on consignment to China and Japan. Dollar himself and his agents in the Far East gradually built up an eastbound, mixed freight business. One 1908 return cargo carried by the *Hazel Dollar,* for example, was made up of 500 tons of Chinese pig iron, 178 packages of tea, and from Japanese ports 1,500 bags of coal, 850 bags of charcoal, 4,000 bags of wheat bran, and smaller items in general cargo.[12]

The closest to a scheduled return voyage for Dollar ships was in a commodity Dollar himself pioneered in the Orient and in California. And even this business, the importation of Chinese iron and steel, was precarious because it depended on the unstable Chinese government, the vagaries of the domestic steel market on the West Coast, competition from the American steel industry, government restrictions on imported iron, and tariff barriers on foreign steel.

Yet Dollar managed to develop a lucrative business in this trade for a number of years. He overcame all obstacles, including the Chinese Revolution of 1912. On a trip to China in 1909 Dollar had made a deal with Han Yeh Ping, China's only iron mining and production company. If he could find a market in the United States,

Bessie Dollar. Built in 1905 as the *J. Abernethy* in Port Glasgow. Acquired by Dollar, she was renamed and placed in trans-Pacific cargo service. Here she is shown sailing with a deckload of lumber. Note her name on the bow in Chinese characters. (APL Archives.)

he agreed to purchase up to 100,000 tons of iron ore each year for the next three years at a price to be determined when he negotiated its resale. Then characteristically, he secured his home base by purchasing sufficient stock in a small independent steel company, Western Steel of Irondale, Washington, to influence its policy. He persuaded the board of Western that he could purchase and transport to Irondale Chinese iron ore and pig iron cheaper than it could be delivered from American sources. Next, he took the works manager of Western, Herbert E. Low, with him to China. There they negotiated an agreement with Han Yeh Ping for 72,000 tons of iron ore each year over a three-year period. Dollar drove such a hard bargain that the Chinese government, which controlled Han Yeh Ping, objected. But after further discussion a compromise was set that satisfied all parties.

Dollar described the advantages of his line to China and to the Pacific Northwest. With some pardonable hyperbole he said:

> They sell and the Western Steel Co. buys for a term of years a minimum of 36,000 tons of pig iron a year, with a maximum amount after one year of 72,000 tons of ore and a like amount of pig iron. This will be shipped from Hankow on the Yangtze River being over 600 miles from the ocean. The magnitude of this deal can be better understood by stating that it will take 35 cargoes of the largest cargo steamers to carry it each year, and the amount of money the Chinese will receive will be three times the amount of the indemnity returned to the United States Government and seeing that the steamer will have to go to the center of China to get the cargoes, it should open up a great trade with the interior of China that is not reached at present.[13]

The importance of Chinese iron ore and pig iron to the economy of the West Coast did not live up to Dollar's grandiose predictions, nor to the extravagant promotional rhetoric in the Seattle, San Francisco, and Los Angeles press.[14] But it did earn revenues for the Dollar Steamship Company. More than that, it opened up profitable connections in China.

As Dollar's trade with the Far East increased, he became more involved with the efforts of the San Francisco Chamber of Commerce to promote the economic growth of the city and state. In addition he was an active member of Merchant's Exchange. Articulate and a born booster, Dollar tirelessly proclaimed the benefits and the potential of the Pacific trade. At the same time he campaigned for a relaxation in regulations that discriminated against Chinese immigrants.

His motives, while expressed in high-minded cadences, were in reality less exalted than they appeared. He knew that anti-Chinese feeling on the West Coast would not tolerate any changes in immigration policy and that state and federal governments were unlikely to change their laws on the subject. But his pro-Chinese stand, well reported in the press, earned him the friendship and support of the Chinese community in California, some of whose members were influential traders. More important than this goodwill was the impression he made on the Chinese government and on the wealthy and influential merchants in Hong Kong, Hangchow, and Shanghai. Moreover, Dollar had another objective in mind. He was combatting a coordinated move of labor unions on the West Coast to prevent shipping interests from hiring Oriental crews, primarily Chinese. Dollar already had the reputation of discriminating against American labor. As the editor of the *Coast Seaman's Journal* remarked, "Captain Dollar has so persistently practiced and encouraged the employment of coolie labor that the very names of his ships have become tainted and malodorous bywords."[15]

Besides these public relations activities that paid off in image-building and, as a result, increased trade, Dollar sought through various ways to combat the longshoremen's unions in the West Coast ports. No amount of savings on Oriental crews or in sharp dealing could alter the fact that cargoes had to be handled in American ports by American workers. Year by year the trend toward unionization among longshoremen and seamen was accelerating. And with the increase in union membership, the incidence of strikes and higher labor costs in American ports accounted for larger segments in the annual budgets of the shipping lines.

Dollar, whose business values were rooted in an earlier age of individualism and of laissez-faire when it came to one's private property, had always frowned upon union activity. If the economic health of his impromptu commercial activities was threatened and the small margin on which he operated between profit and loss seemed in jeopardy from higher labor costs, he could and did take drastic action.[16]

Although the Dollar Line freighters in the Pacific trade were under British registry and operated by foreign crews, its coastal vessels had to be under the American flag. And since the 1890s a large and, indeed, the most profitable share of its business continued to be in local West Coast traffic, primarily the carrying of lumber. In 1913 Andrew Furuseth, the Norwegian-born head of International Seamen's Union, managed to line up Robert La Follette, the progressive senator from Wisconsin, behind a bill to bring much-needed reforms in the working conditions of American merchant seamen.

Dollar joined forces with his erstwhile rival Rennie Schwerin, head of Pacific Mail, to fight the proposed legislation. Both men lobbied unsuccessfully to defeat the bill, which became law in 1915.[17]

Paradoxically, the legislation that he had so bitterly opposed proved to be of great benefit to Dollar. At least in part as a reaction to the law, the Southern Pacific Railroad, the parent company of Pacific Mail, decided to close down the line. It was a rash decision taken without fully considering the immediate future of the shipping business in a world at war. For a brief period the Dollar Line was able to improve its position in the Pacific trade. In a year when the Pacific trade was responding to wartime demands and enjoying a boom, no Pacific Mail vessels called at Japanese and Chinese ports. But numerous freighters flaunted the impudent white Dollar sign on their red stacks.

Despite increases in operating costs due to the virtual elimination of Oriental crews in its coastal trade, the Dollar Line's overall revenues showed sharp increases in 1915 and again in 1916.[18] By now an acute worldwide shortage had developed in shipping. Allied demands, the United States government's preparedness program, and German submarine sinkings of Allied vessels had all created a seller's market for steamers of all ages, designs, and specifications.

Robert Dollar made huge profits buying and selling vessels while the shortage lasted. A prime example of his activities was the old Mexican steamer, the *General Y. Pesqueira*. Enroute to Australia with a cargo of coal, she was purchased through a broker by the mayor of San Francisco, James Rolph, for $200,000. He in turn sold her to the Dollar Line for $225,000. When she reached her destination she had become Japanese property. Dollar had sold her for $275,000, making a profit on this deal alone of $50,000. In May 1916 he sold the *Robert Dollar* for $1,300,000 to the Japanese government. Five years before he had paid A. Rodger and Company of Glasgow $450,000 for her. Dollar himself recorded in his diary that the sale of the *Robert Dollar* was "the highest price on record for a vessel of this class."[19] In 1917 he sold two more ships—the *Melville Dollar*, a small, steel-screw steamer, and a larger vessel, the *Mackinaw*. But he did not invest any of this surplus cash in enlarging his fleet or even in replacing vessels he had sold.

During the United States' participation in the war, the Dollar fleet shrank to its smallest size in a decade. Only two vessels, the *Stanley Dollar* and the *Agnes Dollar*, maintained coastal operations, although both of these ships were also used on the trans-Pacific trade as occasion warranted. Four steamers, the venerable *M.S. Dollar*, formerly the *Arab* and the line's first ship in the Pacific trade, continued to ply between San Francisco and Far Eastern ports. In addition, the *Hazel, Bessie,* and *Harold Dollar,* all freighters slightly over 4,300 tons each, made up the total Dollar commitment to the Pacific routes. Yet these vessels, all under British registry, earned unprecedented profits.

Particularly lucrative was the Russian trade. Freighters loaded with trucks, field kitchens, and railroad flatcars discharged at Vladivostok and returned by way of Chinese, Japanese, and Philippine ports. Each voyage, it was calculated, paid in profits half the original cost of the vessel. Why then did the Dollar Line not expand its fleet? A combination of circumstances had created this conservative policy. Vessels had become too costly to purchase or to build, in Dollar's reckoning. Heightened competition from a revitalized Pacific Mail, along with increased Japanese shipping on these routes, were also factors in the decision.

A new government agency, the U.S. Shipping Board, had been established in 1916. It formed the Emergency Fleet Corporation a year later to build and operate ships for the Allied war effort. While Dollar maintained a close personal relationship with members of the board, he refused to involve his shipping line with government charters, which would require American registry and the employment of American crews. It would likewise require a rapid expansion of personnel and facilities that Robert Dollar was not prepared to undertake. The Dollar organization was a small, tightly controlled family business. Temporary profits from government charters spelled a disruption of traditional practices and a considerable investment of capital funds.

Robert Dollar was quite willing to wait out the war for what he regarded as a much better business proposition, the peace that would throw millions of tons of shipping on the market at bargain prices. Besides these elements, Dollar considered the labor situation on the West Coast too unstable for any sustained enlargement of his fleet. A longshoremen's strike in the summer of 1916 tied up all American ports for a month. The union did not receive the closed shop, its principal demand, but it did wring a wage increase from the stubborn shippers and merchants in San Francisco. Dollar had taken a prominent part in the negotiations, at one point even condoning vigilante action against the strikers.[20]

Despite the failure of the strike, operating costs continued to climb as inflation gripped the war economy. Fuel doubled in price.

The government clamped restrictions on passenger travel and took over ships for military use. Crews were increasingly difficult to enlist on the West Coast since the Shipping Board recruited seagoing personnel for the Atlantic routes. Such uncertainty in the shipping industry dictated caution to a shrewd operator like Dollar. There was money to be made in other ventures not so unpredictable as shipping.[21]

Although his policy regarding the Dollar Line was conservative during 1917 and 1918, Robert Dollar made substantial investments in China and in a new shipping firm, the Pacific Steamship Company, that was operating out of Seattle. With some financial backing from a recent acquaintance, Herbert Fleishhacker, president of the Anglo, London and Paris National Bank and a young, aggressive San Francisco financier, the Dollar Line purchased a controlling interest in the China Import and Export Company for $550,000. Thus the line came into possession of one of the best-located wharves and warehouses in Shanghai.[22] But this too was a speculation. In November 1919 Dollar sold the line's 51 percent interest to Charles E. Dant of Portland, Oregon, for $1 million, almost doubling his investment in less than a year.[23] A few months later he purchased another tract of land that would make an excellent location for terminal facilities on the Shanghai waterfront. In due course this tract became the center of the line's operations in the China trade.[24]

Dollar's eye for choice real estate was not confined to the Far East. When a five-story office building on the corner of California and Battery streets in San Francisco's Financial District came on the market, Dollar purchased it for $425,000. The company's offices, which had outgrown its quarters at 149 California Street, were moved to the new location. Here, at 311 California Street, the executive offices of the Dollar Line remained throughout its active business life. Later, six stories were added at a cost of $245,000. Dollar signs and dolphins formed a design in concrete around the building's flamboyant entrance.[25] That the war years had been most profitable to the Dollar Line and the Dollars personally is shown by the amount of federal income tax the family paid during the war years. On 1918 revenues alone the Dollars paid more than $1 million in taxes.[26]

In late 1918, with the Great War over, Dollar did briefly consider building a fleet of combination passenger and freight steamers, and a public announcement was made to this effect. But he changed his mind, deciding it would be cheaper to wait and purchase ships on what he felt would be a falling market. And then there came an opportunity to invest in an established line, the Pacific Steamship Company, at bargain prices. He and his sons Stanley and Melville met with H. F. Alexander, its president, who was riding high as the shipping tycoon of the West Coast. Alexander was directing the financial fortunes of Pacific Steam, the largest coastal and trans-Pacific fleet then operating under the American flag. But his company was overextended and he was having a difficult time coping with the confusion the immediate postwar period brought to the American shipping industry. Nothing came of the first conference with Alexander except a resolution on the part of the Dollars to begin buying quietly and through proxies stock in Alexander's company, whose shares sharply declined in market value throughout the year 1919. By 1921 the Dollars owned more voting stock in the line than did Alexander. That year Robert Dollar and his sons Stanley and Melville were elected to Pacific Steamship's board. They did not, however, have a controlling interest. Alexander continued to head the management of the company, which was widely known by its trade name, the Admiral Line.[27]

The time now seemed ripe to purchase vessels. But certain moves had to be made if the Dollars were to capitalize on an anticipated postwar expansion in the shipping business. Dollar's third son, Harold, was sent to Shanghai to supervise construction of a wharf and office building. Dollar himself purchased an eighteen-acre tract at Hunt's Point in the Bronx, New York, adjoining other parcels of land that he had acquired earlier. As he announced to the press, the Hunt's Point property would be the terminal for a direct service between Shanghai and New York.[28] That these were not idle words was borne out by the purchase of four freighters over the next year. The ships, all foreign-built and all placed under British registry, were the *Grace Dollar, M.S. Dollar, Esther Dollar,* and *Robert Dollar,* which at 10,883 tons was the largest cargo vessel in the world. When these purchases were made, the Dollars were already formulating plans to inaugurate a "round-the-world" service. On 19 February 1921 Robert Dollar made these plans public. The Dollars took this step in the midst of the short, sharp depression of 1921 when overall freight rates had plummeted to historic lows and cutthroat competition, especially in the Asian market, ruled out any effort to stabilize them through shipping conferences.[29] To a startled commercial community in San Francisco, the Dollar Line seemed to have sprung up suddenly like a white squall, threatening to overturn accustomed ways of doing business.

NOTES

1. *San Francisco Chronicle*, 9 July 1902; Robert Dollar, *Memoirs* (San Francisco: Privately printed, 1917), 30.

2. Robert Dollar, *One hundred thirty Years of Steam Navigation: A History of the Merchant Ship* (San Francisco: Privately printed, 1931), 134.

3. *San Francisco Call*, 21 January 1902.

4. U.S. Congress, House Merchant Marine Committee, Hearings, 58th Cong., 3d sess., 1905, 2:1288.

5. Dollar, *Steam Navigation*, 131.

6. Diary of Robert Dollar, 2, 20 August 1902, Dollar Collection, Bancroft Library, University of California, Berkeley, California.

7. Ibid.

8. *San Francisco Examiner*, 29 December 1902.

9. Gregory C. O'Brien, "The Life of Robert Dollar," Ph.D. diss., Claremont Graduate School, 1968.

10. U.S. Congress, House Merchant Marine Committee, Report, 58th Cong., 3d sess., 1905, 2:1287.

11. O'Brien, "Robert Dollar," 136; *San Francisco Daily Commercial News*, 30 November 1909.

12. *Los Angeles Times*, 27 August 1908.

13. Diary of Robert Dollar, 21, 22 March 1910; Dollar, *Memoirs*, 1:297.

14. See, for instance, *Seattle Post-Intelligencer*, 27, 29 March 1910; *San Francisco Examiner*, 15 May 1910; *Los Angeles Express*, 16 May 1910.

15. *Coast Seaman's Journal*, 22 September 1915.

16. O'Brien, "Robert Dollar," 79–82.

17. *New York Times*, 21 July 1915; O'Brien, "Robert Dollar," 178, 179.

18. O'Brien, "Robert Dollar," 176.

19. Diary of Robert Dollar, 16 May 1916.

20. Dollar, *Memoirs*, 3–4:67.

21. Giles Brown, *Ships That Sail No More* (Lexington: University of Kentucky Press, 1966), 45–50.

22. O'Brien, "Robert Dollar," 19.

23. Diary of Robert Dollar, 13 November 1920.

24. Ibid., 20, 31 July 1917.

25. Ibid., 25 December 1913; 16 December 1918.

26. O'Brien, "Robert Dollar," 205.

27. The Dollars owned 3,767 shares out of the 15,000 shares outstanding. Alexander owned 2,974 shares. See Brown, *Ships That Sail No More*, 84.

28. Diary of Robert Dollar, 29 October, 1 November 1919.

29. O'Brien, "Robert Dollar," 231.

4

DOLLAR TRIUMPHANT

THE two men liked each other. One was tall and spare with rather sharp features and deceptively mild brown eyes. He was Albert D. Lasker, advertising giant of the decade, now chairman of the United States Shipping Board, a post to which he had been recruited in recognition of his part in the election of Warren G. Harding to the presidency. The other man was big and ruddy of face, portly, and self-assured in speech and manner. He was R. Stanley Dollar, a vice president of the family-owned shipping company and next in line to his father, the dominant force in the firm. They had just completed an agreement after a week of conferences with the entire board that would have a pronounced impact on the fortunes of two shipping lines and the economic future of the Northwest.

Dollar had been one of a troop of shipping men who had been calling at the Shipping Board's headquarters in Washington for the past year and a half. They were all eyeing the huge fleet of ships valued at $3.5 billion that the government was building. New ships ordered for the war effort were still coming off the ways. In all the board found itself in 1921 with some 1,740 ships, ranging from the 57,000-gross-ton ex-German liner *Leviathan* through the 535s, the 14,000-gross-tonnage, combination passenger-freight liners, through the ugly, mass-produced Hog Island freighters to tugs and barges.[1]

Since the war's end various shipping lines were operating Shipping Board vessels on a bareboat charter basis or as managing operators. But there had been no definite policy. Finally in 1920 Congress passed and President Wilson signed into law a comprehensive Merchant Marine Act that established a permanent Shipping Board. The act also presaged the sale of the government's huge fleet to private interests. It was so broad in scope that it gave the board a virtual carte blanche over what was to be done with several billion dollars worth of public property. The five men who made up the board could continue its charter policy under terms most advantageous to the shipping industry; or it could operate its own ships; or it could contract with private companies to run ships; or it could sell them below cost on the open market. Nothing was done to implement the act during its first year of existence because the Republican-dominated Congress refused to confirm Wilson's recess appointees to the board. Harding had no such trouble, and by June 1921 the Senate had confirmed a new board, headed by Lasker.[2]

The Merchant Marine Act had been passed as a result of intense lobbying on the part of the shipping industry, other transportation interests, investment bankers, and representatives of port cities and railroads. Now that the business-oriented board was ready to function, its anterooms and offices were crowded with the same group of interested parties. To that place had come H. F. Alexander, president of the Pacific Steamship Company, representing the shipping business of Washington and Oregon, and his competent deputy Ancil F. Haines. And certainly not the man to miss out on any opportunity, old "Captain" Robert Dollar appeared to extol the future of the Far East trade. Buttressing Dollar's arguments was Herbert Fleishhacker, the San Francisco banker. He disclosed the substantial liquid capital he and Dollar were willing to commit if the government would provide the ships. Dollar's son Stanley followed in the wake of his father. He impressed the board with his apparent knowledge of shipping, administrative capacity, and, what most appealed to Lasker the advertising man, his flair for salesmanship.

What the Dollars and Fleishhacker wanted was a chance to strengthen their Pacific service out of San Francisco and to extend it to the entire Northwest. This meant either dealing with or dealing out H. F. Alexander, whose Pacific Steamship Company was expanding its westbound service from Tacoma and Seattle.

Of course the Dollar missions would have been futile had Alexander's Pacific Steamship Company been in a strong financial position. Alexander was not without powerful friends in Washington nor was he without experience. Unlike the Dollars he had devoted a lifetime to the shipping industry. An imposing man with a heavy, square face, he had considerable ability, and, it must be said, some rather grave weaknesses as a businessman. Though his appearance belied it, Alexander was a born gambler with a fatal fascination for quick profits that usually eluded him throughout most of the spec-

Robert Dollar (left), H. F. Alexander (center), and Mrs. Robert Dollar at Pier 36, Seattle. In the background is the steamer *H. F. Alexander.* (Courtesy The Williamson Collection, Puget Sound Maritime Historical Society, Seattle, Washington.)

tacular career that had carried him to the top of the West Coast shipping industry. In 1921 he was overextended. He had expanded his company so rapidly that he found himself without either the staff or more particularly, the financial resources to support his far-flung operations. Perhaps this flaw in an otherwise admirable executive was the result of a poverty-stricken youth spent clawing his way up through the ranks from a longshoreman on the docks to the presiding officer of Pacific Steam.

Born in 1879, Alexander had to forego formal education and at an early age take a job on the docks at twenty cents an hour to help support his family, made destitute by the panic of 1893. Yet five years later he had made the right connections to control the stevedoring company he worked for. After eight years as the head of the Commercial Dock Company of Tacoma, he plowed all of the cash he had saved and all he could borrow into a risky venture that a small group of businessmen from Tacoma and Seattle had put together, the Alaska Pacific Steamship Company.

The new line had nothing to do with Alaska and very little to do with the Pacific except that its one old vessel provided a weekly cargo and freight service from the Puget Sound to San Francisco.[3] Alexander had scarcely moved into the president's office of the new line when he disclosed considerable financial talents. Utilizing his relatively worthless stock in Alaska Pacific as collateral he managed to borrow enough money to purchase control of another fly-by-night shipping concern, the Alaska Coast Company, which at least involved Alaska in its operations since its three small vessels sailed between Seattle and Alaska ports.

For three years Alexander operated these two lines at marginal earnings. He managed to keep his ships in service through aggressive sales efforts that he conducted personally, but, more important, through a strategy of playing his major competitors in the coastal traffic against each other. At the time there were six lines competing for the traffic, all of which were larger and better financed than Alexander's.

The strongest and oldest line was the Pacific Coast Steamship Company, which traced its lineage back to the second coastal line to be established on the West Coast. Founded by Charles Goodall and Chris Nelson in 1860, the Pacific Coast Steamship Company had for years offered the best passenger and freight service from Seattle north to Alaska and south to the California ports.

The Southern Pacific Railroad and later the Great Northern also divided a substantial share of the coastal market. But in 1910 yet another competitor, the Metropolitan Steamship Company, challenged the established lines. Backed by eastern financial interests, Metropolitan sent its two new steamers, the *Harvard* and the *Yale*, to the West Coast. Faster than any of their rivals, these two vessels immediately attracted a sustaining patronage.

In this three-way rivalry Alexander saw his chance. Previously he had combined his two struggling lines under a holding company, Pacific Alaska Navigation. The trade name he gave his reorganized operation was the Admiral Line. Even before the *Harvard* and *Yale* arrived on the West Coast, Alexander had made an arrangement with Metropolitan whereby the two lines would act in concert on schedules, through passenger tickets and bills of lading. From then on the Admiral Line gradually built up its fleet and improved its schedules. By 1916 it merged with its most dangerous rival, the Pacific Coast Steamship Company. Now virtually unchallenged in the coastal shipping business, Alexander changed the name of his holding company to the Pacific Steamship Company.

The entry of the United States in World War I had a crushing impact on coastal traffic, especially on the West Coast. Not only did the government requisition the best ships of the various lines, but it placed restrictions on travel to conserve fuel. In order to keep his line afloat, Alexander decided to experiment with a trans-Pacific route from the Northwest. In this effort he was attempting to improve the revenues of Pacific Steamship by challenging already established lines in the Far East like the Robert Dollar Company, the Pacific Mail Steamship Company, and the Great Northern Steamship Company, as well as Japanese and British lines. Some of these companies did not offer direct service from and to the ports of the Northwest, but all could and did take countermeasures.

On its first voyage to the Far East, Pacific Steamship sent its recently acquired *Senator,* a 2,500-ton coal-burning coastal steamer, to Singapore with a shipment of barrel staves, or box shooks as they were called, and other mixed cargo. This trial voyage was highly profitable. The *Senator* returned fully laden and earned $150,000 net profit for the Admiral Line. From March until December 1918 the *Senator* made three voyages, earning net profits of $343,935. Initial success prompted Alexander to increase his trans-Pacific operations. By the fall of 1918 he had chartered four ships from Libby, McNeil and Libby and had seven vessels on a regularly scheduled service to the Far East from Seattle.[4] A year later the Pacific Steamship Company was sailing eight vessels from Seattle to Yokohama, Kobe, and Hong Kong. Four were sailing on a regular schedule from Portland to the same ports in the Far East. All of these vessels were under bareboat charters from private companies.

When the Shipping Board began to offer its surplus ships under much more favorable charter terms, Alexander quickly replaced his private charters as they completed their voyages with government-owned ships. By the spring of 1920 the Admiral Line was operating seventeen Shipping Board vessels and had expanded its service to the Philippines.[5] With the buoyant optimism that characterized Alexander's style, he applied for preferential rights to the new terminal the city of Seattle was building at a cost of $2.5 million. To accommodate freight operations under the American flag, the Shipping Board established seven foreign feeder services. Alexander secured the inter-island service for the Philippines and the Dollar company was awarded the service between Java and Hong Kong.[6]

The management-operating agreements known as MO4s that the board negotiated with privately owned shipping lines were so generous that the government-owned fleet lost an estimated $200 million over a period of eighteen months.[7] Under typical MO4 agreements, companies and individuals operating government-owned ships were paid a 5 percent fee on the gross revenues of a given voyage. The board underwrote all operating expenses. At great cost, the Shipping Board had achieved its major aim—the scheduled sailings of American-flag ships on major trade routes.

Like other companies Pacific Steam normally inflated the operating costs and either shared them with subcontractors for drydocking, fuel, and stevedoring companies or other suppliers of goods and services. If they performed these services themselves, as many did, the companies pocketed excessive charges. There were also accounting devices whereby gross revenues would be inflated. As the *Seattle Post-Intelligencer* declared, "the M.O. is the most shameful piece of chicanery, inefficiency and looting of the public treasury that the human mind can devise."[8]

During the two-year period ending December 1921, Pacific Steam managed to increase expenses by 80 percent, mainly through doubling its commission on inflated cargo revenues, and to show a loss of $93,301, which it charged to the government.[9] For the year 1919,

Pacific Steam showed net earnings under its MO4 contracts of $337,826.23, divided between an operator's commission of $200,695.77 and a manager's commission of $127,131.16. These two charges were reduced substantially in 1920, but a new entry, an agency fee of $108,527, more than made up the difference. Agency fees were reduced slightly to $99,359.62 in 1921, but at the same time operators' commissions were more than doubled.

If Alexander were to exploit the trans-Pacific traffic and the lucrative Shipping Board operating arrangements, he needed more capital to finance terminal facilities both in the United States and abroad.[10] The Dollars stood ready to supply the need, though, as Alexander would learn, their support carried with it grave risks to his independence.

He also had to expand staff considerably, and his first move in this direction was the employment of Ancil F. Haines as general manager. Haines was an experienced shipping man who had spent many years as an executive with Dodwell and Company, Seattle agents for the British Blue Funnel Line.[11]

Thoroughly familiar with the trans-Pacific trade, Haines rapidly built up an organization in the Far East and in the United States. Pacific Steam had seventeen Shipping Board freighters under operating agreements from the Northwest to the Orient in 1920. Ten of these ships were sailing from Seattle and seven from Portland, sufficient for Haines to establish a regular twenty-eight-day service between Seattle and Singapore by way of Yokohama, Kobe, Hong Kong, and Manila.

George J. McCarthy, San Francisco agent for the company and a Haines appointee, became chief passenger agent in the Far East with headquarters in Shanghai. On 18 March 1920 Earl F. Townsend of Seattle sailed on Pacific Steam's *City of Spokane* to be the company's agent in Singapore. The new sales organization was being directed by E. G. McMicken, general passenger agent, whose responsibilities also included freight.[12]

When the Shipping Board advised Pacific Steam in the winter of 1920 that it would be allocating several of its new 535s for a trade route from the Pacific Northwest to the Orient, Haines had the nucleus of staff to handle the large increase in operations that this implied.[13] At the board's insistence, the new service was to be separated from Pacific Steam's Admiral Line. Another line, the Admiral Oriental Mail, was created under the same management but

Aboard the *President Grant* in Seattle, about 1922. *Left to right:* Captain Mike Jensen, master of the *President Grant;* J. W. Spangler, president of the Seattle Chamber of Commerce; H. F. Alexander, president of the Pacific Steamship Company; Ancil F. Haines, vice president and general manager, Admiral Oriental Line. (Courtesy Allan Yost Collection.)

with a distinct house flag and its own organization. Admiral Oriental Mail would operate Pacific Steam's trans-Pacific service. Throughout 1921, five fast, large ships were delivered to Pacific Steam. The first was the *Wenatchee*, which the board had renamed the *President Jefferson. Silver State* followed her and then *Bay State, Keystone State*, and finally *Pine Tree State*. The ships were renamed, respectively, *President Jackson, President Madison, President McKinley,* and *President Grant.*

The *President* vessels were of the flush-deck type, 535 feet long. Each had accommodations for 257 first-class passengers and 300 in

third class. First-class quarters were comfortable, though not lux-
urious. Staterooms were arranged in pairs with connecting baths
and were fitted with twin beds rather than berths. Cargo capacity
was ample, some 11,000 tons in deadweight. There were seven
hatches, five of which were 30 feet long by 19 feet wide. The remaining two were 19 feet long by 18 feet wide. Fuel-oil tanks had a
capacity of 3,290 tons, sufficient for a round trip at cruising speed of
sixteen knots from Seattle or San Francisco to Yokohama and return.
Turbine-driven power plants developed 12,000 shaft horsepower. At
the time the *President* ships were the most modern, most efficient
cargo passengers liners in the world. Each one had cost the government about $6 million.

Pacific Steam had been presented with a fleet of ships that was
worth about $25 million, even in the depressed shipping market of
1921. Moreover, there was every indication that the board would
eventually dispose of them at a fraction of their original cost. The act
of 1920 provided also for a mail subsidy at rates that were lower than
those established in 1891 but still a factor in the revenue picture.[14]

It was a profit situation in the trans-Pacific routing pattern that
Robert Dollar could not resist,[15] especially when he learned that the
new chairman of the Shipping Board, Albert D. Lasker, was dissatis-
fied with Alexander's operations. As R. B. Bush, treasurer of Pacific
Steam and longtime associate of Ancil Haines remarked, "H. F.
Alexander was 'in dutch' with the USSB." Excessive charges on the
MO4s and considerable duplication of sailings from Portland and
Seattle had been the principal causes of complaint.[16] But Lasker was
also concerned about Alexander's finances.

Dollar and his sons acted swiftly. Stanley spoke confidentially
with Haines and enlisted his support if the Shipping Board decided
to move Alexander out of the trans-Pacific business. Then, after his
father had opened the way with a visit to Washington, Stanley had a
series of conferences with Lasker. The result of these meetings was
that Pacific Steam would form a new corporation, the Admiral Oriental Line, with a capital of $500,000. The Dollars would have complete
control. Haines would stay on as a vice president and general
manager. The other officers would be R. Stanley Dollar as president,
his brother J. Harold Dollar as a vice president, and longtime Dollar
associate and stockholder Hugo Lorber as another vice president.
Alexander was to be excluded completely from the affairs of Admiral
Oriental, which would operate the new 535s and seven additional

President Cleveland [I]. One of the "535" class purchased by Dollar in 1925. Here she is shown in San Francisco Bay sporting the APL stack marking used after 1938. (APL Archives.)

First-class lounge aboard the *President Jackson* [I]. She was a 535 and her designer aimed to give passenger quarters a distinctively American character. (Alfred T. Palmer Collection, APL Archives.)

Shipping Board cargo vessels on the Seattle-Hong Kong-Manila run. To ease any friction and head off a possible battle for control, Alexander would continue as president of Pacific Steam, whose Admiral Line would operate its coastal ships, still an important and profitable enterprise.[17]

When Stanley Dollar informed Alexander of the Shipping Board plans, he was deeply disturbed. He was too experienced a businessman not to realize that the board had become highly critical of some of his past policies. But he had hoped that the reforms Haines had made in charter arrangements and the reduction of sailing schedules would satisfy Washington. Neither he nor his associates were prepared for the Dollar takeover of the most promising part of Pacific Steam's business. Nor were they consoled by promises of support for the expansion of its coastal trade. As Stanley Dollar said, "The message which I brought home with me was a very great shock to Mr. Alexander and his associates, and it took some time for them to realize the situation." At first Alexander balked at any attempt to form a new corporation for the Pacific trade and was particularly adamant about the use of the Admiral Line identity and goodwill for the benefit of the venture. But when he received official confirmation from Lasker that the Shipping Board was determined to back the Dollar interests, he gave in. Lasker had telegraphed on 15 September 1922 that:

> Much to our regret Shipping Board feels conditions within the Pacific Company have made it impossible for Company to give such service to the Government's ships allocated to them both five thirty five's and cargoes as the Government's interests demand STOP Your very commendable expansion on your own account in coastwise trade has undoubtedly demanded so much of your time as to make it understandably impossible and impracticable for you to give the Government's ships that attention which an infant industry so much needs STOP. Therefore much to our regret we hereby give you notice under paragraph (a) of Section sixteen of the Managing Operating Four Agreement dated February one nineteen twenty one of cancellation of said agreement STOP As you know we are about to make M.O.4 contract for operation of the ships with a company to be formed known as the Admiral Oriental Line STOP Until Company has been legally formed we request you to continue operations for us as we cannot make contract until new Company is

duly incorporated in full accordance with law and can give bond
STOP. When this is accomplished and satisfactory arrangements for transfer are concluded between you and Mr. Dollar
we will be guided by your mutual decision as to the day for their
taking over of the boats STOP.[18]

Success in this move merely whetted the appetite of the Dollars
and their San Francisco banking associates. No sooner had the
Admiral Oriental Line been incorporated when Herbert Fleishhacker
journeyed to Washington, where he met with President Harding
and Lasker. Concerned with huge government losses in its merchant fleet, Lasker thought the Shipping Board should promptly sell
off its vessels to private concerns. But mindful of the cost differences
between ships operating under the American flag and those under
foreign aegis, Lasker wanted a subsidy above and beyond that
granted for carrying the mails. He easily convinced President Harding that such a policy would end embarrassing losses for the Shipping Board, would rationalize the nation's shipping, and would be
in line with the Republican party's current notions of aid to private
enterprise.

Thus Fleishhacker met with a favorable response when he proposed that all the shipping lines on the West Coast, admittedly
overextended for the available market, be combined into one concern. What Washington overlooked in initial support of the
Fleishhacker proposal was that the new combination would favor the
Dollar interests over their competitors and the city of San Francisco
over the cities of Los Angeles, Portland, Seattle, and Tacoma as well.
The plan made a splash in the newspapers, and Robert Dollar
headed a committee to work out the details. Strenuous opposition,
however, quickly asserted itself and the scheme eventually was
shelved.[19]

Meanwhile, the Admiral Oriental Line adopted the trade name of
Admiral Oriental Mail for its trans-Pacific service. The new company
took over Pacific Steam's organization in the Far East and purchased
terminal facilities from the Admiral Line. "My associates," wrote
Stanley Dollar, "have impressed upon me the difficult task this [is]
going to be. Father has been keenly interested in this business and
has decided to go to Seattle with me and assist in getting the
business properly started."[20]

And properly started it was. Its 535s were regularly carrying cargo of 10,000 to 12,000 tons of freight and 350 to 400 passengers outward bound. Even return cargoes were good. For example, the *President Jefferson*, which arrived in Seattle in mid-September 1922, carried 79 first-class passengers, 135 in steerage, and 4,000 bales of silk—the equivalent of 5,000 tons in general cargo.[21] This shipment was the forerunner of a significant trade that Admiral Oriental diverted from foreign lines. The great bulk of silk shipments to the United States would soon be carried under American flag to Seattle, where it was transshipped by railroad to the silk textile-producing and consuming centers in the eastern United States. From the fall of 1922 to the fall of 1925, the *President* liners carried over $300 million worth of raw silk.[22] Also during that period they steamed over 720,000 miles while their manifests showed that they carried a total of 36,000 passengers and 435,000 revenue tons of freight. Besides the *President* ships, Admiral Oriental also operated seven freighters on the Pacific route for the Shipping Board. Since the government was responsible for maintenance, the Admiral Oriental was a highly profitable undertaking.

When Lasker took over as chairman of the Shipping Board he tightened up administrative and auditing procedures and consolidated trade routes, which drastically reduced duplication. He also began to develop a policy for selling off the government's fleet. But in his short term as chairman, even as gifted and dynamic a businessman as Lasker could not completely eliminate abuses in the management-operating contracts. While the ships remained government property, the shipping lines that operated them neglected to provide adequate maintenance since the government was still responsible for ship overhaul in the navy yards.

As late as 1924, R. D. Gatewood, West Coast manager for the Shipping Board, complained bitterly about the condition of the *President Jackson*, one of the 535s operated by Admiral Oriental Mail Line. He wrote Ancil F. Haines:

> I had formerly held a high opinion of your port staff, but the condition of this vessel when she was opened up was so truly deplorable and it cost such a large amount to correct this, that I am constrained to modify my views. Nothing could possibly convince me that these vessels had not been operated at entirely too high a speed with entirely too short a turnaround in Seattle. There is entirely too much thought given to traffic and too little attention paid to the technical end of running these vessels.[23]

Another cost-cutting device that attracted much adverse publicity was the policy of Admiral Oriental to increase the ratio of Chinese to Caucasian crew members on the new 535s, in apparent violation of the La Follette Act. Under pressure from the government and the local press, management backed down and removed Chinese seamen from the deck gang, but it continued using them as stewards and as firemen in the engine rooms. The Shipping Board accepted for the time being Haines's explanation that only the most menial jobs in the engine room were assigned to Chinese and that Caucasians supervised them. As for the steward's department, Chinese employees were necessary, he maintained, because "they are used to taking care of the Oriental traffic, which is 90 percent of the total trans-Pacific passenger traffic, [and] because passengers prefer them." By 1924, however, the Shipping Board ruled that no Orientals could serve in either the deck gang or the engine room, and in August of that year it ordered that all Filipinos employed in those departments on the 535s be replaced by American citizens.[24] It would later rescind that order. As late as 1930, despite the Jones Act restriction, the Dollar Lines employed on their ships 2,048 Chinese nationals out of a total of 5,427 employees afloat.

These sharp practices on maintenance and operating costs were the result of policies the Dollars instituted when they gained control of the line. By the beginning of 1921 they were the largest stockholders in Pacific Steam, parent company of the Admiral Line. R. Stanley Dollar had become a vice president and his brother Melville treasurer of the company. Although they did not interfere in management at first, their influence was felt, especially in areas where cost-cutting would improve profit potential even if only a short-term gain was the result.

Alexander's Admiral Line was likewise enjoying unprecedented revenues on its coastal trade. Despite intense competition Pacific Steam had expanded its operations after losing its Pacific trade to the Dollars. Spearheaded by its big new flagship the *H. F. Alexander,* the Admiral Line increased its revenues to $20 million by 1924.[25] Dollar capital, a part of the understanding that purchased Alexander's support, was to some extent responsible for the success of the Admiral Line during the mid-twenties. But Alexander continued to chafe under the restrictions imposed on his exuberant spirit. Supported by Seattle and Portland interests who felt—not without reason—that the Dollars were favoring San Francisco at their expense,

Alexander sought to block the sale of the 535s to Admiral Oriental Mail in 1925.

The Dollars had just concluded arrangements to purchase five 535s that the venerable Pacific Mail was managing for the Shipping Board on the run from San Francisco to the Far East. Stanley had driven a hard bargain with the government. Ships that had cost over $30 million were sold for $5,625,000. And of this sum the Dollar Steamship Company had put up only $140,625, or 2½ percent of the purchase price.

Nothing better illustrates R. Stanley Dollar's audacious style than this deal. He had been negotiating for the Pacific Mail's ships over a two-year period. Opposition had been constant and sometimes intense as Pacific Mail exerted political and financial pressure. Finally, in a preliminary decision on 31 March 1925, the Shipping Board by a close vote of four to three accepted the Dollar Line's bid, ruling that the Pacific Mail's bid was illegal even though it had offered over $1 million more than the Dollar Line for the five ships. Rejection of its bid was ostensibly because Pacific Mail would purchase the ships with a down payment of $1,250,000 in cash, the balance to be paid in the preferred stock of a new company on whose board of directors seven members would be named by the Shipping Board and four members named by Pacific Mail. Provision would be made for dividends on the stock of 4½ percent for the preferred shares, 6 percent for the common. The Dollar offer, if considerably lower, was more straightforward and conformed to the Shipping Board guidelines, being simply a certain amount down, the remainder to be amortized over a ten-year period after a grace period of two years. Whatever the merits or shortcomings of either proposal, the final decision went in favor of the Dollars. On 2 April 1925 three Republicans on the board, its chairman, T. V. O'Connor (who had succeeded Lasker), Meyer Lissner, and Edward Haney, voted to accept the Dollar bid. Vice chairman Edward C. Plumer and W. S. Benson, both Democrats, opposed the decision. Two of the commissioners, one a Democrat and the other a Republican, were absent.[26] According to one man deeply involved in the negotiations on the Pacific Mail side, the cost of the Shipping Board decision in favor of the Dollars was $32,000, which Stanley Dollar "lost" to O'Connor at poker.

The Robert Dollar Company paid R. Stanley Dollar a commission of $281,225 for his share in the acquisition of the ships, and it stood ready to pay another commission when the 535s under bareboat charter to Admiral Oriental Mail came up for purchase. In all, the two companies paid Dollar $698,750 in commissions for negotiating the purchase of the Shipping Board's vessels. These sums were carried on the books of Dollar Steamship and Admiral Oriental as costs of the ships.[27]

The Dollars' influence in Washington had prevailed.[28] So sure of themselves were they that Stanley Dollar made the low offer of $600,000 each or $3 million for an additional five *President* liners operated by Admiral Oriental that were only eight years old and had originally cost over $30 million. Just a few months earlier the Dollar Company paid $5,625,000 for Pacific Mail's 535s, yet Stanley Dollar thought he could get an even better bargain. As he wrote the sales department of the Shipping Board, "It is to be regretted that after reading your advertisement which appeared in the San Francisco papers inviting bids . . . we cannot help but feel that the terms and conditions outlined therein are not conducive to successful operation of the Line and to furnishing the government and the public the adequate service required. . . ." Nevertheless, Admiral Oriental was willing to bid half of what the Shipping Board advertised as the minimum bid. Dollar enclosed a check for $75,000, which was 2.5 percent of the total bid, as the board had stipulated.[29] The Shipping Board rejected Admiral Oriental's bid, but gave the line sixty days to come up with a reasonable offer.[30]

After a series of conferences, the board excluded all would-be rivals on rather flimsy technical grounds, while Admiral Oriental upped its minimum bid to $900,000 for each ship, a figure that was still considerably below what the government had advertised as a minimum. Over the protests of E. E. Crowley, president of the Emergency Fleet Corporation, custodian of the board's vessels, the senators from Washington and Oregon, the Senate Committee on Commerce, and a flurry of injunctions from Pacific Steam and Puget Sound Oriental, the board accepted the Dollars' bid. For a down payment of $112,500, Admiral Oriental purchased the ships. The balance of the cost was amortized over ten years but payments were not to begin until 1928. Interest was set at 2½ percent a year.[31]

Considering the forces arrayed against them, the Dollars had achieved a startling success. An indignant *Seattle Star* charged corruption in high places. In a front-page editorial, the *Star* excoriated the board: "The deal cannot be explained away on the grounds of good business," said the *Star.* "It is bad business. It cannot be explained away on the grounds of politics. It is poor politics to disgruntle the Pacific Northwest. Then why did the Shipping Board sign such a ridiculous contract with R. Stanley Dollar; why did it jam thru a deal that gives the United States all the worst of it? Friendship? Don't make us laugh."[32] Whether or not there was any foundation to these charges, it is a fact that powerful friends, including President Coolidge, did exert themselves for the Dollars.[33]

However the deal was consummated, "Captain" Robert Dollar shared the platform with his erstwhile competitor H. F. Alexander at a celebration in Seattle commemorating the first of the 535s to depart for the Far East under the flag of Admiral Oriental. Dollar assured his Seattle audience that the Dollar Steamship Company would promote and strengthen commercial ties between the Northwest and the Orient. The eighty-two-year-old founder of the Dollar Line may have been sincere, but three months later, to the chagrin of Seattle civic leaders, the home office of Admiral Oriental was transferred to San Francisco. Still the board insisted that the two lines be kept distinct. Admiral Oriental accordingly adopted the trade name of American Mail Line for its service between the ports of the Northwest and the Orient.[34]

NOTES_____

1. John Gunther, *Taken at the Flood: The Story of Albert D. Lasker* (New York: Harper, 1960), 8, 129, 130; Darrell Hevenor Smith and Paul V. Betters, *The United States Shipping Board: Its History, Activities and Organizations,* Institute for Government Research, Service Monographs of the United States Government no. 63 (Washington, D.C.: Brookings Institution, 1931), 63.

2. John D. Hicks, *Republican Ascendancy, 1921–1933* (New York: Harper & Row, 1963), 61; Harrison, "Dollar Steamship Company."

3. Brown, *Ships That Sail No More,* 16.

4. Pacific Steamship Company, "Account Book, 1918," Special Collections, Honnold Library, Claremont Colleges; *Pacific Marine Review,* November 1917; A. R. Lintner and Ralph B. Bush, "History of American Mail Line," Alan Yost Collection, Santa Barbara, Calif.

5. Lintner and Bush, "American Mail Line," Yost Collection.

6. *San Francisco Journal,* 13 June 1921.

7. *Seattle Post-Intelligencer,* 19 August 1921.

8. Ibid.

9. Pacific Steamship Company, "Account Book, 1920–1921," Special Collections, Honnold Library, Claremont, Colleges.

10. *Pacific Marine Review,* April 1920.

11. John Cormode to Allen Yost, 16 February 1966, Yost Collection; *Marine Digest*, 22 May 1937.

12. Lintner and Bush, "American Mail," Yost Collection; *Pacific Marine Review*, April 1920.

13. *Portland Oregonian*, 14 September 1921.

14. Harrison, "Dollar Steamship Company."

15. *Pacific Marine Review*, February 1920.

16. Bush to Yost, 28 December 1963, Yost Collection; *Pacific Marine Review*, July 1920; *Seattle Post-Intelligencer*, 19 August 1921; *Seattle Times*, 27 August 1921; *Portland Oregonian*, 14 September 1927.

17. See Pacific Steamship Company, Annual Report 1922.

18. R. Stanley Dollar to Lasker, 25 September 1922; Lasker to H. F. Alexander, 15 September 1922, Yost Collection.

19. *San Francisco Chronicle*, 28 December 1921; *Los Angeles Examiner*, 29 December 1921; *Seattle Times*, 31 December 1921.

20. Stanley Dollar to Lasker, 15 September 1922, Yost Collection.

21. *Marine Digest*, 12 September 1922.

22. Lintner and Bush, "American Mail," Yost Collection.

23. Gatewood to Haines, 8 December 1924, Yost Collection.

24. "Analysis, Personnel," 12 November 1930, Dollar Collection; *Marine Digest*, 23 August 1924; *Seattle Star*, 4 August 1924; *Seattle Times*, 27 December 1921; *Seattle Union Record*, 10 January 1922; *Newark* [N.J.] *Ledger*, 19 February 1922.

25. Brown, *Ships That Sail No More*, 92, 93.

26. Harrison, "Dollar Steamship Company"; *Shipping Register*, 4 April 1925.

27. Diary of J. H. Kemble, 29 April 1936; U.S. Maritime Commission, 10 April 1939, *Reorganization of American President Lines Ltd.* (Washington, D.C.: U.S. Government Printing Office, 1939), 14.

28. See *Marine Digest*, 16 February 1924, which reported a meeting between President Coolidge and Robert Dollar regarding the purchase of the 535s.

29. Stanley Dollar to Department of Sales, U.S. Shipping Board, 29 January 1926, Dollar Collection.

30. *Railway & Marine News*, November 1925.

31. Ibid., "Minutes of U.S. Shipping Board Meeting," 13 April 1926, Yost Collection.

32. *Seattle Star*, 28 May 1926.

33. See Diary of Robert Dollar, 31 March, 8 April 1926.

34. John Cormode to Allan Yost, 26 October 1944, Yost Collection; Lintner and Bush, "American Mail," 15 June 1926, Yost Collection.

5
ROUND THE WORLD

THE American shipping industry during the early twenties was in a perilous state. This was especially the case with the trans-Pacific trade. Although revival of world trade after the war and the transition of European nations to peacetime consumption patterns increased Pacific traffic an estimated 500 percent over the immediate prewar period, much of the activity was from East Asian and Southeast Asian ports westward through the Suez Canal to Europe. Competition was especially keen from British and Japanese lines and from tramping operations. American lines, some old established concerns and others that had been founded in response to wartime demands, were also battling desperately for sufficient revenues to stay afloat. Particularly onerous for West Coast lines was the routing of East Coast ships through the Panama Canal and direct to the Far East.

Westbound cargoes—raw materials like coal, oil, scrap metal, and also heavy equipment, all of which came out of the mineral-rich, highly industrialized eastern half of the United States—could be shipped by eastern lines cheaper on a direct route through the canal than overland by rail to West Coast ports, even with the preferential rates the West Coast had enjoyed since the late nineteenth century. Shipping lines like Dollar Steamship or Admiral Oriental were forced by circumstances to concentrate on high unit-value cargoes, which of course included passenger traffic.

But R. Stanley Dollar and his father, Robert, believed that some of the handicaps implicit in their base of operations could be reduced through concentration of available traffic on the West Coast in their own hands, a share of the traffic westbound from Eastern ports, and a share of the traffic westbound from Asian ports. These market concepts governed their policies during the twenties, but actually they had been planning for them since their investment in H. F.

Alexander's Pacific Steamship Company. The formation of Admiral Oriental had been a move in this direction. Purchase of Pacific Mail's five 535s and the eventual takeover of its name, flag, and goodwill was another. A third move in their long-range planning was the establishment of the round-the-world service.[1] Finally in 1927 they coordinated the trans-Pacific services of Admiral Oriental and Dollar Line in what was dubbed the horseshoe route.

Before Robert Dollar would commit any resources to the round-the-world service, he decided to make a trial run. During the spring of 1920 he sent the *M.S. Dollar* on such a mission. She returned to San Francisco on 18 February 1921. The experiment provided him and his son Stanley with specific information on what was needed before a full-scale effort was made. Otherwise, the trip of the 9,000-ton freighter incurred a loss. Passenger traffic from Japan, China, the Philippines, India, and Europe to the United States seemed not sufficient to justify employing large combination ships. Considerable sums, more than had been anticipated, would be needed to expand the agency network in Asia as well as Europe. A marketing program was indicated on a scale unprecedented for the Dollars.

The Pacific Mail also started a round-the-world service with Shipping Board freighters under its management in March 1920. The venture, like the trial run of the *M.S. Dollar*, resulted in a loss, and the Pacific Mail discontinued the new service in early 1922.

By then the Dollar company had sent the *Diana Dollar* and the large freighter *Robert Dollar* around the world. Both of these voyages were losses, although again they resulted in valuable information that confirmed for the Dollars that there was a market in the round-the-world concept, provided that certain important factors were figured into the plans.

As the program went through its formative stages, high unit-value freight had to be emphasized from East Asian and South Asian ports westward. Such commodities as silk, rubber, tea, tung oil, tin, and lacquer, topped with whatever mixed cargoes of finished goods Dollar agents could pick up along the way, would make the voyages profitable to Europe. From European Mediterranean ports westward to New York and Baltimore the cargo problem was more difficult. Normally wines would have made up a significant part of European shipments. But with Prohibition in full swing and old Robert Dollar's strict prejudices against alcohol in any form, that lucrative trade was ruled out.

Still there were certain important mitigating factors. A glance at a map will show that the distance westward from Asian and Indian ports to the East Coast of the United States is actually shorter by several thousand miles than shipment by water to San Francisco and Seattle and then by rail to New York. Freight consignments from the Far East could be made to Europe or to North America, depending on the market at any given time. Finally the Dollars would be in a position to claim a share of the traffic moving from East Coast ports through the Panama Canal to Los Angeles and San Francisco. They saw the added flexibility such a service would bring to their operations and with it a maximum utilization of cargo capacity.

Of course all operations would be much more complex, especially in scheduling traffic and in segregating freight. With many more markets in many more nations, there would be an increase in customs and port regulations and documentations. Working with longshoremen of many different nationalities and trade unions would demand close attention on the part of the home office and the ships' officers. Port congestion would be a bigger problem then before, but these factors were more or less tangible, and systems could be readily designed to deal with them.

What was less obvious, and indeed in the hazy realm of speculation, was the future of passenger traffic. Was there a potential for expansion in this area? Would the competition of long-established carriers in the Far East like NYK or the P & O rule out any significant passenger trade from the Far East to Europe or the United States? The trial voyages of Dollar Steamship made it abundantly clear that the passenger business was not profitable at this stage of development. After a suitable infrastructure had been established in Asia and a merchandising program initiated, however, a gradual buildup of passenger traffic could be a reasonable expectation. The bulk of this traffic would in all likelihood be made up of Americans who had the leisure and the funds to enjoy the flexibility the service made possible. A through ticket on one of the round-the-world vessels would guarantee to a passenger that he could stay as long as he liked in one of the many countries the ships called at and pick up at his pleasure another Dollar ship on a regular schedule. Round-the-world ships could count on patronage from the American military and other government service people and from missionaries who were moved about from station to station in the Far East.

It was unquestionably a big move for the Dollars to take, and it was largely at Stanley's urging that it was made. Stanley had been playing an increasingly important role in the management of the Dollar Line. His older brother, Melville, a conservative businessman, objected to Stanley's expansive plans. When their father sided with Stanley, Melville resigned his posts as managing director of the company and treasurer of the Pacific Steamship Company. Thereafter he concerned himself with the lumber business and J. Harold Dollar,[2] the youngest son, took his place in family councils. Harold Dollar never differed from Stanley and his father in important decisions.

Nevertheless, it was decided that the round-the-world service would be contingent on securing Shipping Board freighters at reasonable costs. R. Stanley Dollar had his eye on what were known as the 502s. These ships, each of which was 10,500 gross tons, seemed a good compromise between passenger and cargo capacity. While they had accommodations for about one hundred passengers, they had been designed primarily as freighters. The 502s were also similar in design but about one-third larger than the four Shipping Board freighters, the *Mandarin, Oriental, Celestial,* and *Cathay,* built in China and just purchased by Robert Dollar for $300,000 each. Renamed the *Stuart Dollar, Melville Dollar, Margaret Dollar,* and *Diana Dollar,* these vessels could be operated satisfactorily with the 502s under single, unified operating procedures on round-the-world service. In fact, the *Diana Dollar* was one of the ships that the Dollars had used for their trial runs.[3]

From the spring of 1923 through September of that year, Stanley commuted between Washington and San Francisco. Most of Dollar's meetings in the nation's capital were with Lasker's successor as chairman of the Shipping Board, T. V. O'Connor, who was even more determined than his predecessor to liquidate the government's fleet. Dollar soon established a cordial working relationship with O'Connor, but he ran into opposition from other members of the board who had come under the influence of rival shipping interests, primarily those from the East Coast. An important part of Dollar's strategy was to secure if possible the cargo and passenger traffic of scheduled American flag vessels between New York and London for that leg of the round-the-world service. The United States Lines was then the managing operator of the five 502s Dollar wanted on the route he sought. The other two 502s were being run by the West Coast ship brokerage firm of Swayne and Hoyt through the Panama

Canal to ports on the east coast of South America. He got the seven
ships at the bargain price of about $600,000 each, but he did not get
the northern leg of the European route. His failure to do so required
an alteration in the round-the-world service that omitted the
Gibraltar-to-London run but still provided for calls at the Mediterranean ports of Naples, Genoa, and Marseilles. Such a rearrangement
was a small price to pay for the addition to the Dollar fleet of these
new combination liners.

The seven 502s became the backbone of the Dollar round-the-
world service. Although they were no beauties, with perpendicular
bows and sterns, stacks, and masts, they were comfortable seaboats
and popular with passengers. They were all built by the New York
Shipbuilding Corporation in Camden, New Jersey, in 1920 and 1921.
They measured 502.1 feet long and 62.2 feet in beam. By the time
Dollar acquired them, the Shipping Board had substituted the
names of presidents for the state nicknames that they originally
bore. Thus they entered round-the-world service as *Presidents
Adams, Garfield, Harrison, Hayes, Monroe, Polk,* and *Van Buren,* inau-
gurating the tradition of nomenclature carried on by Dollar and the
American President Lines. They were generally fitted to carry sev-
enty-eight first-class passengers in comfortable cabins, most of
which were fitted with beds rather than berths, and of these, twenty-
four had connecting private showers or baths. In a pinch they could
accommodate 143 passengers. Powered by oil-fired triple-expansion
reciprocating engines, they were good for a sea speed of 14 knots.[4]

Despite the bargain price for the 502s, old Robert Dollar was still
unsure whether the venture would be profitable. As he confided to
his diary in early September 1923, he spent "two days thinking and
figuring upon the proposed purchase of the 502s and the round-the-
world service."[5] Prudent as always, he decided to spread the risk.
The Dollar Steamship Line (it had just been incorporated in California) at its first general meeting came up with the $105,000 required
for the down payment. But it authorized Robert Dollar to seek
financial assistance for meeting the obligation to the government,
which would be at the rate of 5 percent each year after the first two
years for nine years. The balance of $1,135,000 would fall due on or
before 15 March 1936. Dollar managed to obtain a letter of credit for
$866,250, or 22.5 percent of the total cost, from the Anglo London &
Paris National Bank through his associate Herbert Fleishhacker.[6]

The contract R. Stanley Dollar negotiated with the Shipping Board was kept confidential at first. To test public reaction, news of the deal was leaked to the *San Francisco Examiner,* which announced on 13 September 1923 that the ships had been purchased and that the Dollar Line would have eleven vessels on a scheduled round-the-world service, leaving San Francisco every fortnight. The service would begin in late December 1923 or early January 1924.[7] Stanley Dollar immediately was able to reduce the price the Dollar Line paid for the ships by selling their steel ballast on a rising scrap market. The ships had originally been designed as troop transports to carry a minimum of freight, thus they had been heavily ballasted with scrap steel and steel rails.[8]

Robert Dollar, his arrangement with Fleishhacker completed satisfactorily, now banished all qualms about the undertaking. He greeted his son Stanley with great warmth when he returned from Washington. And after studying the contract he brought with him, Robert Dollar thought it "was the best deal on a large scale we ever made."[9] Stanley Dollar was rewarded with a commission of 5 percent on the sale price of the vessels, or $210,000, which was entered on the company books as an addition to the sale price of the 502s.[10]

On 5 January 1924 the *President Harrison,* first of the 502s to be delivered and made ready for sea, sailed from San Francisco to Yokohama on the first leg of her round-the-world voyage. Mayor Rolph of San Francisco and of course an assemblage of Dollars were on hand for the occasion. Robert Dollar, however, was not present. Though nearly eighty years old, his energy and appetite for work undiminished, he had left several weeks earlier for a business tour of the Dollar facilities in Asia and Europe. But it was really Stanley Dollar's show and it was he who made the principal speech. To the spirited march music of John Philip Sousa, the *Harrison* slipped her hawsers and backed slowly into the stream. President Coolidge himself had given the order to cast off when he touched a key, sending a signal from the White House that was picked up on the *Harrison's* radio. The round-the-world schedule took the ships from San Francisco to Honolulu, then to Kobe and on to Shanghai, where there was sometimes a call of three or four days' duration since much ship maintenance was carried out there because wages were dramatically lower than in United States ports. The ships went on to Hong Kong, Manila, Singapore, Penang, and Colombo, through the Suez Canal with calls at both Suez and Port Said, to Alexandria, Naples, Genoa, Marseilles, and then across the Atlantic Ocean to

President Harrison [I]. One of the seven 502-class ships purchased by Dollar from the U.S. Shipping Board in 1923. On 5 January 1924, she inaugurated the popular round-the-world service in passenger-cargo ships. (APL Archives.)

Boston and New York. Thence the voyage was completed with calls at Havana, Cristobal and Balboa at the Panama Canal Zone, and Los Angeles. All told, the schedule called for 106 days to complete the entire voyage.

The sailing of the *Harrison* marked a dramatic change that was occurring in the fortunes of the Dollar lines and of shipping on the West Coast. The next two years witnessed a rapid expansion of the line from what was really a coastal and tramping operation to the largest scheduled liner service in the nation. Seven Dollar vessels on the round-the-world service were in 1925 joined by the five 535s that had formerly sailed under the Pacific Mail's flag. And only a few months later, the Admiral Oriental purchased the five 535s it had been operating for the Shipping Board.

It was announced that beginning in January 1927 a "horseshoe route" would be established with the 535s of the Dollar Line and the American Mail Line operating together. A 535 sailed from San Francisco every two weeks, proceeded west to Honolulu, Yokohama, Kobe, Shanghai, and Hong Kong to Manila, and then reversed her course as far as Yokohama, whence she sailed directly to Seattle. From Seattle she sailed to Manila by way of the usual ports and returned to San Francisco. On the next voyage she went out from

President Adams [I]. A 502 purchased by Dollar in 1923, she received extensive reconstruction in 1929 when the two "islands" of her midships superstructure were joined, thus increasing her passenger accommodations from 96 to 175. (APL Archives.)

San Francisco to Manila and returned to Seattle, and so on.[11] Meanwhile, of course, the 502s in the round-the-world service were sailing westward from San Francisco every fortnight. Thus Dollar could advertise that a ship sailed from San Francisco for the Orient every Saturday afternoon at 4:00 P.M. There was a sailing weekly with San Francisco and Seattle the alternate destinations.[12]

With this new service, with large, modern, terminal facilities constructed at Hunt's Point in New York and in Shanghai, along with a worldwide network of agencies, the Dollar Line was now a force to be reckoned with in American shipping circles and abroad. Dollar may have been considered an interloper, but the imperious established lines between the Far East and Europe soon learned that he was there to stay. A whirlwind of energy despite his age, he concentrated on selling the service of his lines, and his principal sales strategy was the reputation the Dollar Line had already made in punctuality and strict adherence to schedule. Robert Dollar wrote:

> I preceded our first ship in this service, the *President Harrison*, in an effort to get patronage for the new line, but I was confronted with remarks everywhere I called such at this, "You Americans are all 'fly-by-nights,' here today but Heaven knows where tomorrow!" So at the end of my trip round the world it looked as if I had not succeeded. Lord Inchcape [chairman and managing director of the Peninsular & Oriental Steam Navigation Co.] informed me during this trip that I was an interloper and had no right to interfere with his company—the great P. & O. Line. However by playing fair and meeting competition in a clean way, we became the best of friends. We had a struggle to make a success of this service, but finally overcame the obstacles which continually presented themselves, and saw it established with a regular service.[13]

Dollar knew that shippers could effect substantial savings in sailings that adhered strictly to schedules and rapid turnaround time. The fewer days spent at the wharf because Dollar management constantly urged captains to load and unload as rapidly as possible meant savings for exporters in fixed charges like insurance, warehouse costs, and letters of credit. As soon as the lines gained enough experience in port congestion, labor practices, and North American ports for their round-the-world ships, it adopted a system of bonuses and other incentives to those captains who adhered most closely to schedules. The companies also developed special cargo forms for each ship that were color-coded for storage location. And they early placed a premium on wireless communication from ship to port in sequence so that ships' officers could rearrange their stowage plans and thus reduce confusion and delay in port.

These practices were by no means unique to the Dollar Line. Their implementation may have been novel, however, because the companies were suffused with old Robert Dollar's personal philosophy. He set standards for industry and for careful, scrupulous attention to details. A self-made man in the driving nineteenth-century mode, his mode of thought had been tempered in the heat of fierce competition. Work was only second to the Presbyterian God he worshipped. And even the deity, one supposes, had his eye on the balance sheet.

Dollar had no use for college education. The liberal arts were to him simply an excuse for idleness. So although a multimillionaire, when his children came of college age he encouraged his sons to become gainfully employed as soon as they finished high school. Dollar's only concession to higher education was completely practical. He sent his oldest son, Melville, to Heald's Business College in San Francisco for a ten-month course in typing, bookkeeping, and shorthand. Stanley also attended Heald's for six months, but never completed the course. Robert Dollar decided his second son's service in the office was more valuable than any further vocational skills he might acquire in the business school.[14] None of his sons went on for a university degree, yet all became responsible businessmen in the Dollar enterprise. And Stanley came close to sharing his father's ability for management, salesmanship, and financial acumen.

When the Dollar organization became a large and profitable shipping line during the middle twenties, both Robert Dollar and his son Stanley saw the need for training programs to produce engineering and deck officers for their ships and experienced personnel who could handle the complicated paperwork necessary to keep track of cargo at home, sea, and abroad. Beginning in 1925, the Dollar Line set up a cadet program primarily for the training of pursers at its port facilities in San Francisco. The cadets were paid $60 a month and worked on the docks for a year. Once taken on, they worked under the port captain and assisted in loading and unloading. If considered competent, they were sent to sea as assistant pursers where they handled a multitude of assignments such as the stowage of passengers' baggage, the preparation of bills of lading, and the payrolls of the crew.

In the selection of cadets the Dollar Line favored those without college education but insisted on good personal habits (no drinking or smoking). There was no overtime pay, even though they were customarily on the job six days a week and ten hours a day. The Dollar Line had no formal program for deck and engineering officers until the Jones-White Act required that such training be instituted on all American-flag vessels. But captains of vessels were urged to report likely young members of the deck gang or the engine room. Such individuals were given special attention at the home office and were assisted financially if necessary in their studies for license.[15]

These programs reflected the strengthening of the Dollar Line as it responded to the fulsome prosperity of the late twenties. After losing $640,000 during the first year of round-the-world operations, the route became solidly profitable. For the next four years, Dollar Steamship had accumulative net earnings of $2,802,000.[16] By 1929 the company was in strong financial condition, despite the general decline of the American merchant marine. Its round-the-world service, as the Dollars had anticipated, contributed substantially to passenger revenues of the trans-Pacific run.

By combining the large number of vessels on the horseshoe route with those engaged in the round-the-world service, a prospective passenger could book a passage out of San Francisco on any Saturday afternoon and from Seattle every two weeks. He or she could pick up a Dollar liner at any one of a dozen Asian and European ports for short or extended trips. There was sure to be a Dollar *President* calling every two weeks on which he could book a passage, provided of course he was traveling westward. Between Kobe and Manila there were six or seven sailings westbound a month. Freight shipments too became more flexible and their schedules easier to meet, thus enabling the Dollar Line to make its tariffs competitive with foreign shipping lines. For traffic eventually destined to the United States, Dollar ships offered reliable arrival dates for shippers. After some trial runs, the Dollar Line established a 112-day schedule with twenty-three calls at ports that traffic patterns indicated were major concentration and distribution centers. It also soon specialized in the types of cargo that would be most profitable in this deployment of ships. The original decision to compete for high unit-value—or, as they advertised, "the better class of cargo"—proved a sound one and was continued as marketing operations policy throughout the life of the service.

Well before the service was inaugurated Robert Dollar had decided that Boston and New York would be the ports of call on the East Coast of the United States, rather than Baltimore, Philadelphia, or the more southern cities. His reasoning primarily was based on traffic density, but was also because these ports more nearly conformed to a great circle route from the Mediterranean with consequent economies in time and fuel. Manufactured goods, petroleum products, foodstuffs—especially canned and packaged goods, were loaded at these eastern ports for direct shipment to the Orient. Passengers could be ticketed for California ports or for other destinations westward. The Dollar Line actually found that passenger traffic from the East Coast to the West Coast of the United States was profitable, climbing to 25 percent of total passenger revenues by 1929. In effect an early manifest of cruise ship possibilities, the popularity of this run was recognized and exploited by the Dollar management through specialized promotion and advertising campaigns. Freight from California ports that was picked up enroute consisted primarily of refrigerated cargos, animal carcasses, canned fish, fresh vegetables, and fruit.

In laying out the route westward, the Dollars followed the earlier lead of the Pacific Mail by offering direct service between the Pacific Coast of the United States and Burma, Ceylon (Sri Lanka), and India. They also entered the highly competitive carrying trade from Singapore and Malaya, but only for high unit-value cargo such as tin, latex, essential oils, and spices. An example of freight that could only have been profitable on a scheduled route was cashew nuts, where freshness in bulk handling had to be maintained. Dollar ships soon dominated the shipping of this particular commodity between Bombay and New York.[17] If they had not established a relatively fast scheduled service to Europe and the U.S. East Coast, they would have lost out on the lucrative business of South Asia because of the extensive tramping operations of foreign-flag carriers in the region. Of course, not a great deal of time elapsed before rival shipping lines, notably the British P & O, the Japanese NYK, the Isthmian and American Export Line also ran regularly scheduled ships on the rubber and tin trade.[18]

Dollar management discovered that a considerable amount of incidental revenue would be realized through interregional shipments of goods from Japan, China, the Philippine Islands and ports westward.[19] Low handling costs enhanced the profitability of this trade. By 1926 the round-the-world service had so established itself that for the next five years, revenues did not fluctuate more than 7 percent in volume and in earnings.

Such an even pattern in freight shipments, unusual for the carrying trade, meant that management could allocate quite precisely the number of ships needed for a year ahead, with consequent savings in fixed charges like insurance and maintenance costs. By aiming for those high unit-value bulk cargoes whose demand is constant throughout the year such as rubber and tin, the round-the-world ships could be utilized to a maximum capacity on a scheduled routing plan.

When the Dollars began this service, it took a minimum of sixty-five to seventy days to deliver a cargo of rubber or tin to New York. By 1929 the time in transit had been reduced to a range of thirty-seven to forty days.[20] Products like sugar, which depended more heavily on seasonal market conditions and consumption patterns, were strictly avoided unless some particular opportunity presented itself. Nor did management from the very beginning seek out markets of opportunity, however profitable they might have been on given occasions. Experience had shown that deviations from scheduled calls, or "meandering," as it was known in shipping circles, reduced efficiency of officers and crews who were not familiar with the approaches and the facilities of ports off their accustomed routes.[21]

After initial start-up costs during 1924–25, the round-the-world service began showing a net profit before depreciation of $250,000 in 1926.[22] Some 45,231 passengers were carried that year, producing a gross revenue of $6,051,602 that climbed to over $7 million in 1929.[23] Despite the Depression, decline in revenue was not precipitous, except for 1933, when the economy plunged to its lowest point. For the ten-year period 1929–1939, passenger tickets alone accounted for $29,917,454, with an average of 5,825 passengers carried each year.[24] And of surprise to the Dollar management, Asia and the Middle East generated almost 20 percent of the passenger revenue.[25] Between 1924 and 1939, the Dollar Line and its successor averaged a net profit of about $387,000 a year on its round-the-world passenger traffic. Net profits on cargoes before deducting management commission, advertising, and depreciation between 1925 and 1939 were

$17,434,297. Average net profit amounted to $437,000 a year. The Robert Dollar Company, which acted as managing agent for Dollar Steamship, Tacoma Oriental, and American Mail earned, in addition, an average of $638,000 each year in various commissions.[26] Indeed, almost $4 million was paid out between 1925 and 1929 in such management fees. Yet a net profit of over $2 million before depreciation was earned during the same period from the round-the-world service, which carried more passengers and freight than the trans-Pacific service. Passenger revenue of almost $13 million earned during the 1920s dwarfed the sum of $720,511 earned from passenger bookings on the trans-Pacific route for the same period.[27] The problem here, of course, was that cargo carried eastbound from the Orient was far smaller than westbound voyages. The *President Coolidge* during the 1930s, for example, averaged 2,000 to 3,000 tons of unfilled space on her homeward-bound voyages.[28]

With such profits rolling in, R. Stanley Dollar, who had by now assumed a dominant position in the company, determined on a policy of expansion. The buoyant prosperity of the late twenties was certainly a factor in his decision. But equally important was new federal legislation that was aimed at arresting the decline of the American merchant marine.

In 1928, the Congress passed and President Coolidge signed into law the Jones-White Act. Two features of this law were of particular interest to R. Stanley Dollar: a generous mail subsidy for ships under American registry and liberal provisions for financing new construction from a revolving fund of $250 million to be administered by the Shipping Board. Attractive also was the provision that half of the crews of American flag vessels could be aliens during the first four years of any given mail contract. In the late 1920s and early 1930s far more than half the crews of the various Dollar-owned lines were Chinese nationals.[29]

The mail subsidy was to be calculated on a basis of speed and ship tonnage. For completed voyages the postmaster general could pay from $4 to $12 for each nautical mile. He was, however, enjoined to offer the contracts on a bid basis, the assumption being that the lowest bid would be accepted. In practice, the contracts were stabilized in each category and as the act provided, the postmaster general could make an award on the basis of speed alone. The Dollar vessels qualified in the $8 a mile class, but the government would pay only $7 a mile; this amount the line accepted.[30] Accordingly,

Dollar Steamship and American Mail were awarded subsidy contracts, which added over $3 million a year to the revenues of the lines.[31]

Once the mail subsidy rates had been settled, Dollar began negotiations with the Shipping Board to underwrite the construction of new vessels, as the Act required. Discussions on a building program already had been underway in the executive offices of the Dollar Building at 311 California Street. The most important conferences took place in Robert Dollar's office around his heavy Japanese oak table that matched the wall paneling. The eighty-four-year-old gentleman himself, his faculties undimmed by age, chaired the meetings. The point at issue was the Shipping Board's request, backed up by the navy, that the Dollars build four new vessels that would be larger and faster than the 535s for the trans-Pacific trade.

At various times the Dollars had talked about four or five new vessels in press releases. Stanley Dollar had announced expansively that the company would build a new fleet at a cost of $35 million.[32] Despite all this advance publicity, the Dollars committed themselves only to building two ships in the first phase of the construction program. These vessels, they thought, would complement their round-the-world service. Should circumstances warrant they would seek government underwriting for the construction of several more.[33] Stanley Dollar's preliminary surveys indicated that two liners, much larger than the 535s and with more luxurious passenger accommodations, would be more profitable than four smaller ships.

Experience with the round-the-world service had shown that—with proper merchandising techniques—fast, new liners would attract passenger traffic even on the trans-Pacific routes. Nor was Stanley Dollar unaware of the prestige the line would enjoy from owning and operating the largest liners built up to that time in the United States. This prestige would, of course, be translated into increased patronage for all Dollar vessels. The heady business optimism of the late twenties also entered into the plans being considered at 311 California Street, an optimism that even the cautious Robert Dollar shared. At Stanley's behest, Ferguson and Peterson, naval architects of Newport News, drew up plans for 33,000-ton turbo-electric liners.

Persuasive as always, R. Stanley Dollar, over several months of personal lobbying in Washington, managed to convince the Shipping Board and other government agencies that two larger liners at this stage would be much more advantagous to the merchant marine and to defense needs than four smaller vessels. He appealed to their patriotism and sense of nationalism, pointing out the prestige that would be gained in the Orient from these compelling examples of American design and technology.

There was at the time a sense of urgency in Washington that R. Stanley Dollar skillfully played upon. The 502s and 535s that were the basic components of the merchant navy were becoming obsolete. Germany and Japan with their fast new liners had become world leaders in the transoceanic passenger business. While Stanley Dollar was making his case before the Shipping Board, the North German Lloyd liner *Bremen* broke all speed records in the trans-Atlantic route. Nippon Yusen Kaisha (NYK) and Osaka Shosen Kaisha (OSK), the two great Japanese shipping syndicates, were building new liners. The 792-foot, 42,450-ton *Ile de France* had a year earlier made her maiden voyage to the United States, and the French Line had just announced that it would build an 80,000-ton liner to be named the *Normandie*. The British Cunard White Star Line was also reported to be about to begin construction on a comparable vessel.

It was the high point of the transoceanic liners when national prestige seemed as much at stake as passenger revenue miles. And Stanley Dollar meant to capitalize on the boom. But he did not neglect to present figures on speed and size that impressed doubting admirals. He stressed safety and efficiency in his proposal and the ease with which these ships could be converted to troop carriers in national emergencies. And he promised to follow up this construction program with two additional vessels of unspecified size and design.

By mid-1929 Dollar had secured a contract whereby the board would lend $14 million or 75 percent of the construction costs for the two vessels. The Dollar Line would be responsible for 25 percent of the cost, or $3,525,000. The same ratio would apply to expenditures for outfitting the ships such as furniture, carpets, interior decoration, swimming pools and the like, estimated at another $3 million. Contractual arrangements were worked out in a series of interest-bearing promissory notes. These "temporary" notes were to be accompanied by a mortgage or deed of trust with the board as the mortgagor. When the ships were completed the temporary notes would be canceled. Twenty "permanent" notes would take their place. First mortgages on the ships held by the government served as collateral. These notes with interest were to be paid off at the rate of one each year for the next twenty years.[34]

As soon as these arrangements were completed the Dollar Line accepted bids from the Newport News Ship Building and Drydock Company for construction of the two liners. On 6 December 1930 Mrs. Herbert Hoover smashed a bottle of water that the Dollar public relations department claimed had been collected from the seven seas across the bow of the *President Hoover* as she slid down the ways at Newport News. A little over a year later, Mrs. Calvin Coolidge christened the *President Coolidge* at her launching with a bottle of water taken from the Black River, which ran through the former president's Vermont farm. On such public occasions during Prohibition water flowed as champagne had done earlier.[35]

During the same period R. Stanley Dollar secured from the Shipping Board a government loan of $1,250,000 to cover work already accomplished in reconditioning four of the Dollar Line's 502s. These vessels, all in the round-the-world route, were the *Presidents Adams, Harrison, Garfield,* and *Polk*. The loan equivalent to three-fourths of the expenditures was to be paid back over a fifteen-year period. In addition, he borrowed a like sum to purchase from the International Mercantile Marine Company the 15,000-ton cargo liners *Manchuria* and *Mongolia*, which were renamed the *President Johnson* and the *President Fillmore*.[36]

With expansive prospects for the future and dramatic increases in its business, the Dollar Line needed far more capital and a far more flexible corporate organization. Over some grumbling from his father, R. Stanley Dollar brought outsiders for the first time into the organization. Herbert Fleishhacker, whose bank had put up the million-dollar bond the government demanded on its construction loans, became a director in the new company, which was incorporated as Dollar Steamship Lines, Inc., Ltd. under Delaware law. All of the Dollar shipping assets were consolidated under Dollar Steamship, which was authorized to issue 260,000 shares of Class A nonvoting stock, 2,100,000 shares of Class B voting stock, and 40,000 shares of noncumulative preferred stock.[37] The Dollars retained a controlling interest in the new company, but Herbert Fleishhacker and his brother Mortimer became major shareowners. The company was launched in May 1929 with considerable publicity, which forecast a buoyant future for the American merchant marine and abundant profits for the Dollar lines.

Just four months later came the Wall Street panic that presaged the Great Depression. But neither the crash itself nor the next year of rapid decline in the economy seemed to affect the fortunes of Dollar Steamship. True, the Depression put an end to the passenger boom, but government financing continued until the completion of the *President Coolidge* in 1931. In addition, R. Stanley Dollar secured yet another loan from the Shipping Board at most favorable terms to outfit the two liners. The extravagant plans for two or three additional liners, however, were shelved when the board terminated its loan program.[38]

In an effort to halt a threatened rate war on world trade routes, Dollar Steamship joined in a conference with North German Lloyd, Hamburg America and the Luckenbach Line to maintain a minimum rate structure. Three months later it participated in a conference with its Japanese competitors on the trans-Pacific routes to put a floor under commodity rate schedules. The Shipping Board approved both agreements. Neither conference was able to withstand the pressure of steeply declining world trade, however. By 1932, the Dollar Line's round-the-world service was forced to cut rates across the board on passengers and freight to meet unrestricted competition. But profits continued to be made. A significant factor in earnings was the mail subsidy, which rose to $8 million a year after the *Presidents Hoover* and *Coolidge* went into service and earned the maximum mail rate under the Jones-White Act.

Storm clouds were indeed on the economic horizon, though R. Stanley Dollar, the proverbial optimist, chose to regard them as a temporary phase, and with some justification. Luxury passenger traffic may have been greatly reduced, but it was still earning revenue. Experiments with special cruises seemed to indicate that the two big new liners could meet expenses and turn in modest profits. The round-the-world service also continued to operate in the black. Trans-Pacific trade and the coastal business were the weak elements in the Dollar financial picture. Yet R. Stanley Dollar persuaded his board to buy control of the Tacoma Oriental Steamship Company in 1932 since it competed with American Mail in the Pacific Northwest.

After two profitable years in the trans-Pacific trade with its seven ships and a ten-year mail subsidy contract, the Tacoma line had been in precarious financial condition.[39] American Mail, a Dollar subsidiary, had run these ships as a managing operator for the Shipping Board during the mid-twenties. In 1928, when the board decided to put the vessels and the route up for sale, American Mail bid for them. But this time Dollar influence in Washington did not succeed over pressure from the Seattle-Tacoma business community. The ships and the route were awarded to the newly formed Tacoma Oriental Steamship Company, which became directly competitive with the Dollar Line and American Mail.[40]

For strategic reasons it seemed right to consolidate most of the shipping business of the Pacific Northwest under Dollar control. But with labor problems looming and traffic on the horseshoe route falling away, it was unquestionably a rash decision to take over the responsibilities and the liabilities of a near-bankrupt company. Had old "Captain" Dollar been his usual perceptive self, he probably would have restrained his impetuous son. But the elder Dollar was in frail health and for the past two years had relinquished direct control of the business.

Stanley Dollar, unfortunately, did not read the signs of the times correctly. Even when the Depression began sweeping away outworn concepts, he persisted in following the paternalistic policies his father had instituted and ruled the increasingly complex and far-flung activities of Dollar Steamship, American Mail, Tacoma Oriental and a dozen or more interconnected service companies like a benevolent despot.

NOTES

1. Walter A. Radius, *United States Shipping in Trans-Pacific Trade, 1922–1938* (Palo Alto, Calif.: Stanford University Press, 1944), 16.

2. O'Brien, "Robert Dollar," 239.

3. Ibid., 235.

4. Arnold Kludas, *Great Passenger Ships of the World* (Cambridge: Patrick Stephens, 1976), II, 128–35.

5. Diary of Robert Dollar, 8–10 September 1923.

6. O'Brien, "Robert Dollar," 272.

7. *San Francisco Examiner,* 25 December 1923.

8. O'Brien, "Robert Dollar," 274.

9. Diary of Robert Dollar, 1 October 1923.

10. U.S. Maritime Commission, *Reorganization of American President Lines Ltd.* (Washington, D.C., 1939), 14.

11. Lintner and Bush, "American Mail," 4 January 1927, Yost Collection.

12. Dollar Steamship Line and American Mail Line, Trans-Pacific and Round the World Sailing Schedule No. 8, Issued 30 November 1926, Effective 25 January 1927; *Railway and Marine News,* October 1926.

13. Dollar, *Steam Navigation,* 136–37.

14. Undated transcript of an interview with R. Stanley Dollar, Dollar Collection.

15. A medical fee of $1.50 was deducted each month from their pay. Eugene Lukes, "Oral History Transcript," p. 2, APL Archives, Oakland, Calif.

16. U.S. Maritime Commission, *Reorganization*, 14, 15.

17. "Reply of American President Lines Ltd. to Memorandum Entitled 'Suggested Program for Realigning the APL Service,'" 24 April 1940, p. 33, APL Archives.

18. Ibid., 37.

19. Ibid.

20. Ibid., 136.

21. Ibid., 34.

22. Ibid., 10.

23. Memorandum, "Total Passenger Revenue all Classes 1929," Dollar Collection.

24. "Reply," 47.

25. Ibid., 46.

26. Figures are calculated for 1925–38. The average earnings would have been much higher had the losses of 1937 and 1938 not been included; "Reply," 13.

27. "Reply," 29.

28. Ibid., 42.

29. For example, see "Analysis, Personnel," Dollar Collection.

30. "Summary of Historical Events in the Development of Dollar Steamship Lines," Dollar Collection.

31. Zeis, *American Shipping Policy*, 145–49; John H. Kemble and Lane C. Kendall, "The Years Between the Wars: 1919–1939," in *America's Maritime Legacy*, ed. Robert A. Kilmarx (Boulder, Colo.: Westview Press, 1979), 160.

32. *New York Times*, 31 May 1928.

33. O'Brien, "Robert Dollar," 321.

34. Construction Loan Agreement with U.S. Shipping Board, U.S. Shipping Board, *Sixteen Annual Report* (Washington D.C., 1930), 47, 339–40. Copy in Dollar Collection.

35. *New York Times*, 7 December 1930; 20 February 1931.

36. Ibid., 29, 30 May 1929; *Manchuria* and *Mongolia*, passenger-cargo ships, 13,635 gross tons, 600 feet by 65 feet, operated between San Francisco and the Orient for the Pacific Mail 1904–15. They were sold to the Atlantic Transport Line in 1915 and operated trans-Atlantic and intercoastal until purchased by Dollar in 1929. They were extensively refitted to carry 146 first-class and 48 special-class passengers.

37. American President Lines, Ltd., Annual Report 1938, APL Archives.

38. *New York Times*, 7 August, 6 September, 13, 16 October 1931.

39. The ships were originally named the *City of Spokane, Cuprum, Edmore, Eldridge, West Himrod, West Ison*, and *Wheatland Montana*. These vessels were renamed the *Olympia, Shelton, Grays Harbor, Tacoma, Bellingham, Everett*, and *Seattle*. The Tacoma line paid $696,000 for these ships and the goodwill of the service. Only 2.5 percent of this sum, or $17,422.65, was paid in on the successful bid. At the delivery of the ships the company paid the government 22.5 percent of the cost, the balance to be liquidated over a period of seven and one-half years at 4½ percent interest, to be paid semiannually. See Frank A. Clapp, "Tacoma Oriental Steamship Company," *Steamboat Bill*, March 1962.

40. Clapp, "Tacoma Oriental Steamship Company"; Lintner and Bush, "American Mail," February 1928, Yost Collection. Memorandum, "Tacoma Steamship Co.," 21 February, April 1928, Dollar Collection; C. K. Hale to Allan Yost, 21 October 1963, Yost Collection.

6

A CHANGE IN MANAGEMENT

WHEN the flag-bedecked new liner *President Hoover* arrived in her home port of San Francisco on 26 August 1931, the city turned out to welcome her. A splendid ship, the largest passenger liner ever built in American yards, she represented the nation's technological achievements in naval architecture and marine engineering and its continuing belief in the importance of the Pacific traffic for passengers and for freight. To the San Francisco Chamber of Commerce, the *President Hoover* and her sistership the *President Coolidge*, which was to follow in October, guaranteed a prosperous future for the port and all those industries dependent on its economic well-being. She was 654 feet 3 inches long, 81 feet in beam, drew 34 feet of water, and measured 21,936 tons gross. Her turbo-electric engines were rated at 32,000 shaft horsepower and drove her twin screws at a cruising speed of 21 knots. She had accommodations for 988 passengers (307 in first class, 133 in special class, 170 in third class, and 378 in steerage), and her crew numbered 324. Citizens of San Francisco, who strolled over the *President Hoover's* broad decks and through her spacious public rooms, were impressed by her two outdoor swimming pools and the fully equipped gymnasium, as well as the tasteful furniture and fabrics in her staterooms and lounges in first and special classes.

No money had been spared in making her art deco furnishings the equivalent of the best hotels of the day. Every room had its own telephone. All first-class and many special-class quarters had private or connecting baths. The first-class dining salon was two decks high and seated 272 persons. Adjoining it was a private dining room seating 18. The special-class dining room seated 120, at small tables. Special attention had been paid to forced ventilation in all public spaces as well as in passenger staterooms although this was before the era of air conditioning. Nor had the safety of the passengers

President Coolidge [I]. The pride of the Dollar Line was transferred to APL in 1938. (APL Archives.)

The Continental Lounge in first class aboard the *President Coolidge* [I]. Her passenger accommodations were noted for their spaciousness. (APL Archives.)

been neglected. A flip of a switch on the bridge closed all watertight doors in thirty seconds. Each of the twenty lifeboats was equipped with a special shortwave magneto-powered radio that could transmit messages over one thousand miles.[1] Even old Captain Dollar, who was far from well at the time, was quite overwhelmed by the *President Hoover.* After saying a few words to the thousand or more visitors who crowded the liner's main lounge, an effort that caused him considerable pain, he wrote in his diary, "The ship is a wonder."[2]

While San Francisco was heaping praise on the Dollars for their leadership in the maritime industry, Stanley was involved in two negotiations that would triple the size and, he hoped, the business of the Dollar Line. The Shipping Board, now headed by a longtime Dollar friend, T. V. O'Connor, had suggested that the line take over the United States Lines, which was in financial difficulties. Though his father and the Fleishhackers were skeptical, Stanley went ahead and offered $3,190,000 for the stock of the line. The Shipping Board approved the deal, but when Stanley Dollar went to Washington to close it, he ran into a situation that Dollar influence could not overcome. The huge shipping combine that J. P. Morgan had put together, the International Mercantile Marine Company, or IMM as it was known in business circles, wanted the United States Lines, too. Talks continued during which various Dollar enterprises purchased a substantial but not a controlling interest in the United States Lines. Eventually, the declining national economy and the continued opposition of IMM forced Stanley Dollar to dispose of the stock at a substantial gain and back out of the purposed acquisition.

While he was attempting to purchase the United States Lines, Dollar was also seeking to acquire the American–Hawaiian Steamship Company. For some time the Dollars had eyed enviously the profits another San Francisco firm, the Matson Navigation Company, was reaping from the Hawaiian trade. American–Hawaiian, the Dollars thought, would give them just the entree they needed to expand their business in the islands. But two formidable obstacles stood in the way. The Matson line itself, backed by wealthy and powerful Hawaiian interests, opposed the merger. Likewise, American–Hawaiian's president and chief shareholder, Roger Lapham, set himself squarely against the Dollars. Talks broke down. Then Matson prepared to challenge the Dollar interests in the trans-Pacific and round-the-world trade.

For the second time in his aggressive, ebullient career, R. Stanley Dollar not only realized that he was beaten, but more than that, he became concerned at the probability of ruinous competition from an organization with far more resources than he could command. The result was a complete capitulation. The Dollar lines agreed to pay Matson 50 percent of the annual gross passenger and freight revenue generated between California ports and Honolulu, an amount roughly equivalent to $120,000 a year. The deal also stopped the Dollars from soliciting short-haul passenger business between the mainland and Hawaii in the absence of long-haul passenger business. In return, Matson would refrain from entering the trans-Pacific trade. The agreement that went into effect on 23 April 1930 lasted for ten years.[3] Thus the Dollars were forced to limit their operations in a lucrative market area at a time when revenues were declining and costs for the financing of new construction were mounting.[4]

In another sphere of business strategy, shortwave radio communications, Dollar Steamship was more successful. And for a period of time it was among the leaders in an industry that was rapidly becoming an indispensable tool for all long-distance communications. While planning for expansion in the Pacific and round-the-world routes, R. Stanley Dollar had acquired the radio patents of Frederick G. Simpson, a brilliant inventor whose laboratory in Seattle had developed the first practical shortwave transmitter capable of broadcasting relatively static-free signals over great distances. With Simpson's cooperation, Dollar set up what became the Pacific Radio Company and eventually Globe Wireless. Dollar then secured from the U.S. Department of Commerce exclusive use of certain wavelengths between experimental stations in the Far East and the U.S. West Coast.[5]

As a next step Dollar employed Ralph Heintz, whose consulting firm was engaged in research on ship-to-shore communications, to develop a reliable system. Dollar's major interest in radio had been to reduce cable costs that were claiming an ever-larger share of Dollar Steamship's operating budgets. But he was also keenly aware of the flexibility radio communication provided over cable in controlling and coordinating the movement of ships, passengers, and cargoes. After a year of experiments with antennae, transmitters, and receivers, Heintz perfected what was known as the MC system, which worked well in sending and receiving signals over thousands of miles with three shifts of frequency during each twenty-four hour period. By 1929 new stations built to Heintz's specifications had been completed in South San Francisco, followed by others in Manila, Port Apra, Guam, Honolulu, Garden City, Long Island, Portland, Seattle, and Los Angeles. Known as DOLLARADIO, this network was in full operation when the *President Hoover*, equipped with a Simpson shortwave radio system, sailed into San Francisco Harbor on her maiden voyage.

To the casual onlooker Dollar Steamship had never appeared more prosperous, with its sure grip on the Pacific trade of California and the Northwest, its round-the-world service, and its mail subsidy that brought in over $3 million a year. But in reality the lines were overextended, their debt to the federal government and to the Anglo-California Bank of San Francisco climbing to over $20 million.

Passenger bookings for the two new liners fell far short of expectations. Built to accommodate 988 passengers, the *President Hoover* carried only 400 on her maiden voyage, despite an elaborate public relations and merchandising campaign. Similarly when the *President Coolidge* sailed on her first voyage to the Orient she carried scarcely one-third of her capacity.[6] Nor were these exceptions. A general decline in passenger business had set in during 1930 and dropped even more sharply during 1931.

On 16 May 1932 and in his 88th year, Robert Dollar died. As late as 28 April he was still going to the office in San Francisco from his San Anselmo home, visiting ships when they were in port, and giving lectures on the evils of dope and liquor to their officers.[7] His death symbolized the end of an era when personal control of a family-owned business could and did function with reasonable efficiency. But such management had become obsolete well before Captain Dollar's death, and only the prosperity of the 1920s and the largesse of the government had made it seem practical.

Though Stanley Dollar conducted affairs as usual, he was certainly very much aware of a perilous situation that was rapidly developing in the American shipping industry as the Depression began to take its toll. Competition, especially in the passenger area, was forcing the Dollar Line and its subsidiaries Pacific Steamship, Tacoma Oriental, and American Mail to cut rates and reduce overhead wherever possible, which meant in many instances deferring needed repairs. Even the intervals between scheduled overhauls were lengthened while turnaround time, in the past always too short for proper maintenance, was reduced further.

The bulk of the Dollar fleet, the 535s and 502s, were now from twelve to fourteen years old. They were becoming obsolete and their physical condition was deteriorating. Breakdowns at sea and greater consumption of fuel per mile because of lower engine efficiency had to be balanced against the time and money required for essential repairs. From time to time the Shipping Board complained, but in effect it had no real power as mortgagor to enforce high standards of maintenance.[8] The Bureau of Marine Inspection and the American Bureau of Shipping were no more successful in compelling any change in policies.

While the Dollar lines were retrenching, their principal competitors—the two Japanese lines NYK and OSK and the Canadian Pacific Railroad—were building fast combination ships whose passenger accommodations were far superior to those of the older Dollar vessels. The *Empress of Japan*, which went into service during 1930, dazzled AML's general passenger agent, Dean Hanscom. He wrote a long letter to Ancil F. Haines, the line's general manager, recommending a complete modernization program for its 535s. In his comparison of AML's combination vessels and those of the competing lines, he laid bare a policy that had long neglected improvements for passenger comfort. Such attractions as telephones in staterooms, gymnasiums, tiled swimming pools, passenger elevators, and even sound motion-picture projectors, all standard equipment on the *Empress of Japan* or the *Empress of Canada*, were not available on any of the *President* ships except the *President Coolidge* and the *President Hoover*.

Wood paneling graced the staterooms and public rooms of the *Empresses*, but painted and stippled plaster and beaverboard divided compartments on the *President* liners. Hanscom also complained about the monotonous white color scheme that prevailed on all Dollar and AML ships. Competing vessels had varied colors in passenger compartments, modern furniture, and forty-inch-wide beds of polished nickel, compared to the twenty-six-inch-wide white-painted steel beds in the staterooms of the 502s and 535s. Despite the desperate need to modernize if the company were to meet the competition, Hanscom's recommendations were ignored because of more pressing needs for cash.[9]

In 1931 Dollar did make a major change in scheduling. The horseshoe route was abandoned, and four of the 535s were placed in the Seattle-Manila trade under the aegis of the American Mail Line. The

other six 535s plus the new *Presidents Hoover* and *Coolidge* operated
from New York, through the Panama Canal to San Francisco, and
thence to the Orient. The round-the-world ships already provided
westbound service via the Panama Canal, but now Dollar offered
sailings eastbound every two weeks in addition to the now-weekly
westbound service. This change placed them in a position to compete effectively with the Panama Pacific Line and the Grace Line,
which were already in the trade.

From the outset the *Presidents Hoover* and *Coolidge* were fitted to
carry passengers in four classes: first class, special class (a euphe-
mism for what was generally known as tourist class), third class, and
steerage for Orientals. In 1932 the 535s were altered to carry tourist
as well as first class. This modification was accomplished by setting
aside some of the less desirable staterooms and deck space, parti-
tioning off part of the dining salon, and fitting up small lounges
and smoking rooms for tourist-class passengers. The 502s continued
to carry first class only, and *Presidents Adams, Garfield, Harrison,* and
Polk had alterations made to their superstructures to provide twenty
additional staterooms. By this time all the Dollar passenger steamers
had outdoor swimming tanks for passengers in first class and special class.

Fares were reduced in order to stimulate travel. In 1927 round-the-
world fares ranged from $1,000 for a room without private bath to
$1,260 for private bath to $3,500 for a suite. A few years later the fare
was $749 for a room without bath, $907 for a room with bath, and
$1,867 for a two- to three-room suite. In 1936 Dollar offered a round-
the-world rate of $567. This fare covered a voyage of 110 days, calling
at twenty-two ports and traveling 26,000 miles. Trans-Pacific passenger rates did not change drastically, however. In 1925 the first-
class fare from California to Yokohama was $300 and to Hong Kong
$375. In 1937 these fares were still unchanged.

Until 1930 the Dollar Steamship and American Mail had managed
to keep up interest and principal payments to the Anglo-California
Bank and the United States government. In 1931, however, the lines
requested a two-year moratorium on payments to the government.
The Shipping Board agreed to the extension, but Dollar Steamship
had a net loss of $1 million in 1932 and almost as great a loss in 1933.
Even before reporting its 1933 loss, the company's cash flow had
declined so precipitously that its financial condition became critical.
Obviously it could not meet its obligations to the government with

its working capital so gravely impaired. Besides defaulting on notes that came due in 1931 and in 1932, it was unable to meet its obligations maturing in 1933.

At this point the comptroller general of the United States stepped in. He insisted that the deliquencies be made up either from the mail subsidy or from a tighter financial control over the company's management. From various sources the comptroller general had learned that Dollar management had been diverting large sums from the working capital of the lines through the seventeen service companies it controlled. In 1932, for example, one of these subsidiaries, the Robert Dollar Company—which acted as managing agent for all the lines—reported a profit of $60,000 and an outlay for executive salaries of $135,000. Yet that year, the Dollar Steamship Company reported a loss of $1 million and in 1931, when it received a two-year extension for payments on its government debts, R. Stanley Dollar received in salaries alone $216,447 from Dollar Steamship, American Mail, and Tacoma Oriental. His brother J. Harold Dollar, H. M. Lorber, and Herbert Fleishhacker of the Anglo-California Bank divided an additional $202,759. Altogether, from 1923 when the Dollars first began acquiring ships from the government, these four individuals were paid almost $5 million, with the lion's share of over two-and-one-half million dollars going to R. Stanley Dollar.[10]

Considering the deteriorating condition of the Dollar-controlled fleet and the failure to modernize, it seemed the height of poor administration and personal irresponsibility, if not unethical behavior on the part of the managers, to divert 10 percent of the mail subsidy to their own pockets through the Robert Dollar agency. This particular charge on working capital, of course, was only a part of the systematic draining of company assets that had been going on for ten years before it became evident to Washington.

However wasteful the practices that the government auditors uncovered, it was obvious to the Shipping Board that mere reform alone would not solve the cash-flow problem. And if the mail subsidy were applied to the debt, the Dollar Line and its subsidiaries faced bankruptcy. Thus the government chose the option of more direct control over the budgets of the debt-ridden lines. On 11 April 1933 the Shipping Board adopted a resolution to that effect and implemented it with a memorandum that stipulated how joint control would work. When the Dollar companies accepted the mandate they in effect entered into a contract with the board that permitted oversight of their financial operations. As Max O'Rell Truitt, a member of the Maritime Commission, outlined it in a report of 27 September 1938, the contract provided

> That all transfers from the joint account (namely, the mail revenue account) to general funds of the company could only be effected upon countersignature of a representative of the Shipping Board. It also provided for complete inspection of the books of the operation and all subsidiaries and affiliates. The theory of the joint account was that ordinary revenues should first be used to meet operating expenses and that such operating expenses should be subject to government control, the mail revenue was to be used to pay, first, interest on the government loans, then to meet emergency operating requirements and the balance to reduce the principal of the government loans.

Two Shipping Board financial men were sent to San Francisco to ensure compliance.

But the Dollar management resisted their efforts to make changes in disbursements. Nor would Stanley Dollar and Hugo Lorber, the only executives with this authority, permit the Shipping Board to examine the books of the subsidiary companies. As the government auditors reported to Washington, "on no less than seven different occasions they refused to give information regarding these items or to permit verification through the books of subsidiaries and affiliates." Only after a direct order from the comptroller general did Dollar and Lorber relent, but they still rejected any effort to audit the books of the Robert Dollar Company.[11]

An accident that claimed two lives and caused damages of about $500,000 to one of AML's 535s oddly enough briefly eased the financial pressure. On 24 March 1933 the *President Madison*, which was undergoing repairs at her pier in Seattle, capsized in sixty feet of water. After R. Stanley Dollar learned that the insurance settlement would be $1 million, he telephoned Admiral H. I. Cone of the Shipping Board that AML would accept payment but would not repair the *President Madison* and put her into service. As he explained to Cone, AML would use the funds to pay off completely the $360,000 mortgage on the vessel and settle past-due notes on all of AML's 535s, an additional $315,000. The balance would be applied to working capital. Moreover, AML would be able to make their mail contracts without the use of the *President Madison*.[12]

The *Madison* settlement bought only temporary relief. Yet despite government pressure and sharply declining revenues, Stanley Dollar continued to draw funds for his personal account at a higher rate than he had in either of the two preceding years. For the first six months of 1934 Dollar and Lorber were paid $92,000.[13] In addition to this income from the Robert Dollar Company and from the other service companies under family control, American Mail paid him almost $50,000. He collected a similar amount from Dollar Steamship. Even Herbert Fleishhacker, whose managerial duties at American Mail were nonexistent, drew a salary of $12,000 a year and was listed as a vice president of the line.[14]

Many of these facts were drawn out in an investigation of mail subsidies Senator Hugo Black of Alabama conducted during the spring and summer of 1933. Dollar Line and American Mail Line executives testified frequently during the hearings. The investigation may have had a partisan tone, and it surely was directed against the Republican-sponsored Jones-White Act of 1928, but it did uncover wholesale diversions of mail funds to the personal accounts of shipping executives. And that section of the Jones-White Act that required new construction as a condition for the mail subsidy had been largely evaded after the crash in 1929. The Dollars, for example, had agreed to construct four new vessels but had built only two, the *President Hoover* and the *President Coolidge*. Other shipping lines were, if anything, more delinquent than the Dollar Line.

As a direct result of the Black hearings and the resulting publicity, President Roosevelt directed Postmaster General James A. Farley to make another investigation of the mail contracts. Farley's report, which was released in early 1935 and like the Black hearings had a partisan tone, was a severe indictment of the shipping industry's policies on mail subsidies. Roosevelt had also appointed an interdepartmental committee for policy guidance on the merchant marine. Its report, made at the same time as the report from the postmaster general, was more favorable to the shipping lines. It singled out various economic factors like the decline of world trade due to the Depression, costly strikes that hampered operations, and especially the differentials in labor, construction, and ship repair costs that provided a competitive edge to foreign operators. The report recommended that the mail subsidy arrangement be discarded and that the government pay differential subsidies for trade routes that were in the national interest as defined by defense and economic needs.

President Roosevelt accepted most of these recommendations. In general terms he suggested a direct subsidy policy for the merchant marine. He emphasized three points in his message to Congress on 4 March 1935. First, he noted that foreign nations had no qualms about granting subsidies or rebates to their flag carriers and that these practices ruled out fair competition for American shippers. His other two points underscored the importance of a strong merchant marine in time of war or threatened war as cargo and troop carriers and as maintainers of vital trade routes. To implement this policy he advised that Congress replace mail contract subsidies with direct subsidies that "should cover first the difference in the cost of building ships; second, the difference in the cost of operating ships; and finally, it should take into consideration the liberal subsidies that many foreign governments provide for their shipping."[15]

Through two sessions of Congress, various bills looking to the reconstruction of the merchant marine were introduced and debated on Capitol Hill and in the nation's press. Everyone supported the idea that the United States should have a strong merchant navy, but sharp differences arose over how this was to be achieved. The shipping industry favored government support, direct and unequivocal, with few strings attached. Liberal New Dealers in and out of Congress favored a government-owned and operated merchant marine, along the lines of such utilities as the Tennessee Valley Authority. Eventually a compromise emerged that embodied the direct subsidy idea for both construction and operation on designated routes.[16] But the Merchant Marine Act that passed Congress in 1936 and that President Roosevelt signed into law sidestepped the sticky question of public or private ownership. Instead, the act abolished the Shipping Board and replaced it with the Federal Maritime Commission, which was given broad discretionary powers.

The new commission could build, own, and operate merchant ships directly or under charter arrangements if private interests were unable to undertake the program of modernization the act contemplated. But the clear implication was that existing shipping lines would be encouraged through subsidies, not penalized by either the threat of government ownership or outright competition from government-owned and operated lines.[17] Throughout the debates on the Merchant Marine bill of 1936, there was an awareness that defense needs were as important in determining policy as were the economic aspects of international trade.

The rise of fascism and communism in Europe and the belligerent posture of Japan in the Far East greatly concerned the Roosevelt Administration. And the strengthening of the merchant marine, especially in the Pacific, was a factor in granting such broad powers to the commission. Finally, Congress appropriated funds to finance a program that envisaged the construction of sixty-five vessels. Later, as the Sino-Japanese War broke out and the situation in Europe became more menacing, the building program was accelerated.

The commission was to be nonpartisan. Roosevelt appointed Joseph P. Kennedy to be its first chairman, and through the force of his personality as well as his business acumen he forged a policy that assumed the public interest would have priority over private interests. Efficient and economical maintenance of the Pacific trade routes was uppermost in his mind. If existing privately owned lines on the West Coast could not measure up to the standards of business practice he deemed essential, Kennedy had no compunction in withholding assistance or even foreclosure in the case of debt owed to the government. His successor in 1938, Admiral Emory S. Land, continued this policy.[18]

Meanwhile the outlook for Dollar Steamship and its subsidiary companies American Mail and Tacoma Oriental was becoming progressively worse. In the spring of 1934, San Francisco longshoremen sought control of hiring procedures, a closed shop, higher wages, and improved working conditions. Heretofore, company unions had represented longshoremen and ships' crews. A well-financed and aggressive owners' association had held the line against any change since the waterfront strike of 1920.

From the mid-twenties on, W. P. Bannister had been Dollar Steamship's labor relations director. A blunt, gruff person, Bannister made no bones about his antiunion attitude. In this respect he was simply reflecting management's policy, which had remained relatively unchanged since the turn of the century. Working conditions and pay on the Dollar ships were superior to those of seamen from other maritime nations, but could not compare with such competitors as the Matson or the States lines, neither of whose employee policies was especially enlightened. All were opposed to unionization and clung to absolute control over hiring, whether it be for ships' crews or for longshoremen gangs.[19]

Inspired by the labor provisions of NRA codes and well organized by the Australian-born union leader Harry Bridges, the longshoremen of San Francisco demanded a union shop. When the

Waterfront Employers Association refused, the longshoremen decided to strike. The Roosevelt Administration managed to delay action for arbitration. While bargaining was going on, the International Seamen's Union sought union recognition and improved working conditions. The Steamship Owners' Association rejected all demands. When arbitration of the longshoremen's grievances failed on 6 May 1934, they went on strike. Six days later, the seamen struck, not just in San Francisco, but along the entire West Coast. In addition, a two-day city-wide general strike in San Francisco was called to show sympathy for the longshoremen and the seamen.

During the month of July all commercial activity ceased. Sporadic violence occurred in San Francisco and in other ports. In mid-July President Roosevelt appointed a board headed by Secretary of Labor Frances Perkins to investigate and recommend a course of action. The association and the unions accepted the board's report, which called for binding arbitration. On 31 July 1934 the strike was over but not before it had dealt a damaging blow to the already-weakened Dollar lines.

As a result of arbitration and pressure from the National Labor Relations Board, a settlement was reached in April 1935 that granted almost all of the unions' demands.[20] The faltering Dollar companies were now faced with sharply increased operating costs at a time when they were unable to meet the interest, let alone reduce the principal on their debts to the government, and were barely able to stave off default on their debts to banks in San Francisco and Seattle. In fact, the Anglo-California Bank came under sharp criticism from the comptroller of the currency for not having adequate collateral to secure its loans to the Dollar lines and for its failure to have the principal of these loans reduced during the past year.[21]

The Shipping Board again exerted pressure on the bank and the Dollars to place the debt position on a sounder footing. After lengthy talks, R. Stanley Dollar finally agreed to pledge some of the company's nonoperating assets as collateral for $3 million in bank loans and $1 million of indebtedness to the government that was past due. The company instituted a program of strict economy and a schedule for payment of debts under Shipping Board guidelines. By these means the Dollar company managed to keep their debt on a current basis, but only at the expense of new debt incurred for the construction of the *President Hoover* and *President Coolidge*. The first installment to be paid on these mortgages was about to come due.

Interest and principal on the total unfunded debt grew rapidly so that by October 1935, the Dollar lines were $3 million in arrears to the government on a debt of $15 million. Some $3 million was owed the Anglo-California Bank and $2.5 million to other creditors, primarily suppliers.

The Anglo-California Bank had so much of its assets tied up in the Dollar lines that if the latter went bankrupt, they might very well carry down the bank as well. Yet under the pay-back arrangement of the Shipping Board, the working capital of the lines became progressively impaired.[22] As Max O'Rell Truitt said, "Under the policy adopted in 1934 the government incurred substantial repayment which, however, was at the expense of working assets . . . the payments made to the government, therefore, merely shifted the burden to the other creditors."[23]

This was the situation when the Dollar lines sustained in quick succession a series of heavy blows to its already gravely weakened financial structure. The agreement between shipowners and the unions that followed the 1934 strike expired on 30 September 1936. The seafaring unions were now pressing new demands. First, they wanted the hiring-hall system to be continued; second, they insisted on the elimination of optional overtime and cash to be paid for all overtime; third, they demanded a wage increase of 20 percent across the board with a 55 percent increase in hourly overtime rates; fourth, a union shop; and fifth, all other demands to be adjusted by the Maritime Administration, whose decision would be final. The cooks' and stewards' union had similar demands, as did the longshoremen's union. Thus the West Coast unions were acting together.[24]

West Coast shipping owners were unwilling to accept any of these demands. R. Stanley Dollar, reporting to his board of directors, estimated that in wage costs alone, acceptance of the union's demands would increase operating expenses "nearly $1,800,000 yearly." "It would be entirely impractical," he added, "to continue operation if the demands of the unions were granted, although it appears the only alternative is a general marine strike involving dock operators as well as ships."[25]

The newly appointed Maritime Commission managed to postpone any action on either side for a month. Secretary of Labor Perkins sent her Under Secretary Edward F. McGrady to the West Coast as a conciliator. But he was unable to secure an agreement and in mid-October 1936 all of the maritime unions on the West Coast struck. Dollar estimated that 232 vessels were idled at ports up and down the coast. Almost immediately Dollar Steamship, American Mail, and Tacoma Oriental had to refund passenger tickets and return stranded passengers from ships that were tied up. The Dollar Line, for instance, paid $3,500 to the Matson line for transporting passengers on board the *President Pierce* from Honolulu to San Francisco. Various Dollar lines endorsed tickets worth $125,980 to Nippon Yusen Kaisha and the Canadian Pacific Company.[26]

Although there was none of the violence that characterized the 1934 strike, the consequences for the Dollar lines were much more serious. Their ships were tied up for over three months, and, as Dollar had predicted, the settlement that in almost every respect met the unions' demands increased operating costs significantly at a time when freight and passenger traffic on their Pacific routes was still far below pre-Depression levels.[27] The first casualty was the Tacoma Oriental Line, a majority of whose stock was owned by Dollar-controlled Admiral Oriental Line.

Operations of Tacoma Oriental's fleet of seven vessels had been synchronized with those of American Mail, although it remained a separate company. On 18 November 1936, Tacoma Oriental filed for bankruptcy in the U.S. District Court for the Western Division of Washington.

On 30 January 1937 the court ordered the sale of its assets to satisfy creditors and the eventual dissolution of the company.[28] Loss of Tacoma Oriental did not so much impair the financial situation of the Dollar companies as it injured their credit status among banks and created further doubts about their management in Washington.

The collapse of Pacific Steam's Admiral Line in March 1937 was more serious. The Admiral Line, which operated an extensive coastal business, had been one of the first shipping lines on the West Coast to feel the effects of the Depression. For the three years 1929–1931 the line lost well over $2 million and was forced to default on its marine equipment mortgage. H. F. Alexander resigned in 1931, but R. Stanley Dollar decided that the line must continue operations. J. Harold Dollar became its new president with the task of protecting the heavy investment the family had in the line through utilizing its ships as feeders for the trans-Pacific fleet.

The Admiral Line continued to lose money, however. In 1932 it sustained a loss of $1,359,804. And in 1933 the trustee for the bondholders sold its ships worth over $1 million for slightly over $500,000 to the Dollars. Stanley Dollar tried various means to reorganize Pacific Steam, but when they failed to improve its financial picture, he began to liquidate the family's interest in the company. This process was not complete when his brother J. Harold died of cancer on 7 April 1936, leaving the line without an executive head. Then in October the maritime strike dealt a crippling blow. All operations ceased in June 1938 and to all intents and purposes Pacific Steam and its Admiral Line went out of existence. As Joseph P. Kennedy remarked, "Much as I oppose government ownership, nevertheless, as a practical matter to me it is inevitable because of the impossible situation we have today. We have old ships; they are mostly in the hands of people who have no money."[29]

A far greater blow to the Dollar enterprises came at about the same time in the form of a wireless message to company headquarters at 311 California Street. The *President Hoover* had run aground off the east coast of Taiwan and it seemed likely that she would have to be abandoned. For the past several months the trade of the various Dollar companies with China had been interrupted by a sharp escalation of the Sino-Japanese War. Japanese armies occupied Peking, Tientsin, Shanghai, and Nanking. Not only had freight and passenger traffic from Chinese ports declined and insurance rates risen sharply, but with the major port of Shanghai closed, Dollar vessels had to be rerouted.

The *President Hoover* was in Kobe when her captain, George W. Yardley, received a wireless message from the home office that the fighting between Japanese and Chinese forces around Shanghai had brought all operations in that busy port to a complete halt. He was instructed to sail directly to Manila, omitting Shanghai. Yardley decided to cut time and distance by sailing east of Taiwan rather than following the traditional course south through the Formosa (Taiwan) Strait. The new course involved some risk because of shoal waters and dozens of small islands off the coast. But Yardley had good charts, from which he concluded that the Japanese government had marked the sea routes off the eastern coast of Taiwan with ample navigational aids.

The *President Hoover* left Kobe on a stormy morning and as she steamed south encountered rain squalls and low visibility. When she arrived in the vicinity of Taiwan's northeast coast, Yardley discovered that the Japanese had extinguished most of the lights and removed many of the other navigational aids on the mainland of Taiwan and the islands offshore. Despite these hindrances to a safe passage and the fact that because of weather conditions the *President Hoover* was proceeding on dead reckoning in shallow waters with tricky currents, Captain Yardley maintained his cruising speed of twenty knots. At midnight on 11 December 1937 Eugene Lukes, an assistant purser on the vessel at the time, recalled that he was awakened by a heavy jarring and bumping. "If you had that feeling once," said Lukes, "you would recognize it. She had stranded. We had come to a halt. Even with flood lights we could not see anything. Apparently we were in the middle of the ocean, but we could hear surf."[30]

Captain Yardley immediately ordered soundings at number three hatch forward under the bridge. Soundings revealed twenty feet of water in the hold and the same depth of water surrounding the vessel from the bow to amidships. The *President Hoover* was not only hard aground but had lost her bottom plates almost to her firerooms, approximately half of the ship. Moreover, soon after stranding she had broached on Hoishoto Island. Since no immediate damage was posed to crew and passengers, Captain Yardley waited until there was enough light to disembark without unnecessary hazard. He ordered oil spread on the lee of the huge ship, which smoothed out the choppy waves. And then he had several lines taken ashore so that the lifeboats could make their way through the surf. In about two hours, all of the passengers and most of the crew were landed safely. Yardley himself and a skeleton force remained aboard. He hoped to get the *President Hoover* off and radioed to Kobe for divers and a salvage tug. The following message went to the home office:[31]

Aboard Hoover: Stranded north-west point Hoishoto Island resting rotten coral heading 104 degrees with 7½ degree list to port. Present weather strong northeast monsoon. Pounding slightly. Soundings forward average 3½ fathoms both inshore offshore to break forward house; about 3 fathoms inshore 4 offshore to after part midship deck; from there aft 3 to 5 inshore, 4 to 5½ offshore. No divers have been down yet. Seawater rising falling with tide in all cargoholds, deep tanks. Vessel set up in no. 3. Forward boiler room bulkhead leaking. Port motor strained. Engine and boiler rooms kept dry by vessel's pumps.

The *President Hoover* aground on Hoishoto Island off the northeast coast of Taiwan in 1937. Adjudged a total loss, she was broken up by Japanese salvors. (Courtesy United States Salvage Association.)

> Estimate 60% cargo damaged oil and seawater. Salvage depends largely upon condition weather.

Salvage proved not to be feasible and the *President Hoover* was adjudged a total loss. The Japanese salvagers, who got an estimated 14,000 tons of scrap metal from the hulk, eventually paid the insurance underwriters $50,000.

At one stroke revenues for Dollar Steamship were cut by about one-fourth. The *President Hoover* and the *President Coolidge* were the most profitable ships of the line. Most of the insurance money would go for the reduction of indebtedness and since Dollar Steam-

ship and American Mail were on the brink of bankruptcy, the loss of
the *President Hoover* seemed likely to take them both under. The
Maritime Commission was faced with the gravest crisis yet in the
tangled affairs of the Dollar companies.

As the government began to phase out of the mail subsidy program and prepared to institute a direct subsidy, it became apparent
that unless quick action were taken to supply funds, Dollar Steamship and American Mail would follow Tacoma Oriental and Pacific
Steam's Admiral Line into receivership. But the Maritime Commission was unwilling to grant a long-term subsidy until it was satisfied
that Dollar management was sound and that Dollar resources were
sufficient to meet long-deferred repairs, not to mention new construction that was required under the terms of the 1936 act.

The commission also decided to apply impounded mail subsidy
funds to the principal and interest of the Dollar indebtedness. In
response to a frantic telegram of protest from the Dollar board of
directors, Max Truitt wrote Stanley Dollar disclaiming any responsibility for the commission's action. He said:

> For several weeks, we have tried without success to obtain
> sufficient financial information to negotiate for a settlement of
> our various claims and to grant an operating differential subsidy
> that would enable you to compete with your foreign com-
> petitors as provided in the act. If the information had been
> furnished promptly the matter would long since have been
> concluded. Financial relief has been delayed only because your
> company has deliberately failed to cooperate with the commis-
> sion in these matters.[32]

The commission realized that withholding of the mail subsidy
from Dollar Steamship and American Mail might well force both
companies into receivership. Dollar, who had come to Washington,
thought that bankruptcy was the only alternative. The Anglo-California Bank disagreed. Its vice president, Paul Hoover, hurried to
Washington and convinced the commission that a 77 B reorganization (bankruptcy) would be "a long-drawn-out, expensive and
complex procedure and that representatives of the company desired
to have an opportunity to work out a voluntary reorganization."[33]

Dollar thereupon devised a plan to capitalize a portion of the debt
through the issue of preferred stock and debentures that would
cover all private obligations. When he presented it to the board,

however, he encountered spirited opposition. Herbert Fleishhacker, for one, refused to go along. He was worried about the future plans of the commission and concerned that his personal stake in the Dollar companies would lose most of its value. "This Shipping Board [Maritime Commission] is here today and gone tomorrow," he said. "Kennedy is already talking of resigning."[34] The commission decided it would extend a temporary differential subsidy with the possibility of loans from the Reconstruction Finance Corporation for essential repairs and eventually a new construction. But before taking any of these steps it sent a team of legal and financial experts to San Francisco where they would work out with Dollar and Lorber a fourfold program. First the plan would seek an adjustment of the intercompany bank and trade debts, possibly through a new issue of stock. Second, the commission would attempt to reach an accommodation with Dollar and Lorber whereby they would supply from their other private assets sufficient cash ($500,000 was mentioned) to ease the strain on working capital. Third, the plan contemplated the removal of the Robert Dollar Company from its role as managing agent while the temporary subsidy was in effect. Fourth, the team would study and report whether there should be any changes in management.

An immediate result of the team's work in San Francisco was Herbert Fleishhacker's change of stance on Stanley Dollar's plan for issuing preferred shares and bonds as a partial settlement with the Anglo-California Bank and the trade creditors. Dollar Steamship would issue 33,595 shares of preferred stock along with $377,300 in 3 percent debentures. From its all-but-empty cash reserves the company scraped up $261,086. Trade creditors got $1,468,586 in cash, debentures, and preferred stock, $1,338,900 in preferred stock was issued to settle intercompany claims, and finally, the Anglo-California Bank received $1,140,494 in preferred stock, which paid off about one-half of the principal owed.[35]

While its team was in San Francisco, Joseph P. Kennedy telephoned Secretary of State Cordell Hall about the situation in Asia and the consequences of a suspension of the Dollar lines. Hull thought any stoppage of Dollar service should be avoided. "The existing hostilities between Japan and China," he said, "which are now threatening the safety of thousands of American citizens located in other Asiatic cities . . . the suspension of the service in view of the present precarious condition might seriously endanger the lives of Americans in Asia."[36] As a result of this conversation and the report of the commission's team in San Francisco, which indicated apparent agreement of Dollar Steamship, Kennedy and his colleagues promised a temporary subsidy. They also agreed to advance $1 million for repairs, the money to be secured by a blanket mortgage on the Dollar fleet.

It was at this point, just as a policy seemed to have been worked out, that the *President Hoover* was lost off Taiwan. Dollar and the board of Dollar Steamship now began to feel that any compromise with the government would entail the pledge of all their resources, including their private fortunes, to what might well be a dubious enterprise. Neither Dollar nor Lorber nor Fleishhacker was prepared to gamble his own and his family's future on the mere promise of a government subsidy. What they wanted was some means whereby the huge debts that hung over them would be discharged without any personal liability. Thus they were unresponsive to the commission's offer.

On 22 December 1937 Joseph R. Sheehan, Kennedy's executive assistant, telephoned Dollar and suggested that he might also consider the sale of the company's fleet to another line. Dollar lost no time in contacting William Roth, president of the Matson line. Roth was "definitely interested." "We have not arrived at any number yet," said Dollar in a later conversation with Sheehan. "We have been talking about the *Coolidge* and maybe 3, 4 or 5 of the 535s that would relieve the pressure and I am sure we could work out a plan that would be satisfactory to everyone." But negotiations between Matson and the Maritime Commission over subsidies, as a condition of sale, did not work out.[37]

Twelve days later Kennedy himself, his assistant Joseph Sheehan, and Max Truitt, at the time the commission's general counsel, arrived in San Francisco. In response to a call from Reginald Laughlin, a member of the commission staff in the city, Dollar agreed to meet with Kennedy and Truitt. Dollar summoned the senior executives of his company, who all went over to Laughlin's office, where Kennedy was waiting. "Who are all these men?" asked Kennedy of Dollar. "I want to talk with you and you alone." Kennedy's rather curt remark did not faze Dollar, who responded, "I would like Mr. H. M. Lorber to stay, and I would like my nephew, Mr. Robert Dollar II to stay." "That is all right," said Kennedy. The other executives remained in the reception room while the conference took place.

Kennedy took the lead in the discussion. He told Dollar that he and his associates would have "to come up with $500,000 in cash and have it in the bank by the next morning or there was nothing to talk about; that he would throw us into bankruptcy." Dollar said he would have to call the Fleishhackers at the Anglo-California Bank and ask them to join the conference. When they arrived Kennedy repeated what he had said. Dollar then said that they would have to discuss the matter privately. Everyone assented. The Dollar group moved to the other side of the office. Addressing the Fleishhackers in muted tones, Dollar offered to put up $250,000 if they would put up the other $250,000. After some hesitation both Fleishhackers agreed. As soon as Kennedy learned of their decision, he asked Truitt and Laughlin to draft a letter embodying their acceptance of the cash requirement and the appointment of a commission nominee to be vice president-finance of Dollar Steamship. While the letter was being written, Dollar asked Kennedy if there would be further demands.

"No," he replied.

"Will this qualify us for a subsidy?" Dollar queried.

"Yes, it will," said Kennedy, "and I am going to give you a six-month temporary subsidy, and I will give you a long-range subsidy."

"What will it be—a twenty-year subsidy?" asked Dollar.

"No, I can't do that," Kennedy said, "but I will give you a ten-year subsidy."

"Have we a meeting of the minds on this?" asked Dollar. "Is this thing final?"

"Yes it is final," said Kennedy.

By now the letter had been drafted. Dollar thought he should consult with his board and the company's attorneys but Kennedy was adamant. Dollar signed. He had no other choice, but he kept to himself certain reservations.[38] That evening Kennedy attended a dinner at the Bohemian Club in San Francisco, where it had been arranged for him to give a speech on the government's maritime policy. Among the guests was R. Stanley Dollar, a member of the club.

Kennedy's manner was completely different from what it had been a few hours earlier. He greeted Dollar warmly and in the course of his remarks alluded in cautiously optimistic terms to the meeting in Laughlin's office. In his speech he said:

I am happy to announce that the Commission has just today reached an agreement with the Dollar interests with regard to its continued operation in foreign commerce. Under the agreement, the line will be given a temporary operating subsidy pending an effort on the part of all interested parties to work out an ultimate solution of the problem involved.

I want to point out, however, that this is not to be regarded as a permanent or satisfactory solution of the Dollar situation. This solution does not provide new capital which is necessary for the replacement of the obsolete vessels which make up a large part of the Dollar fleet.[39]

Before the speech that evening Kennedy had begun to implement the understanding he thought he had with Dollar with regard to the appointment of a new vice president of finance for the company. He already had a person in mind for the position, Arthur Poole, a distinguished accountant whom he had known for many years.

Poole had worked with Kennedy since 1927. He had impressed that shrewd and immensely capable financier with his ability to evaluate accurately the economic status and future prospects of ailing corporations that Kennedy thought had investment potential. In fact, at Kennedy's behest Poole had examined the reports and other documents the Dollar Line had submitted to the commission. It had been Poole's opinion that at the very least the Dollar interests should provide $500,000 in new capital before any subsidy was granted.

When Dollar, Lorber, and Herbert Fleishhacker agreed to the Poole appointment, Joseph Sheehan called Poole in New York offering him the post but requiring a prompt decision. As soon as Poole accepted, Sheehan asked if he could be present at a special board meeting of the Dollar Line on Monday, January 12. "I went into New York," Poole recalled. "I had an office there and closed out my affairs . . . on Sunday afternoon, I took a plane to come out here. It was a Douglas DC-3. I think we came down six or seven times for fuel on the way out but we got here 9:34 on the dot Monday morning, April 12." There was barely enough time for a scant briefing from Kennedy and his associates before Poole attended the special meeting of Dollar Steamship at 2:30 that afternoon. The board elected him vice president and treasurer of Dollar Steamship and a member of its board of directors.[40]

After a month of hard work, Poole found that the company was in a far more difficult position than either he or the commission had thought. The temporary operating subsidy of $1.4 million would only meet an estimated 53.63 percent of repair costs mandated by the "safety-at-sea" requirement of the shipping act.[41] The remainder, he felt, could be covered from the *President Hoover* insurance money. Nor was the $500,000 in new capital that Dollar and Herbert Fleishhacker had promised sufficient to keep the trade creditors at bay, let alone make any payment on arrears of the huge debt owed the government.[42] By now the line owed its trade creditors almost $2 million and management was fearful that those few ships still operating would be libeled.[43] The cash position throughout the spring and summer of 1938 remained dangerously low. Moreover, a commission investigation of shoreside management uncovered serious deficiencies in administration and policymaking. The lower echelons of organization, however, were deemed sound, and indeed were complimented for their ability and resourcefulness under trying conditions.[44]

Utilizing Poole's examinations, reports, and other data the commission, now headed by Admiral Emory S. Land, decided that it could not refinance the company and grant a five-year subsidy unless the Dollar interests pledged their stock for collateral. But confronted with a liability of about $17 million, an obsolete fleet worth at most about $11 million, and interest charges accumulating at the rate of $80,000 a month, they capitulated. As R. Stanley Dollar said, "For a man and his family to turn over all they have and lose control of the company and not know whether the people operating it will operate it successfully—they could break it very easily, I don't think it is fair of anyone to ask me to do that, that is my opinion of it."[45] Hugo Lorber thought that the subsidy arrangement offered was simply tantamount to an eventual takeover by the government. As he reviewed the past seven years of decline, he said:

> The business has always been more or less closely held. If we had the means, we bought ships and carried on our business in that manner. We got to the point with the subsidy business and building obligations that we could not, with our means, carry on a big program like that. If we expanded we would have to expand so that the general public could participate and the stock be sold on the exchange.
>
> With that thought in mind the Delaware Corporation was formed. It was arranged so stock could be put on the market.

> We contracted for the *President Hoover* and *President Coolidge*, which were necessary to carry out our subsidy obligations and the Bank underwrote 25 percent of the down payment.
>
> We had hardly put our name on the contract when the stock market crash of '29 came, and we had no chance to float the stock. Now the Maritime Commission is proposing to load the company with a further loan of 3½ million and don't know how we can pay it back. Then there is a building program that will further keep us in debt . . . I don't know how we could borrow more money. Even with the subsidy I don't feel the round-the-world ships can make money.[46]

On 15 August 1938, in return for release of all liability, the Dollar interests assigned their voting stock to the commission. Dollar did insist that "the employees be retained." He also stipulated that whatever organization succeeded Dollar Steamship it would not use the Dollar name. "It is our family name," he remarked later, "and I didn't know what kind of management was going in." The commission was happy to comply with these requests. It had already decided that the Dollar organization below the top executive level must be kept intact at all costs. And as far as the Dollar name, goodwill, and house flag were concerned, Land and his fellow commissioners felt that the past several years of neglect and mismanagement had, if anything, produced a negative image.

Under the financial terms of the agreement, the Dollar interests surrendered about 90 percent of the common stock. The commission then arranged for a loan from the Reconstruction Finance Corporation of $2.5 million for working capital. Out of its own appropriations, it advanced $2 million for repairs, and it granted a twelve-year operating differential subsidy that would provide payments of about $3 million a year. The commission felt that these funds, together with the anticipated earnings of the line, were sufficient to discharge the debts to the Anglo-California Bank, the trade creditors, and the United States government.[47] Contrary to what he would maintain at a later date, Dollar did not simply pledge the common stock he and his group relinquished to the government; they transferred ownership. In a letter to W. T. Mitchell, a shipping agent in London, Dollar confirmed this fact: "Under our agreement with the Maritime Commission," he wrote, "we surrendered our stock, and in return were relieved of our obligations under the mortgages. The outcome is that the Maritime Commission now *owns* approximately 90 percent of the stock in the new Company and thus are in a position to control the Directorate."[48]

Meanwhile, American Mail was experiencing similar difficulties. When Ancil Haines became critically ill (he died on 15 May 1937), the company had been finding it increasingly difficult to meet its obligations, let alone make a profit.[49] John Cormode, Haines's assistant, had taken over as general manager. Though a capable shipping man, Cormode was unable to improve the capital position of the line, which between 1926 and 1933 had paid out to R. Stanley Dollar, his brother Harold, H. M. Lorber, and Herbert Fleishhacker the sum of almost $2 million in salaries.[50] Yet so dependent had American Mail become on government support that an adjustment in the payment schedule of the mail subsidy in the winter of 1935 required a bank loan of $50,000 to meet its monthly operating costs.[51]

Under the authority of the Merchant Marine Act of 1936, American Mail had been granted a temporary operating subsidy. It quickly became apparent, however, that these payments were not sufficient to place the line on a break-even basis. Since January 1938 American Mail had unsuccessfully sought an increase in the subsidy of $9,000 for each voyage.

At a special board meeting on 10 May 1938, the directors decided to advise the commission that all operations would have to be terminated when its temporary subsidy contract expired on 22 June. Before taking this step, however, a sharp argument developed between Fleishhacker and Dollar. Fleishhacker thought that the commission should be informed that the current subsidy was inadequate and that American Mail would lose about $300,000 after depreciation for the year 1938. What he wanted was a new subsidy contract that would improve American Mail's bargaining position in the sale of its ships to Seattle interests. Dollar disagreed with this strategy. "We will have to continue under our contract with them until June 24," he said. "If we ask for a new contract it is going to bring up the question of invested capital and they will say we have to put up more money and a lot of other things and it is not going to get us anywhere. In the light of past experience I feel we should not ask for a new contract." Cormode reminded the board that the commission would not award a long-term contract without being assured of a new construction program to replace American Mail's aging 535s. Reluctantly the board agreed to go along with Fleishhacker's suggestion. Cormode was directed to send a telegram to the commission requesting a new contract and stating that "under existing conditions and the subsidy allowances now in effect, it would be impossible for the company to continue its operation after the termination of the present contract on June 22, 1938."[52] Three weeks later the board received its answer from the commission. After 3 June 1938 operations of American Mail and the Dollar Steamship Line were to be suspended.

At the time all seven of the Dollar Line's round-the-world ships were at sea. Its three remaining 535s and the *President Coolidge* were completing their trans-Pacific runs. The *President Wilson* and the *President Lincoln* were in San Francisco. All of American Mail's vessels were in Seattle. Because of its mortgage obligations, Dollar Steamship sent its last vessel, the *President Adams*, on the round-the-world run. The *Presidents Pierce, Coolidge,* and *Cleveland* made their last trans-Pacific voyages during the summer and fall of 1938. By then, the Dollar Line was no more. Dollar, Lorber, Charles King (its operations head), and E. H. Hall (its treasurer) had all resigned on 26 October 1938. American Mail, its four 535s tied up in Seattle (the *President Madison,* its fifth 535, had never been repaired), awaited the results of bankruptcy proceedings in the Federal District Court at Seattle.

In announcing the reorganization of the Dollar Line the commission emphasized that it would be operated as a private company. William Gibbs McAdoo replaced Dollar as chairman of the board and Joseph Sheehan, now executive director of the Maritime Commission, became president of the corporation. At its first meeting in San Francisco on 1 November 1938, the new management voted to change the name of the company to American President Lines, Ltd. A white eagle would replace the white dollar sign that had for the past thirty-four years marked the stacks and the house flag of a merchant fleet that had fallen victim to economic depression and to the flawed management policies of a bygone era.[53]

NOTES_____

1. *Pacific Marine Review,* August 1931, 310–39; *New York Times,* 7 December 1930; *San Francisco Chronicle,* 16 December 1930.

2. Diary of Robert Dollar, 27 August 1931.

3. Ibid., 13, 14, January, 8 May 1930; U.S. Maritime Commission, *Reorganization,*

49; "Transcript, R. Stanley Dollar v. Emory S. Land et al.," 744 (San Francisco, California Historical Society).

4. "Minutes, Regular Meeting of the Board of Directors, April 15, 1936," APL Corporate Files, Oakland, Calif.

5. Roger W. Bunce, transcript, "The Dollar Steamship Radio System," Robert Dollar Collection; "Pacific Radio Company," Robert Dollar Collection.

6. *New York Times,* 7 August, 6 September, 13, 16 October 1931.

7. O'Brien, "Robert Dollar," 387; Diary of Robert Dollar, 28 April 1932.

8. Dollar v. Land, transcript, 734–38, U.S. Maritime Commission, *Reorganization,* 45.

9. General Passenger Agent to A. F. Haines, 25 September 1930, Yost Collection.

10. U.S. Maritime Commission, *Reorganization,* 15–17.

11. Ibid., 18–19.

12. Transcript of a telephone conversation between R. Stanley Dollar and Rear Admiral H. I. Cone, 4 Aug. 1933; Telegram, *S.S. President Madison,* Shipping Board Settlement, 24 March 1933; Telegram 4 August 1933; Cone to Dollar, 4 August 1933, Dollar Collection.

13. J. Harold Dollar received approximately $43,000. See U.S. Maritime Commission, *Reorganization,* 15–16.

14. "Pacific Steamship Statistics," Honnold Library.

15. House Committee on Merchant Marine and Fisheries, *Hearings to Develop an American Merchant Marine,* 74th Cong; 1st sess., 1935, 1122, 1123, 1093–95.

16. Radius, *United States Shipping in Trans-Pacific Trade, 1922–1938,* 173, 174.

17. Ibid., 174, 175.

18. Admiral E. T. Cochrane, affidavit in Dollar v. Land, transcript.

19. Don S. Burrows, Chief Planning Section to Executive Director, U.S. Maritime Administration, "Memo," 13 September 1938, APL Corporate Files.

20. Kemble and Kendall, "The Years Between the Wars," 164, 165.

21. U.S. Maritime Commission, *Reorganization,* 19.

22. Ibid., 19, 20.

23. Ibid., 21.

24. W. P. Bannister to R. Stanley Dollar, 28 October 1936, APL Archives.

25. "Statement of R. Stanley Dollar, in Minutes," Board of Directors Regular Meeting, 26 October 1936, APL Corporate Files.

26. "Minutes, Board of Directors Regular Meeting, Dec. 16, 1936," APL Archives.

27. Kemble and Kendall, "Years Between the Wars," 165, 166.

28. Frank A. Clapp, "Tacoma Oriental Steamship Co.," *Steamboat Bill,* March 1962; "Tacoma Oriental Steamship Company," Dollar Collection; Seattle *Post-Intelligencer,* 12 January 1936.

29. Quoted in Brown, *Ships That Sail No More,* 217.

30. Lukes, "Oral History Transcript," 16–19, APL Archives.

31. C. Bradford Mitchell, *Touching the Adventures & Perils: A Semicentennial History* (New York: American Hull Insurance Syndicate, 1970), 81.

32. Truitt to Dollar, June 1937, in "Minutes of the Board of Directors of Dollar Steamship Lines, Inc., 16 June, 1937," APL Corporate Files.

33. U.S. Maritime Commission, *Reorganization,* 29.

34. "Minutes, Board of Directors Meeting, 3 Sept. 1937," APL Corporate Files.

35. U.S. Maritime Commission, *Reorganization,* 31; Dollar Steamship Lines Inc., Ltd.; "Statement showing creditors who signed agreements as of October 28, 1937, and the amount of cash, bonds and stock to be issued in settlement," Dollar Collection; U.S. Maritime Commission, *Financial Readjustment in Dollar Steamship Lines Inc., Ltd.* (Washington, D.C., 1938); 68–73.

36. Dollar v. Land, transcript, 246.

37. Ibid., 352, 353, 526, 527.

38. Ibid., 533, 537, 551.

39. Ibid., p. 921.

40. Arthur Poole, "Oral History Transcript," 1–7, APL Archives.

41. "Minutes of Special Meeting of Board of Directors, Dollar Steamship Inc., Ltd.," 10 January 1938, APL Corporate Files.

42. *Time Magazine,* 11 February, 29 August 1938.

43. U.S. Maritime Commission, *Reorganization,* 103.

44. Don S. Burrows, Chief Planning Section, "Organization Report—Dollar Steamship Company, 13 September 1938, APL Corporate Files.

45. Dollar v. Land, transcript, 635.

46. Ibid., 141.

47. U.S. Maritime Commission, *Reorganization,* 78, 79.

48. Dollar to W. T. Mitchell, 23 January 1939, Dollar Collection.

49. Extracts from letters to R. B. Bush, Seattle, 19 February 1936, Dollar Collection; *Marine Digest,* 22 May 1937.

50. Memorandum, "American Mail Line, Ltd.," 30 June 1934, Dollar Collection.

51. J. Harold Dollar to R. B. Butterfield, 13 March 1935; J. G. Peacock to J. Harold Dollar, 16 March 1935; R. Stanley Dollar to M. A. Arnold, 22 March 1935, Dollar Collection.

52. "Minutes, Board of Directors Meeting," American Mail Line, 10 May 1938, Dollar Collection.

53. "Minutes of the Special Meeting of the Board of Directors, Dollar Steamship Lines Inc., Nov. 1, 1938," APL Corporate Files; Harrison, "Dollar Steamship Company"; U.S. Maritime Commission, "News Release, Washington, September 27, 1938," in Dollar v. Land, transcript.

7
THE REORGANIZED COMPANIES
AND THE WAR EFFORT

A t 4:00 P.M. on 1 November 1938 at 311 California Street in San Francisco's Financial District, William Gibbs McAdoo, the new chairman of Dollar Steamship, declared to the assembled directors that a quorum existed and that "the meeting was duly convened and qualified to transact business." At seventy-five years old, McAdoo was continuing a distinguished career that stretched back almost half a century to when, as a young lawyer in New York City, he successfully promoted the first railroad tunnels under the Hudson River. McAdoo had been Woodrow Wilson's secretary of the treasury and his premier advisor on banking and economic affairs. A brilliant organizer, McAdoo not only directed the nation's financial and fiscal policies with signal ability, but when the United States entered World War I, he managed its railroads as well. After failing to secure the Democratic nomination for the presidency in 1924, McAdoo remained active in party politics and had been largely responsible for shifting the California delegation to Franklin D. Roosevelt in the 1932 convention.

When the Maritime Commission selected him to succeed R. Stanley Dollar, he had just completed a term as U.S. senator from California. Lean, tall, and possessing distinctive aquiline features, McAdoo fitted the popular perception of an American statesman. He was an ideal choice to restore the public confidence in the largest shipping line on the West Coast. Moreover, his connections with the Roosevelt administration would be most helpful at this crucial junction in the Dollar Line's affairs.

In decided contrast to McAdoo was the new president of the line, Joseph R. Sheehan, a short, thickset lawyer whose Boston Irish background was evident in his accent and in his direct manner. Sheehan too had legal training and considerable knowledge of ship-

William Gibbs McAdoo, chairman of the board, American President Lines, 1938–40. (Courtesy *San Francisco Chronicle*.)

ping gained during his tenure as a staff member of the Maritime Commission for the past two years. Other members of the reconstituted board were Arthur Poole, whom Kennedy had brought in to reorganize the financial side of the Dollar Line, J. Hugh Jackson, a San Francisco businessman, Paul Hoover, who represented the Anglo-California Bank, and Grant H. Wren, spokesman for the local creditors.

The first item of business was an amendment to the corporate charter changing the name of the line from Dollar Steamship to American President Lines, Ltd. Ironically, while the board was discussing this proposal, on the same floor of the building R. Stanley Dollar, the former chairman, was preparing to leave for the day. As a stockholder he would have known that the meeting was taking place and that the board was erasing his family name from an enterprise that his father had founded and that he had managed for a decade. His feelings must have been mixed—a sense of relief that his personal liability for millions of dollars of debt had been assumed by the Maritime Commission and the new management, and a sense also of loss that this, the most notable of his family's properties, was now in other hands.

Yet there must have been some comfort in the fact that the Dollar organization that he and his father had built up would continue to function. Dollar had many faults as a businessman, but like his father he was a thoroughgoing paternalist in his attitude toward his employees. In fact, one of the stipulations he had made with the commission as a condition of the takeover had been assurances that personnel in good standing could remain with the company. "I wanted a clause," he said, "that the employees be taken care of, that they would take them over, and keep them and run the organization . . . and while I was getting nothing out of it myself, I wanted a definite obligation from them, that they would take care of these employees."[1]

Whatever the feelings expressed or withheld on the top floor of 311 California Street, the business of the new company went ahead with dispatch. The board decided that a special meeting of stockholders would be called for 18 November at which time the name change to American President Lines would be acted upon and new bylaws that were being prepared to conform with the requirements of the commission and the Reconstruction Finance Corporation would be voted upon. President Sheehan displayed the new insignia that had been designed for the line. The board voted unanimously to accept it, along with the new house flag—a white, stylized eagle on a red background with a white star in each corner.

Arthur Poole reported that the entire $4.5 million in government loans had been received and was on deposit. Further, he announced that all passenger refunds had been made, all cargo claims paid, and that the most significant of the debts owed to private creditors and not covered by preferred stock had likewise been paid off, as had the current interest on the *President Coolidge* mortgages. The long-over-due repair and rehabilitation program for the Dollar fleet was under-way.

With the approval of the name change and new bylaws by the stockholders and the directors at the special meeting in November, American President Lines, or APL, as it became known to the public, was officially launched. Dollar Steamship, so long a potent force in American shipping, became part of maritime history.[2]

It was imperative that operations be resumed as quickly as possi-ble. The Dollar fleet was either laid up or undergoing repairs. Morale of both seagoing and shore personnel was at low ebb. Very soon after the special meeting, Sheehan visited all the former Dollar agencies in New York, Los Angeles, Chicago, Boston, Washington, D.C., Cleveland, and Seattle. Longtime Dollar executives M. J. Buckley, vice president of freight traffic, and Hugh Mackenzie, vice president of passenger traffic, accompanied him. Sheehan perceived his role at this point as one of clarification about the intentions of the new management and its plans, reassurance about the future, and above all stimulation of the district agents to greater efforts in retain-ing old customers and soliciting new business. When the Sheehan group returned to San Francisco, they planned meetings with Oscar A. Steen, a veteran of the Dollar organization in the Far East and recently appointed APL's vice president for the Orient.

Readying the *President* steamers for sea was in the hands of a new employee, H. E. Frick, who had seen many years service at sea as a captain and as an operations executive with several lines on both coasts. W. J. Bush, who had been Stanley Dollar's assistant for oper-ations, became assistant operations manager and shared vice-presi-dential status with Frick. With the financial logjam broken by gov-ernment loans specifically earmarked for repairs, Frick and Bush developed a system of priorities for overhaul, depending on the material state of the vessels. Those judged in the best condition, like the *President Coolidge*, were sent to sea, while the remainder went into West Coast yards. They determined that for the time being the *President Lincoln* and the *President Wilson* were in such a bad state of repair that they could not meet subsidy requirements and were accordingly laid up. The *President Hayes* was to be repaired only to the extent necessary for her to sail as a cargo carrier. The other eight ships would be operated as they had been before on the trans-Pacific and round-the-world service. This determination required a change in the subsidy agreement, which the commission approved at a later date, though it insisted that these vessels be replaced as soon as possible with new construction.[3] By the spring of 1939, American President Lines had eleven ships in service.[4]

Management also determined on a policy of disposing and writing off inactive properties. The steamers *President Fillmore* and *President Johnson* had been considered unfit for service and had been put up for sale. But since there had been no takers, it was decided to carry them on the books for scrap value only. This action resulted in a write-down of $1,814,415 after mortgage indebtedness had been satisfied to the Anglo-California Bank, the Maritime Commission, and Dollar Steamship Lines of California. The President Terminal Steamship Company, a wholly owned subsidiary and the owner of the old coastal steamer the *Ruth Alexander,* and the Hunt's Point property in the Bronx, New York, was also deemed an inactive property. In fact, President Terminal had been losing money since its incorporation in 1937, and its debt on the books stood at $698,942. As yet management had not been able to determine an accurate market value for President Terminal. The two properties were carried on the books for $1,721,589, but Arthur Poole recommended that the capital stock of the company be written down to cover the losses while efforts were being made to dispose of the properties.[5] The board accepted his judgment.

Besides reflecting the assets of the line more accurately on the books and making efforts to sell inactive properties, the new management took steps to improve working conditions of its employees, especially its seagoing personnel. The Dollar Line had its own medical service, but unlike other shipping companies on the West Coast, it had no group insurance and no pension plan. The policy had been wholly paternalistic, and some employees were kept on in some sort of job long after they served any usefulness to the company, while others who failed to maintain their connections within the company were usually let go at some point before they reached their sixty-fifth birthdays.

Favoritism and nepotism more frequently than not determined tenure. Thus turnover rate had been high among shipboard personnel. There were far too many instances when well over half the men in a given crew left the employ of the line after a single voyage termination. Sheehan believed that fringe benefits like insurance, pensions, and longevity pay would reduce this wasteful loss of experienced seamen and corresponding costs of recruitment and training of replacements.[6] A fringe-benefit policy for all personnel was finally put into place by the end of 1939.[7]

While these efforts to rejuvenate the line were being made, management became increasingly concerned about the impact of war, which was threatening in Europe during the summer of 1939. Problems had already arisen in the Far East as the Sino-Japanese War flared up in 1938, resulting in some rerouting, which had claimed the *President Hoover* off the east coast of Taiwan as she steamed south on an unfamiliar course. An additional problem had risen during the spring of 1939, when the Japanese government refused to repatriate yen surpluses that stood at the company's credit. It took forceful State Department intervention before the money, some $250,000, was released in the fall of 1939. By then Europe had been plunged into war and the round-the-world vessels were being held up in Suez by British inspection for contraband.

After a month or so of uncertainty the delays were eased, but by the summer of 1940, when Italy came into the war and France collapsed, the round-the-world vessels had to be rerouted around the Cape of Good Hope. Operating costs began to escalate sharply because of war bonuses for ship's companies and war risk insurance. Both categories of expenditure were covered by differential subsidies, but there was always a delay of from three to four months before payment, which put a strain on the line's cash position. Other increases in overhead were not balanced by subsidy. Fuel oil, for example, doubled in cost between the Allied declaration of war in September 1939 and the end of the year.[8] But the uncertainties of the new war situation were more than compensated by a sharp rise in passenger and freight traffic.

During the first few months under new management, increases in revenue were offset by a disproportionate rise in operating costs. Beginning in September 1939, however, and continuing for the last quarter of the year, three of the round-the-world vessels, the *President Polk, President Adams,* and *President Van Buren* each grossed about $500,000 on a terminated voyage. Even the trans-Pacific vessels were doing a heavy freight and passenger business outward bound and homeward bound as well. In response to State Department warnings, the families of American businessmen, missionaries, and army and navy dependents crowded into American President vessels for passage to the United States. The *President Coolidge* sailed from Manila in September 1939 with the largest number of passengers ever carried from that port. The *President Coolidge*'s purser department managed to improvise sufficient linens, china, and tableware for such an unprecedented number of passengers. Despite increases in passenger fares that went into effect during the late summer of 1939, Sheehan reported to the board that "passenger business has been exceptionally good and we have over 350 people on the waiting list."[9]

Freight traffic also responded to the stimulus of war. American exports to the Allies in Europe and to Southeast Asia were exceptionally strong in the high-unit value freight that was the specialty of APL, as it had been of the Dollar Line. And the United States government as well as American industry stepped up its purchase of commodities like tin and rubber that might be cut off or in short supply due to wartime conditions. Cargo revenues for the first quarter of 1940 on the round-the-world and trans-Pacific routes were running from 35 percent to 40 percent above the average revenues since the change in management. Tin and rubber shipments from the Straits were exceptionally strong. Despite initial problems connected with the resumption of operations, APL carried 500,000 tons of American exports during its first year of operations.[10]

Although it had written off various properties, APL was not only meeting its obligation to its creditors but was earning net profits that were steadily increasing. Allied purchases of commodities and finished goods in the United States, the stockpiling of strategic resources by the Allies and the United States, and the flight of British, French, and American nationals from the Far East were all combining to push up revenues.

The advent of the war also created a sellers' market for ships. The thirty-six-year-old *President Johnson* and twenty-seven-year-old *Ruth Alexander,* both of which had been written down to scrap value, suddenly became valuable assets. During 1940 the *President Lincoln,*

President Wilson, and *President Fillmore,* laid up since the summer of 1938, were sold for $1,529,000.[11] After much discussion as to whether the *President Johnson* and the *Ruth Alexander* also ought to be sold or refurbished, management finally decided they were worth more as operating units in the company fleet than what they would bring even on a rising market for ships. The financial position of the company was strong enough, they felt, to carry the new construction that the commission required and an expansion of activities in the Northwest. In 1939 the line entered into an agreement with the Baltimore Mail Steamship Company for the charter of four vessels for scheduled service between New York and the Malaysian Straits.

At the commission's behest, APL made a nominal bid for the name and goodwill of the Puget Sound Line, a Seattle company that had just begun operating under charter four Hog Island freighters. As a part of its bid, APL agreed to a basic rate of $12,343 a month for these vessels. It also agreed to replace them with five new ships of the C1 or C3 design.[12] As it turned out, however, APL did not enter the shipping business of the Northwest at this time. The two reasons why the commission had requested the line to take over Puget Sound were now irrelevant.

A deadlock had developed between two conflicting groups in Seattle for control of the shipping business out of the Seattle-Tacoma area. For national security as well as for the economic health of the region the commission wanted a reputable line in which it had confidence handling the oceangoing traffic from the Northwest. Hence its request that APL take over Puget Sound.

After American Mail suspended operations in the summer of 1938, a group of Seattle businessmen formed the Pacific Northwest Oriental Company, which in turn created the Puget Sound Line. With American Mail's vessels tied up and the company involved in litigation with creditors, the commission appointed Puget Sound as its agent and made available four Hog Island–type freighters on a charter basis. These vessels, the *Capillo, Coldbrook, Collingsworth,* and *Sartatia,* were not ready for sea until the late summer of 1939. Indeed, the first of the Hog Islanders to sail from Seattle for the Far East was the *Coldbrook,* which departed on 4 September 1939.

That the commission was not satisfied with this arrangement was obvious from the beginning; in fact, it felt uneasy about the use of Hog Islanders on such a strategically and economically important route. Its predecessor, the Shipping Board, had mass-produced these ugly little freighters during 1918 and 1919. Hog Islanders were "three-island"–type freighters, completely without sheer. Their name, after the Pennsylvania shipyard where many of them were built, portrayed accurately their awkward appearance. Although they seemed unstable to the untutored eye and when fully loaded had very little freeboard, they were sturdy vessels and surprisingly seaworthy. Slow and comparatively expensive to operate, each Hog Islander had a tonnage of 5,100 gross.[13]

The commission regarded the Hog Islanders as a temporary expedient and was anxious to replace them with their new C-series freighters or combination passenger freighters. They were almost twice the size of the Hog Islanders but consumed about 30 percent less fuel per nautical mile. At a cruising speed of 16.5 knots, the C3s, for instance, burned 350 barrels of oil a day. Smaller Hog Islanders burned 850 barrels at the slower cruising speed of 10 knots.[14]

Closely associated with the replacement issue was the ability of Pacific Northwest Oriental, the holding company for the Puget Sound Line, to finance the purchase of these new vessels. American Mail may have been inoperative and in the process of reorganization, but it had an estimated net worth of $1,350,000, far more capital than Pacific Northwest Oriental could command. These assets included equities in the *President McKinley,* the *President Jackson,* and the *President Jefferson.* Though the commission had taken over these 535s, they represented a substantial balance to the credit of American Mail after all mortgage indebtedness had been paid. The *President Madison* had been sold to a Manila buyer for $350,000 and renamed the *President Quezon,* while the trustee for American Mail was negotiating for the sale of the *President Grant,* a deal that was never consummated.[15]

Admiral Land may have been dubious about the financial resources of Pacific Northwest Oriental, but he was satisfied that American Mail was in a far stronger position. The reorganization of American Mail, which was completed on 15 December 1939, simplified the commission's decision in one way but complicated it in another. American Mail's new management immediately challenged the Pacific Northwest Oriental group, which gave no indication of backing down. If this did not create problems enough for the commission, another factor emerged to muddy the issue: the Dollar interest.

Federal District Judge John C. Bowers, who had presided over the reorganization, ordered the trustee for American Mail to recapitalize the company and divide its new stock into three categories, Class A and Class B common shares and preferred shares. Through their holding company Admiral Oriental, the Dollars controlled the preferred stock and the Class B common.

The court had followed the advice of the Seattle law firm of Bogle, Bogle and Gates, which had drawn up a voting trust. As Lawrence Bogle described it, the trust would pool sufficient Class A stock "to insure that neither the Dollars nor any other outside interest could get control of the management."[16] And since Class A was issued primarily to satisfy the claims of Seattle creditors, it was assumed that control of the company would be in the hands of the Seattle business community. Yet at first the new management of American Mail and several members of the commission feared that R. Stanley Dollar through a silent partner would acquire enough Class A shares, combined with his Class B and preferred shares, to control the company.[17] At the first annual meeting, the new board of directors consisted of six members representing primarily Seattle creditors and three members representing the Dollar interests. Under the terms of Judge Bowers's order, the Class B stockholders were entitled to one director and the preferred stockholders to two directors.[18]

R. H. Drumheller, a Seattle businessman and president of Pacific Northwest Oriental, used just this argument to rally community opinion against American Mail. In a long letter to the board of the Seattle Chamber of Commerce, Drumheller recounted all the evidences of Dollar mismanagement and personal exploitation of American Mail. "If the reorganized American Mail Line succeeds in its plan," said Drumheller, "the result will be that Mr. Dollar, discharged of all the mortgage and other indebtedness of the American Mail Line, gets rid of the old ships, now obsolete and so not eligible for Government subsidies, by turning them over to the Maritime Commission as a down payment on new tonnage and emerges as the majority stockholder in the reorganized company."[19] He also sought to raise the bugbear of Dollar ownership with the commission and he very nearly succeeded. Underscoring community opposition to "the reestablishment of Mr. Dollar's dominance in Puget Sound shipping," Drumheller claimed the "the vast majority of the businessmen with whom I came in contact are uncompromisingly opposed to the present set up of the American Mail Line."[20]

Lawrence Calvert, new president of American Mail, reacted strenuously. He sent John Ambler, a partner of the Seattle law firm of Grosscup, Morrow and Ambler, to Washington to counter Pacific Northwest Oriental's campaign and to lobby for the subsidized trans-Pacific route from the Northwest. Ambler was also charged with following up a lead that Richard J. Reynolds, the tobacco millionaire from Winston-Salem, North Carolina, might be willing to provide enough capital to buy the Dollar interests out and to supply funds for the initial financing of new ships. Ambler, a perceptive lawyer and energetic spokesman for American Mail, immediately began a series of interviews with members of the commission, the congressional committee on Maritime Affairs, and the state of Washington's House and Senate delegation.

At first Admiral Land seemed rather distant. He already had in hand APL's bid for the Puget Sound Line; but when Ambler presented American Mail's position and explained "to him our plans had just cleared the court and we are only now in a position to go ahead, he seemed pleased and anxious that we get action at once." "Labor trouble in Seattle," continued Ambler, "and an apparent lack of support from the chamber of commerce and state congressional delegation worried him a lot." It was obvious to Ambler that Pacific Northwest Oriental's campaign, emphasizing as it had Dollar holdings in American Mail, had succeeded to a considerable extent in Washington, D.C. A third factor to be considered were the influential men in Washington who favored public ownership. Edward C. Moran, a former Democratic congressman from Maine and a newly appointed commissioner, represented the public ownership advocates. He could not be moved from this position throughout the controversy.[21] Of the other commissioners, Max Truitt and Thomas M. Woodward were favorable to American Mail, and Admiral Henry A. Wiley, the fifth member, was noncommittal but clearly concerned about congressional and community opinion. Washington senator Lewis Schwellenbach had urged the commission to support Pacific Northwest Oriental.

Ambler spent a busy two weeks in early December presenting American Mail's case and canvassing opinion. By 13 December he concluded that it would be a hard fight, even though a majority of the commission did not think that Pacific Northwest Oriental could comply with bid requirements that called for the purchase of new tonnage. "For this reason," Ambler advised Calvert, "they think they (the commission) should get the united support of the community which they ask for. Otherwise, everyone in Seattle is likely to lose out."[22]

Since the bids for the route would be opened on 14 February 1940, both groups redoubled their activities. W. Walter Williams, president of the Seattle Chamber of Commerce, tried unsuccessfully to bring them together for the good of the community. In a letter to Calvert and Drumheller, Williams appealed for harmony and cooperation.[23] And on three subsequent occasions, Drumheller approached American Mail with offers for consolidation that in effect would have made the line subordinate to Pacific Northwest Oriental. Needless to say, Calvert and his board rejected all these overtures. By then the Seattle Chamber of Commerce had become so apprehensive that R. Stanley Dollar was actually in control of American Mail that it brought pressure to bear on Admiral Land in favor of Pacific Northwest Oriental. "It is my belief," wrote Walter Williams, "if our citizens were made aware, through a hearing or otherwise, that Dollar and his California associates own approximately 56 percent of the stock issued in the American Mail reorganization they would strongly protest the Commission's entering into a contract for a subsidized operation by that company (American Mail) on this route."[24]

Meanwhile Ambler had been having talks with Rayford W. Alley, a New York attorney acting for Richard Reynolds. The tobacco magnate, who had long been interested in shipping lines and was an experienced sailor, was quite willing to buy out the Dollars if they would sell at a reasonable price. Through Alley, Reynolds indicated that he might also put up another $200,000 in new capital if that became necessary. This additional sum would be secured by a new issue of preferred shares as permitted in the reorganization settlement. At some future date the preferred shares and the Class B stock would be converted into Class A voting stock. As Ambler explained the deal to Lawrence Calvert, such an eventuality would give Reynolds control of the company. "But," said Ambler, "he is not really interested in control, being primarily interested in the business and in competent operation."

Ambler did not think that American Mail needed new capital. Land, however, continued to stress the fact that no new capital was going into the company. American Mail was asking the commission to finance an entirely new program of ship construction while it was only offering, he said, "a scant $250,000 or $300,000 working capital." Clearly American Mail had to have the backing of Reynolds or some other outside source of capital to satisfy the commission and the public ownership advocates that the Dollars would not regain control. Ambler again reinforced this view only more urgently in a telegram to Calvert on 2 March:

> Feel sure Reynolds won't be interested unless he has positive assurance he can exchange any stock purchased share for share. Has many other interests and this is sort of hobby. Unless you positively call off PNO [Pacific Northwest Oriental] or work some deal with Reynolds going will be tough. Important to have some rabbit to pull out if possible Monday [4 March].[25]

Reynolds himself was now in direct touch with Ambler. The two men worked out a deal whereby American Mail would sell to Reynolds 25,500 shares of authorized but unissued Class A stock for $8 a share for a total of $204,000. The company would use these funds to call in its entire issue of preferred shares, all owned by Dollar-controlled Admiral Oriental at the redemption price of $10 a share or $203,833. In addition Reynolds would have a six-month option to purchase 10,000 shares of Class A stock at $10 a share if the Maritime Commission insisted on additional capital. Ambler related these details to Calvert over the phone and got his agreement.

When the commission met on 4 March, Ambler presented the new arrangement. Moran objected strenuously, claiming that the bid for the route was too low; that the Dollars still controlled the company; and that the commission was being asked to take the obsolete 535s at inflated wartime prices. All of these criticisms had been anticipated and were answered fully. It appeared from the questions asked by the chairman and other commissioners that the Reynolds deal had banished all qualms. Still Ambler fretted about the pressures that were being exerted on the commission. As he described the situation:

> The Chairman is trying very hard to keep the Commission together and is allowing in every case opposing views to be thoroughly discussed and made a matter of record. This is particularly important as the Commission is now being threatened by Senator Clark of Missouri with a Congressional investigation . . . to add to the confusion, Senator Wheeler of Montana is pressing a bill to place the entire Commission under

the I.C.C. [Interstate Commerce Commission]. The President apparently recently indicated his approval of such plan.[26]

The threatened public takeover never materialized, nor did a last-minute barrage of arguments from Drumheller and others favoring Pacific Northwest Oriental prevail. On 7 March 1940 the commission, with Moran voting in the negative, accepted the company's bid for the trade name and goodwill of the Puget Sound Line and the bareboat charter of its Hog Islanders. The commission made three conditions, however. First, all earnings over 10 percent on capital investment had to be deposited in a capital reserve fund. Second, these deposits were to be applied toward the purchase of replacement vessels as provided in Chapter V of the Merchant Marine Act of 1936. Third, American Mail had to agree to place these replacement vessels in operation when the commission made them available.

A special board meeting of American Mail on 12 March confirmed the deal made with Reynolds, and, over the objection of E. H. Hall, who represented the Dollar interests, voted to call in the preferred shares. Dollar representation was now reduced to one director. And with the huge financial resources Reynolds could command behind American Mail, R. Stanley Dollar agreed to dispose of the Class B shares at a figure that was acceptable to all concerned.[27]

Ambler had been correct in assessing Reynold's intentions regarding American Mail. Although he now held a controlling interest in the line, he did not interfere in its management. At first he was concerned whether Calvert and his colleagues could provide a competent chief executive and so he had the firm hire as a consultant Angelo L. Ruspini, a veteran captain and former executive of the Italia Line. But once Reynolds had taken stock of A. R. Lintner, the new general manager American Mail had acquired, he was satisfied that the operations of the line were in capable hands.

Lintner, a short wiry man, had that kind of decisive personality that commanded respect on the ships as well as on the docks and in the boardroom. A veteran of the navy's Construction Bureau, he had been ship superintendent at Portsmouth, at Newport News, and at New York in 1916, then he briefly headed the technical staff of the Seattle Construction and Dry Dock Company. Two years later he joined the Shipping Board, where he supervised all marine engineering and design in the government's West Coast shipbuilding

A. R. Lintner, president of American Mail Line, 1946–59. (APL Archives.)

program. In 1922 he moved into Shipping Board operations as executive assistant to the North Pacific district director, and in 1927 he became district director. When the Shipping Board began to phase out its operating division in 1929, Lintner joined the States Steamship Company to head up its Far Eastern Division in Kobe, Japan. He was stationed in the Far East for six years. In 1934 he returned to the Northwest, where he assumed the post of Seattle manager for the States line and during the next six years directed all of that company's activities in the Puget Sound area.

Lintner had been an ideal choice for the reorganized American Mail Line. Over the years he had built up good relations in Washington, D.C., with the navy and key members of the Maritime Commission. He was well known in the shipping world of the West Coast. Equally important for the future of American Mail, Lintner had the confidence of the business community in Portland and Seattle.[28]

One of Lintner's first acts was to hire as his assistant John Cormode, the last manager of Dollar-owned American Mail. While Cormode concerned himself with the sale of the 535s, three of which were still in the hands of the Maritime Commission, he began preparations for the transfer of Puget Sound's vessels to American Mail, the joining of the Pacific Westbound Conference, revision of forms and documents, publishing sailing schedules, negotiations for stevedoring contracts, and all the myriad details essential to start-up operations of a shipping line.[29]

Lintner and Calvert also employed the former treasurer of the American Mail Line, R. B. Bush, to handle the financial side of the business. Like Lintner, Bush had a background in both shipping and government. A hardy professional who was seldom seen without his pipe clamped firmly in his jaw, Bush had thirty years of accounting experience behind him. He was considered as adept at coping with the procedures and policies of the Maritime Commission as he was in imposing strict financial controls that were essential if the reorganized line were to prosper.[30]

Once it completed its new financing, which included a loan from Reynolds of $200,000, the payment of $60,478 from the Maritime Commission in long-deferred subsidy payments, and another loan of $50,000 from the Pacific National Bank of Seattle, American Mail began an ambitious replacement program.[31] By May Lintner had sold the *President Grant* and *President Jackson* to the navy and the

An American Mail Liner in wartime. The *President McKinley* [I] became the attack transport *J. Franklin Bell* during World War II. (W. G. MacDonald Collection, APL Archives.)

President Jefferson and *President McKinley* to the army for $500,000 each.[32] The funds received from these vessels remained on deposit with the commission as a down payment for the purchase of six C2 class freighters. In early 1941, American Mail replaced three Hog Islanders that were being chartered with three C1s, the *Cape Alava, Cape Fairweather,* and *Cape Flattery,* also under a charter arrangement with the Maritime Commission. These ships were the first in a series of Maritime Commission designs. The commission had established a technical branch that prepared plans and specifications for standard ship types built under its auspices. The letter C preceded the designation of these ships. By 26 July three of the new freighters, the *China Mail, Island Mail,* and *Japan Mail,* had been launched for American Mail at Chester, Pennsylvania.

American President Lines was also making significant progress from near-bankruptcy. In 1939 the Maritime Commission was interested in building two or three large, fast steamers to be operated in the trans-Pacific trade. For a time they thought in terms of ships comparable in size and speed to the *America,* which was under construction for the United States Lines' trans-Atlantic express service in 1939. In February 1940 the commission invited bids for two liners that would be 759 feet in length with displacements of 35,000 tons. They would be designed to carry 1,000 passengers, a crew of 500, and cargo space for 535,000 bale cubic feet. The ships could quickly convert into aircraft carriers in the event of need. They were never built, however.[33]

On 28 March 1940 Joseph Sheehan died suddenly. It was evidence of the line's intrinsic strength that despite the loss of its president and an interval of nine months before he was replaced, operations continued smoothly. Indeed, APL took delivery of two C3 combination freighter-passenger vessels, named the *President Polk* and the *President Monroe.* These new ships had a capacity of 10,900 cubic tons of general cargo and 1,080 cubic tons of refrigerated cargo. They could also carry 1,050 cubic tons of commercial bulk oil in tanks and had accommodations for ninety-six passengers each.[34]

The *Polk* and the *Monroe* were placed in the round-the-world service just when Italy invaded France and President Roosevelt declared the Mediterranean an additional combat area. Most of the round-the-world ships were rerouted around the Cape of Good Hope or returned to their home port of San Francisco across the Pacific.

Despite the interruption in world trade patterns after the fall of France in June 1940 and the American embargoes of strategic exports to Japan, APL earned a net income of $4.6 million during the year. It had made the required down payment of $1.14 million on the *Presidents Polk* and *Monroe* and an additional $1 million down payment on two more C3s. At the same time its earnings were sufficient to cover the payment of over $4 million on its debt to the government and to banks.[35]

Although he was nearing eighty, McAdoo had borne the triple burden of formulating policy, acting as the company's chief liaison in Washington, and shouldering much of the responsibility for running the business after the death of Sheehan while the slow wheels of government came around to naming a successor. It had not been

President Monroe [II]. One of seven C3-type passenger-cargo ships built in 1940 to replace the aging 502s in the round-the-world trade. Only she and the *President Polk* [II] returned to APL service after World War II. (APL Archives.)

until May, well over a month after Sheehan's death, that Admiral Land sent McAdoo a list of candidates for the presidency of the company. Land wrote that the commission would welcome nominees for the post from the board at its earliest convenience. In mid-May Land himself brought up the subject with McAdoo while he was visiting San Francisco. A leading contender was Max Truitt, now one of Land's fellow commissioners. Truitt had been a prominent figure in effecting the changeover from Dollar management. He was thoroughly familiar with the shipping business on the West Coast and with APL, but he was undecided for personal reasons. Moreover, there were political factors why it might be inadvisable for a person so prominently identified with the commission to be made operating head of a presumably independent enterprise. The charge of conflict of interest could be made and 1940 was a presidential election year.

On 15 July Land again requested that the board make nominations within one month. When McAdoo tried to reach Land, however, he found that the admiral was on vacation and could not be reached until the second week in August. Though several members of the board thought that Truitt would be a satisfactory choice, McAdoo urged delay until he could communicate directly with Land.[36]

Truitt eventually removed himself as a candidate. The commission and the board of APL then settled on a president who was willing to take on the responsibilities and whose training and experience in government and industry qualified him for the post. Their choice was Henry F. Grady, who had just resigned his position as under secretary of state. Grady had been an outstanding dean of the business school at the University of California, Berkeley, before he became Cordell Hull's deputy in 1937. Considered an expert on international trade as well as business management, Grady would not be as controversial an appointment as Truitt would have been.

After sizing up the situation, he accepted the post in November 1940. But before he took charge, he saw to it that three key management officials were made members of the board. At the same time that he was made president on 30 December 1940, the board elected to its membership H. E. Frick, vice president of operations, M. J. Buckley, vice president of freight, and Hugh Mackenzie, vice president of passenger traffic.[37] Grady further coordinated policy and management when he proposed and the board accepted the appointment of an executive committee. It consisted of himself, Buckley, Poole, Mackenzie, and Frick. In addition, he employed E. Russell Lutz to be his executive assistant. Lutz, like Grady, came from government service. A member of the legal staff of the Maritime Commission, he had demonstrated a talent for administrative work in managing the many bareboat charter contracts the government had made with private shipping lines.[38]

These moves reflected an urgent need to strengthen the management of the line. There had been no single operating head since the death of Joseph Sheehan. Though McAdoo had spared what time he could from his busy schedule to manage the company, he simply did not have the time, nor at his age the energy, to oversee day-to-day operations. And no sooner had Grady taken over than McAdoo died of a heart attack in Washington on 1 February 1941. It was a

Henry F. Grady, president of American President Lines, 1940–48. (APL Archives.)

severe loss to the line, yet there was no pause in the modernization of the fleet.

By November 1940 the third of the C3-Ps, the *President Jackson*, had been placed in round-the-world service, to be followed by *President Hayes*, *President Garfield*, and *President Van Buren*.[39] These were sisterships to the *President Monroe* and *President Polk* and would complete the reequipment of the round-the-world service. The war in Europe was now entering a critical phase and the United States responded with the Lend-Lease Act and stepped up rearmament. It appeared unlikely that the military would allow delivery of any additional vessels.

After President Roosevelt proclaimed a state of national emergency on 27 May 1941, the Maritime Commission refused to permit the sale of the *Ruth Alexander*. The navy requisitioned the *President Adams* while she was being completed at the Newport News Shipbuilding and Dry Dock Company.[40] Both the army and navy began purchasing or chartering the company's 502s and 535s as the round-the-world and trans-Pacific services were curtailed by increasing wartime disruption of normal trade routes and American economic sanctions against Japan. During the fall and winter of 1940–41, Pacific trade was primarily military, though shipments of lend-lease aid were going to China by way of Rangoon. In the West, when General Erwin Rommel and his Afrika Korps drove the British back into Egypt, the problem of supply became critical. Churchill appealed to Roosevelt for assistance. He responded by ordering the Maritime Commission to secure vessels for the transport of military supplies through the Red Sea to Egypt.

APL's *President Fillmore* made one trip and the *President Buchanan* two trips to Alexandria, Egypt, during 1941–42. The commission fixed very generous charter rates because of possible hazards in a war zone. When experience indicated that the danger had been exaggerated, the commission reduced the rates it would pay. And in December of 1941 it worked out entirely different arrangements through a ship warrant system. The three voyages of the *President Fillmore* and *President Buchanan* earned $776,487 in clear profit to APL. In 1942, Admiral Land, under pressure from the Truman committee investigating excessive wartime profits, asked all the American shipping executives whose ships were utilized in the Red Sea operation to agree voluntarily to a revision of rates, and he indicated clearly that it was in their interest to do so. Grady advised the board to make a refund of $289,758, which would leave the company an amount equal to what was now being paid for bareboat charters of vessels of this type. As he reminded the board,

> It must be remembered that many of the vessels in this war emergency service for the government enjoyed profits greatly in excess of those which they had earned in preceding commercial operations or by subsequent charter hire from the government. . . . Members of Congress, the Maritime Commission, and the public to a great extent, consider the profits as excessive and unjustifiably so as earnings from government war contracts. . . . The future of the various companies comprising the American Merchant Marine, particularly those serving routes in foreign commerce, is inexorably woven into such national policies as may be adopted in the future through laws, treaties and governmental administrative decisions. The self-interest of the industry will be served by taking cognizance of the fact that governmental authorities who will participate in determining such matters may be seriously influenced by a failure of the

industry to agree to profits for war and emergency services which are not excessive particularly in connection with the Red Sea voyages.[41]

Excess profits may have been one thing, but the tightening of government controls was certainly another as American involvement in the war became more obvious. American Mail took delivery under charter from the commission of three C1 freighters during 1941, the *Cape Alava*, the *Cape Fairweather*, and the *Cape Flattery*. But of the three C2s on order, only the *Island Mail* was delivered to the company. The government requisitioned the other ships while they were still on the building ways at the Sun Shipbuilding and Drydock Company's yard at Chester, Pennsylvania, the Seattle-Tacoma Shipyard, and the Bethlehem Yard, Beaumont, Texas.[42]

By midsummer of 1941 APL suspended all trans-Pacific schedules, a move that American Mail quickly followed. Limited round-the-world service was continued until 11 October 1941, when the *President Buchanan*, formerly the *President Monroe*, left San Francisco. From the beginning of the year to December 1941, the government took over eight of the thirteen vessels that APL was operating, including all its new ships. On 10 July 1941 Henry Grady negotiated a general agency agreement with the commission for APL's operation of government ships.[43] Likewise, the army and navy had requisitioned American Mail's four 535s. The company continued to operate its new C1 freighters under Maritime Commission charter.

All but two round-the-world ships were in American ports when the Japanese struck at Pearl Harbor on 7 December 1941. The *President Harrison* and the *President Madison* were in the Philippines under military control. Commanded by a veteran skipper, Captain Orel Pierson, the *President Harrison* had docked at Manila in late November 1941. The navy port authorities ordered Pierson to take his ship to Hong Kong where she would be refitted as a transport and then sail to Shanghai to evacuate a marine battalion. With the *President Madison* assisting, the marines were removed and transported to the Philippines on 4 December 1941. When they had disembarked, Pierson was ordered to sail with the tide for Chingwangtao on the north China coast to evacuate the Peking and Tientsin legation guard.

As the *President Harrison* sailed north through the China Sea, Captain Pierson gave some thought to what he would do if war should begin between the United States and Japan. He might alter course to the south for Australia or to the northwest in a great circle course to the United States. Both options seemed remote because the vessel was within easy reach of Japanese sea and air power and was even then under surveillance. About 3:30 A.M. on 8 December (7 December in the United States), Pierson heard on the ship's radio that Pearl Harbor had been attacked. The *President Harrison* at that moment was close to the China coast, north of the Yangtze estuary. At dawn a Japanese patrol plane circled the *Harrison* and signaled her to stop. When Pierson continued on his course, the plane strafed the *Harrison* with machine-gun fire. Very soon thereafter a Japanese destroyer appeared on the horizon. Pierson realized that escape was now impossible so he headed the *Harrison* at full speed for land, hoping to tear out her bottom on the reefs he knew were near the estuary. He succeeded in stranding the vessel but did not damage her as extensively as he had hoped. Still, it took the Japanese salvage crews and repair units almost six months to make her seaworthy. Utilized as a troop transport, the *Harrison* was later torpedoed and sunk by an American submarine on 14 September 1944.[44] The Japanese interned Pierson, his officers, and crew for the duration of the war. Sixteen members of the crew died in prison camps.[45]

The *President Grant* and the *Ruth Alexander* were luckier than the *President Harrison*. Both ships were in Manila when the Japanese attacked, but both managed to survive bombing attacks (which sank American Mail's Hog Islander the *Capillo*) and made their way safely out of the harbor. Some of their crew members who were on liberty, however, had to be left behind and became prisoners for the remainder of the war. The *Ruth Alexander* was later sunk in the Makassar Strait, a casualty of a Japanese dive-bombing attack.[46]

The greatest loss to APL or American Mail during the war fortunately caused the least loss of life when the *President Coolidge* struck a mine on 26 October 1942 off the harbor of Espiritu Santo, one of the New Hebrides islands south of Guadalcanal. Crammed with over 5,000 American troops, the 21,000-ton *President Coolidge* went down in about an hour and one half. Yet Captain Henry Nelson and the ship's company of the *Coolidge* organized the rescue so well that only two men were lost, a sterling example of calm, effective leadership under extremely adverse conditions.[47]

Altogether, APL lost nine vessels during the war by enemy action

Loss of the second of the fated *Presidents*. On 26 October 1942, the *President Coolidge* [I] struck a mine in the harbor of Espiritu Santo. She sank quickly, but of the over 5,000 men aboard, only two were known lost. (Courtesy World Wide Photos, New York.)

or stranding in war zones, precisely one-third of its prewar fleet. Three of American Mail's Hog Islanders that it operated under charter from the commission were sunk—two from enemy action, and the other abandoned after stranding off the Alaskan coast. None of these ships were owned by APL or American Mail.

After Pearl Harbor, the armed forces took over all ships that still remained in private hands, some outright, the remainder on a bareboat charter basis. On 21 February 1942, President Roosevelt created by proclamation the War Shipping Administration, which assumed the duties of the Maritime Commission in building, organizing, and coordinating the shipbuilding and shipping industries.

Like other shipping lines, APL and American Mail became general agents for the War Shipping Administration. In this role they performed all their normal shoreside and seagoing activities such as manning, equipping, overhaul and repair, handling of cargo and passengers, fueling, and other dockside requirements. In addition, APL and American Mail were designated berth subagents for the War Shipping Administration. Husbanding activities for various government-owned vessels from time to time were assigned to the lines under contract. The same provisions were made for the administration's vessels assigned to the British Ministry of Transport or those under the Chinese flag. Most of these berthing arrangements were for voyages beginning and terminating on the West Coast. But not infrequently the lines were assigned responsibility for East Coast berthings. American President Lines was more involved in East Coast operations than American Mail because of its prewar round-the-world and Atlantic/Straits service, both of which used company-owned terminals in Jersey City. The lines on occasion acted as subagents for other carriers when they used port facilities on the West Coast. They did not, of course, control either the sailings or the destinations of their own and other vessels under general agency agreement. The branch offices of the War Shipping Administration and the army and navy port personnel had this responsibility.

As the momentum of the war effort built up, as hundreds of Liberty ships, standardized 10,800-ton gross freighters, C-type freighters, and vessels of other designs and tonnages came off the ways, so the general agency and berthing responsibilities of APL and American Mail increased accordingly. By August 1945, when the war in the Pacific came to an end, the War Shipping Administration's fleet had climbed from 900 dry cargo vessels and 440 tankers to 4,221 freighters, tankers, and troop carriers, and from 11,850,000 tons of shipping to 45 million tons.[48]

In 1944 2,727 planes, 1,223 vehicles, 9,993 boats and 296 amphibious craft were shipped out as deck cargo alone from Pacific ports. American Mail and APL accounted for most of the dockside loading and shipment of this cargo.[49] An increase in operations of this size required a substantial increase in personnel. American Mail, for instance, from December 1941 to December 1944, increased its shoreside and its seagoing complement from 457 to 2,507 employees.[50]

There were also shifts of responsibility in the management of the two lines. The government now and then required Henry Grady's services for special wartime missions in North Africa and in Italy. In

1943 E. Russell Lutz was elected executive vice president and acted as chief executive officer in Grady's absence.

Another executive whose responsibilities grew rapidly as a result of rearmament and wartime expansion was Thomas C. Cuffe, who had joined Dollar Steamship in the early twenties.[51] Cuffe was a solidly built, self-assured person who early mastered the intricacies of soliciting and moving freight. Outgoing and aggressive, he quickly caught the eye of Stanley Dollar, who moved him up in the organization. As San Francisco freight manager, Cuffe not only built up dramatically the business of the Dollar Line, but he developed a legion of personal contacts within the shipping world—especially in Washington, D.C.

When McAdoo and Sheehan replaced Dollar and Lorber, they gave Cuffe additional duties in connection with the round-the-world service that took him frequently to Washington and to East Coast ports. He soon became one of the company's chief negotiators with the commission on the sale of its aging fleet and its replacement with the new C-series vessels. Not long after Henry Grady became president in November 1940, he promoted Cuffe to assistant vice president of freight traffic. Less than a year later he made Cuffe vice president of eastern U.S. territory, an organizational change that reflected management's awareness of the United States' imminent participation in World War II and the need for an experienced person with proper connections in Washington. Cuffe seemed an ideal choice, and indeed he proved to be worthy of the confidence, if not the trust, imparted to him. While he saw to it that APL got its share of general agency and berthing contracts, he was also busy lining up prospects for himself in what he judged accurately would be great opportunities to establish an independent shipping line of his own when the government disbanded its fleet after the war.[52]

Unlike APL, American Mail's management structure continued largely unchanged despite the rapid expansion of the company's operations in response to wartime demands. Lawrence Calvert remained president throughout the war, but his other business responsibilities claimed a major share of his time. A. R. Lintner, the very capable general manager, ran the line with the assistance of Adrian Raynaud as port superintendent in Seattle and chief coordinator of operations on both coasts. R. B. Bush handled the financial duties of the line with his accustomed skill, despite the increasing tempo and complexities of business in wartime.

During 1944, for instance, American Mail operated on a general agency contract the Liberty ships assigned to it but owned by the War Shipping Administration. American Mail still owned five vessels, three of which were C1s and two C2s—the *Island Mail* and the *China Mail*. But all of these vessels were managed under a bareboat charter agreement with the War Shipping Administration.[53]

In early 1942 Lintner joined the War Shipping Administration, first as Pacific Northwest representative with headquarters in Seattle, and on 1 July 1942, as director of all West Coast operations. He moved his office to San Francisco, where he was immediately confronted with the immense responsibilities of coordinating all cargo and troop movements by ship to the Pacific Ocean theaters of war. Working closely with the port staffs of APL, Lykes, Matson, States, and other West Coast shipping firms as well as his own company, American Mail, Lintner had a smoothly running operation by early 1943.

Nor did this man of driving energy find it at all difficult to continue as vice president and general manager of American Mail, which he operated with conspicuous ability and no apparent conflict of interest during the war. On 15 November 1945 he resigned his post with the War Shipping Administration. At the same time, Calvert relinquished the presidency of American Mail and Lintner took over as president and chief executive officer.[54]

Both companies earned substantial revenues during the war, more than sufficient to liquidate their debts to the government and to pay a modest dividend. American Mail declared a $1.00 annual dividend throughout the war years to its stockholders. The government was the major recipient of American President Lines' profits through its ownership of 90 percent of the stock. Under subsidy agreements both lines were required to deposit in reserve accounts all earnings beyond 10 percent per year on invested capital required for operations. The Maritime Commission and its wartime agent the War Shipping Administration jointly controlled the reserve funds with the companies for eventual purchase of replacement vessels. There was also a provision whereby half of the profits over and above 10 percent could be recaptured by the government. Funds subject to recapture could not be used for the payment of dividends, long-term bank indebtedness, payments into sinking funds or port facilities, and equipment beyond depreciation accruals. Annual net profits of 10 percent on capital, or "free earnings," could be paid out in dividends. It was not until the end of 1942 that APL paid a dividend. On 30 December of that year the company declared its first dividend of $1.25 a share on its five percent noncumulative preferred stock.[55]

By the war's end, American President Lines had almost $12 million in its capital reserve fund and almost $9 million in its special reserve fund subject to recapture of about $6.5 million. Its fleet, reduced to six ships free of debt, was valued at $9.6 million after depreciation. Real estate included the Shanghai wharf property, which was estimated to be worth about $1 million. In all, the line had assets of almost $40 million, an incredible improvement in its financial position since the dark days of 1938.[56]

Similarly, though on a much smaller scale, American Mail Line emerged from the war as a valuable property. Over half of R. J. Reynolds's initial investment in 1940 and 1941 had been paid back in dividends alone. And he all but owned a shipping line worth more than $10 million with a profitable future ahead. The fleets of both lines had been built in 1940 and 1941 and, with the exception of APL's venerable *President Johnson* of 1904 vintage, had long lives of efficient service ahead of them.[57]

The management of the lines had been preparing for the expansion of their respective fleets and renewal of their subsidized routes, which had been suspended in 1942. Company planners were confident that trade with the Far East—so long disrupted by war— would be much greater than it had been in the past. Besides their traditional markets, there was also the rehabilitation of war-torn China and Japan to be considered. Southeast Asia and the subcontinent of India would not only be the source of raw materials essential to the reconstruction of the European economy, but would constitute enormous markets for coal, grain, and timber from the West Coast. APL's Atlantic/Straits and round-the-world services, it was thought, would be important adjuncts to the recovery of Europe in the postwar world. Passenger and freight traffic on the trans-Pacific route would also justify significant expansion of the fleets of both APL and American Mail.[58] At Henry Grady's direction the board of APL during the summer of 1944 approved application to the Maritime Commission for the purchase of ten C3 freighters under Title V of the Merchant Marine Act of 1936.[59]

When Grady filed the application with the Maritime Commission, which had retained its legal status during the war, he and Cuffe had lengthy discussions with Vice Admiral Howard Vickery, Land's deputy in the War Shipping Administration.[60] The result of their talks had been that APL agreed to charter four P-2s, large (16,000 tons) combination ships for the trans-Pacific service. These vessels, whose hulls would be modified to meet the line's special requirements, would have accommodations for 177 first-class, 130 tourist, and 250 third-class passengers. They would have approximately 250,000 cubic feet for dry cargo, 60,000 cubic feet for refrigerated cargo, and 35,000 cubic feet for cargo oil.[61]

Lawrence Calvert in his last annual report as president of American Mail announced similar plans for replacement and expansion, though on a more modest scale. "The backbone of our purchased fleet," he wrote, "is expected to be vessels capable of a nominal or maintained schedule speed of not less than 16½ knots and of approximately 10,500 deadweight tons with limited passenger facilities on several of them. . . . Our basic fleet alone, owing to larger size and faster speed of vessels will at least double any service heretofore available to this northwest area."[62]

With all these plans for expansion, with bright prospects for American-flag carriers in a postwar world starved for manufactured goods and raw materials, with the balance sheets of both shipping lines showing substantial assets on the credit side and little or no debt, it was not surprising that R. Stanley Dollar should have suddenly developed a renewed interest in APL. Now that the debts had been discharged, Dollar felt that the line should be returned to the Dollar interests. It was no secret that the commission wanted to disengage itself from the ownership of the company. In the midst of the war, on 6 July 1943, it had issued a press release to this effect and urged private interests to submit comprehensive and definite proposals. Nothing came of this early announcement, though R. Stanley Dollar at the time did engage a Wall Street legal firm to keep an eye on American President Lines, and of course he continued to retain a stock interest in the firm so that he could personally follow its earnings.[63]

In the fall of 1945, the commission again solicited proposals for the return of the line to private ownership. This time Dollar acted with dispatch. Through his lawyers he instituted legal proceedings to halt the sale of the commission-owned stock.[64] In addition, he asked for a writ of *mandamus* ordering the commission to transfer its shares to the Robert Dollar Company. The District Court for Northern California issued a temporary restraining order on the commission preparatory to a hearing in San Francisco on 15 November. For the next seven years, one of the longest and costliest suits in the annals of American shipping clogged the federal courts.[65]

NOTES

1. Dollar v. Land, transcript, 872, 873.
2. "Minutes of Special Meeting of Board of Directors of Dollar Steamship Lines, Inc., Nov. 1, 1938"; "Minutes of Special Stockholders Meeting," 18 November 1938, APL Corporate Files.
3. "Minutes, Special Meeting of the Board of Directors," 6 June 1939, APL Corporate Files. *President Lincoln* and *President Wilson* were sold to Spanish owners in 1940.
4. "Minutes, Regular Meeting of the Board of Directors," 16 April 1939, APL Corporate Files.
5. Ibid.
6. "Minutes, Regular Meeting of the Board of Directors," June 1939, APL Corporate Files.
7. Ibid., 24 August 1939.
8. "Minutes of Regular Meeting of the Board of Directors," 28 December 1939, APL Corporate Files.
9. Ibid., 28 December 1939.
10. Ibid., 23 November 1939.
11. "Minutes, Special Meeting of Board of Directors," 12 April 1940, p. 183; American President Lines, Ltd., Annual Report 1940, APL Corporate Files.
12. "Draft, Minutes of Board of Directors Meeting, Feb. 21, 1940," APL Corporate Files.
13. *Seattle Post-Intelligencer,* 30 March 1939; see also Captain Gunnar Obsborg's description of the *Sartatia* in *Sea Chest,* a publication of the Puget Sound Maritime Historical Society (December 1973).
14. John Cormode, "Memorandum, re. C1 and C2 cargo steamers and C3 passenger and cargo steamers," APL Corporate Files.
15. *Seattle Post-Intelligencer,* 1 December 1939.
16. Lawrence Bogle to Thomas M. Pelly, 26 December 1939 (copy), APL Corporate Files.
17. *Seattle Post-Intelligencer,* 15 December 1939; *Seattle Star,* 14 December 1939.
18. "Minutes of Annual Meeting of Shareholders of American Mail Line Ltd.," 30 June 1940, APL Corporate Files.
19. R. H. Drumheller to Board of Trustees, Seattle Chamber of Commerce, 15 December 1939 (copy), APL Corporate Files.
20. Drumheller to Admiral E. S. Land, 28 February 1940 (copy), APL Corporate Files.
21. John Ambler to Earl D. Doran, 1 March 1940, APL Corporate Files.
22. John Ambler, Memorandum to the president and board of directors of the American Mail Line, "Maritime Commission," 18 December 1939, APL Corporate Files.
23. W. Walter Williams to Lawrence Calvert and Roscoe Drumheller, 18 December 1939, APL Corporate Files.

24. W. Walter Williams to Admiral Emory S. Land, 26 February 1940 (copy), APL Corporate Files.

25. John Ambler to Lawrence Calvert, telegram, 2 March 1940, APL Corporate Files.

26. John Ambler to Lawrence Calvert, 4 March 1940, APL Corporate Files.

27. W. C. Peet, Jr., secretary of the U.S. Maritime Commission to American Mail Line, Ltd., 9 March 1940, APL Archives; "Special Meeting of the Board of Directors, American Mail Line, Ltd.," 12 March 1940, APL Corporate Files.

28. American Mail Line Staff, mimeograph copy, "History of American Mail Line, 1850–1946" (Seattle, 1947), 38. Yost Collection.

29. See John Cormode to Lawrence Calvert, 9 March 1940; ibid. to S. L. Barnes (undated), APL Corporate Files.

30. John Cormode to S. L. Barnes (undated), APL Archives.

31. "Minutes of Special Meeting of Board of Directors of American Mail Line Ltd.," 17 April 1940, APL Corporate Files.

32. These vessels became transports and were renamed, respectively, the *Harris, Zeilin, Henry T. Allen,* and *J. Franklin Bell;* "Regular Meeting of the Board of Directors of American Mail Line, Ltd.," 18 June 1940, APL Corporate Files.

33. *New York Journal of Commerce,* 28 April, 4 May 1939; *Los Angeles Times,* 14 February 1940.

34. Both were built by the Newport News Shipbuilding and Drydock Co. Their gross tonnage was 9,261 and their dimensions 492 feet by 69 feet. They were single-screw turbine engine ships with a speed of 16.5 knots.

35. American President Lines, Ltd., Annual Report 1940, APL Archives.

36. "Minutes, Regular Meeting of the Board of Directors, American President Lines, Ltd.," 11 July 1940, APL Corporate Files.

37. American President Lines, Ltd., "Chronology of Important Events of the Company," APL Archives.

38. "Minutes, Regular Meeting of Board of Directors, American President Lines, Ltd.," 13 February 1941, APL Corporate Files.

39. *President Jackson* was requisitioned by the War Shipping Administration on 30 June 1941, the *President Hayes* on 7 July 1941, and the *President Garfield* on 1 May 1942 after being operated by APL under charter to the War Shipping Administration from 28 March 1941 to 1 May 1942. The *President Van Buren* was delivered to the navy on 14 January 1942. None of these ships ever returned to civilian service for the American President Lines.

40. "Minutes, Regular Meeting of the Board of Directors, American President Lines, Ltd.," 9 June 1942, APL Corporate Files.

41. "Minutes, Special Meeting of the Board of Directors American President Lines, Ltd.," 10 May 1943, APL Corporate Files.

42. American Mail Line, Ltd., Annual Report 1940; Lintner and Bush, "American Mail," Yost Collection; "Minutes, Special Meeting of the Board of Directors of American Mail Line, Ltd.," 14 October 1941, Yost Collection; Harrison, "American Mail."

43. American President Lines, Ltd., Annual Report 1945, APL Archives.

44. W. G. MacDonald, "American President Lines—President Liners," APL Archives.

45. Orel Pierson, Memorandum, "Loss of *Harrison*—Dec. 8, 1941," APL Archives.

46. *Marine Digest,* 7 May 1983; Eugene F. Hoffman, *American President Lines' Role in World War II* (pamphlet) (San Francisco: APL, 1957), 13.

47. Ibid.

48. War Shipping Administration, *The United States Merchant Marine at War* (Washington, D.C.: U.S. Government Printing Office, 1944), 33–40.

49. Ibid., 42.

50. American Mail Line, Ltd., Annual Report 1944, APL Archives.

51. Don S. Burrows, "Organization Survey Report, Dollar Steamship Line, Inc., September 13, 1938," 6, 9, APL Corporate Files.

52. See annual reports of the American President Lines, Ltd., 1941–45; "Minutes, Special Meeting of the Board of Directors of American President Lines, Ltd.," 9 August 1944, APL Corporate Files.

53. Finance Office, American Mail Line, "Tabulation of ships of U.S. War Shipping Administration, American Mail Line," Yost Collection.

54. American Mail Line, *Annals*, APL Archives; Lintner and Bush, "American Mail," 21 February, 1 July 1942; 5 November 1945, Yost Collection.

55. American President Lines, Ltd., Annual Reports 1941, 1942, APL Archives.

56. Ibid., Annual Report 1945.

57. American Mail Line, Ltd., Annual Report 1945, Yost Collection.

58. "Minutes, Regular Meeting of the Board of Directors of American President Lines, Ltd.," 23 August 1945, APL Corporate Files.

59. Ibid., 4, 9 August 1944, APL Corporate Files.

60. Emory S. Land, *The United States Merchant Marine at War* (Washington, D.C.: U.S. Government Printing Office, 1946), 73–74.

61. "Minutes, Regular Meeting of the Board of Directors of American President Lines, Ltd.," 28 September 1944, APL Corporate Files.

62. American Mail Line, Ltd., Annual Report 1945, Yost Collection.

63. "Minutes, Regular Meeting of the Board of Directors of American President Lines, Ltd.," 8 July 1943, APL Archives; U.S. Maritime Commission press release, 6 July 1943, in Dollar v. Land transcript, APL Corporate Files.

64. Clinton M. Hester to U.S. Maritime Commission, 25 July 1945; Emory S. Land to Clinton M. Hester, 30 July 1945, Dollar v. Land, transcript, California Historical Society.

65. "Minutes, Regular Meeting of the Board of Directors of American President Lines, Ltd.," 8 November 1945, APL Archives.

8
RETURN TO PRIVATE OWNERSHIP

"APL is engaged in the world-wide operation of a major steamship line. These operations are complex and difficult in any circumstances and are made the more exacting by the present demand for emergency shipping. A major upheaval in the directorate and top management of the line, symbolized to the world by change of name and of flag could not fail to be costly." So said Ralph Davies, president of the American Independent Oil Company, speaking for the line's minority stockholders. Warner Gardner, Davies's counsel, wise in the ways of events and governments, had drafted the remarks and suggested the plan of action, that of appearing as *amici curiae* or friends of the court in filing a brief against the Dollar interests during the final phases of the litigation that had been going on for more than six years in the federal courts.[1]

The *amici curiae* shrewdly took advantage of the uncertainties inherent in the wartime situation during the fall of 1951, a frustrating stalemate that existed between the United Nations forces and those of China and North Korea. APL was one of the principal links in the supply route from the West Coast of the United States to the war theater. Anything that might interrupt schedules or even disturb shipments to the Far East and the return was well calculated to upset a federal judge sufficiently for him to find for the government in its efforts to retain its controlling interest in APL.

Even without the urgencies of wartime, Gardner could have made a strong case for continuity of management no matter who gained control. In the thousands of pages of hearings on motions, testimony and arguments by opposing counsel on technical and substantive points, there had been no criticism of the management since the partial reorganization in 1938. Under the capable leadership of McAdoo and Sheehan, Grady and Lutz, and always the prudent financial management of Arthur Poole, APL had performed admirably under the extreme pressures of World War II. Although operations had been profitable there had been no excessive salaries and no systematic draining of assets as in the days of the Dollars. The results had been clear and positive: The shipping line was free of debt in 1945, its planning well advanced for the resumption of its traditional trade routes with new and improved carriers for peacetime commerce.

In the years immediately following the end of hostilities, the APL fleet was almost completely renewed. The last of the vessels of World War I vintage, the *President Tyler* (ex *President Hayes*), a 502, was sold to the War Shipping Administration on 20 March 1945. At that time the company-owned fleet was reduced to three vessels, one of which, the *President Johnson* (ex *Manchuria*), a 16,000-ton ship built in 1904, was up for sale. The other two ships were the *President Monroe* and *President Polk*, C3-P–type ships designed for the round-the-world passenger and cargo service and built in 1940 and 1941. They reentered service in 1946 after being completely reconditioned and modernized following wartime operation as transports. For the next two years, under Henry Grady's presidency, APL acquired a new fleet of C3s, the *President Grant, President Pierce,* and *President Taft* in 1945, and the *President Madison, President McKinley,* and *President Jefferson* in 1946. Three more C3s were on order.

For the trans-Pacific express passenger and cargo service, APL had to acquire a new fleet, since the *President Coolidge* and *President Hoover* had both been lost. In 1946 and 1947 service was provided by chartered transports, the *General M. C. Meigs, General W. H. Gordon, Marine Adder,* and *Marine Swallow.* They had been partly converted for commercial passenger service but in no sense represented the standard that APL aimed to achieve.

To serve fully the requirements of the California-Orient route, two hulls under construction at Bethlehem-Alameda Shipyards were redesigned to improve the passenger accommodations. They were of the transport type similar to the *General* ships but were caught early enough in construction so that troop-type accommodations did not have to be altered for civilian passengers. Completed for the War Shipping Administration but conforming to APL's specifications, they were bareboat-chartered from WSA by APL.

Named the *President Cleveland* and *President Wilson*, these ships had an overall length of 608 feet 6 inches and a beam of 75 feet 6

The Victory-class ships of World War II were not likely to win any beauty contests, but they were good, efficient cargo carriers. Here is *President Garfield* [III], one of six owned by APL, 1951–58. (Alfred T. Palmer Collection, APL Archives.)

President Wilson [II] and *President Cleveland* [II] *(right)* passing in San Francisco Bay. They provided the backbone of APL's trans-Pacific passenger service from 1948 until 1973. (APL Archives.)

inches. Their gross tonnage was 15,359, or about one-quarter less than the *President Coolidge* and *President Hoover.* On her trials the *President Cleveland* developed 20,460-shaft horsepower with her turbo-electric engines driving twin screws. The ships had two complete engine rooms, one for each propeller, which was a desirable feature for a transport subject to wartime torpedo attack but which considerably increased the cost of peacetime operations. The ships were designed for a sustained sea speed of 19 knots, and on her trials the *Cleveland* developed 22 knots.

The vessels were designed to carry about 550 passengers in three classes—first, tourist, and economy. As it turned out, they never carried tourist class since the demand for first-class passage was so great that the accommodations originally designated for tourist were assigned to first class. As they entered service the ships carried some 326 passengers in first class and 506 in economy. First-class public rooms were handsomely finished, and staterooms were spacious and comfortable. Passenger accommodations were air-conditioned throughout. The crews of each ship numbered 352.[2]

President Cleveland sailed from San Francisco on her maiden voyage on 27 December 1947 and was followed by the *President Wilson* on 1 May 1948. The announced intention of APL in 1947 had been to withdraw the two *General* ships for refurbishment after the new ships were in service. When returned to the line they would be similar to the new vessels and the four ships would offer sailings to the Orient every two weeks. This was never accomplished, however, and the *Gordon* and *Meigs* were phased out in early 1949.[3] But under the terms of the Merchant Ship Sales Act, APL purchased three additional C3s and five freighters of the Victory design, 7,652-ton, 16½-knot vessels, all built during 1944 and 1945.[4]

When Henry Grady resigned the presidency on 12 August 1947 to become the United States' first ambassador to India, APL owned fifteen ships, none older than eight years and most either new or but one or two years old. In addition, thirty-six more were being operated under bareboat charter or general agency agreement. The company had ample funds for further replacement and expansion. Its capital reserve fund totaled $12 million and its special reserve fund $1.1 million.

Management had made substantial progress in implementing the program the Maritime Commission had outlined in its *Report on Essential Foreign Trade Routes and Services Recommended for United States*

The California Room, the first-class dining salon aboard the *President Cleveland* [II] or *President Wilson* [II]. (APL Archives.)

Flag Operations that was issued on 22 May 1946. This document had a profound impact on American peacetime commerce since it gave a manifest of the government's intentions and described the limits of its support to the merchant marine. Within the meaning of the Merchant Marine Act of 1936 the report defined thirty-one trade routes, within which were specified seventy-four services, including itineraries, sailing frequencies, and number and type of ships for these routes. Prominently displayed were APL's three traditional prewar services—trans-Pacific, round-the-world, and Atlantic/Straits. The report declared that subsidy arrangements on the trans-Pacific and round-the-world services that had been suspended during the war would be reestablished and would reflect changed labor and economic conditions. It also included the Atlantic/Straits service

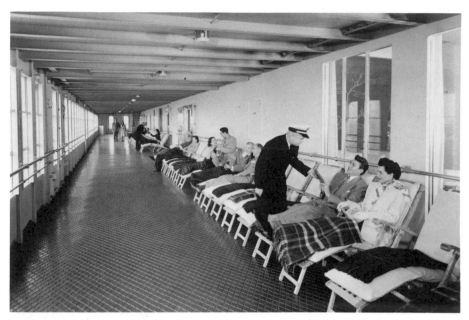

The first-class promenade deck aboard the *President Cleveland* [II] or *President Wilson* [II]. Notice that rubber tile has replaced the traditional teak decking. (Alfred T. Palmer Collection, APL Archives.)

The first class lounge aboard the *President Cleveland* (II) or *President Wilson* (II). (Alfred T. Palmer Collection, APL Archives.)

as essential to the foreign commerce of the nation and implied that a subsidy agreement also would be worked out for these voyages.

The commission's report specified the minimum number of ships and their types and speeds for all subsidized services. For example, for the trans-Pacific trade route no. 29, there were three services. Service E, passenger and freight with a sailing every two weeks (twenty-six sailings a year), would require four P2-type (15- to 16,000-ton combination) vessels. Freight service E1 was determined to be exclusively cargo and would be maintained by four improved 19-knot C3s. Similarly, freight service F would supplement the cargo capacity of E and E1 on the trans-Pacific route with five C3s. The commission contemplated, therefore, a minimum of thirteen vessels on route 29.

APL would expect a substantial share of this market, but not all, as the commission plainly stated. In the round-the-world service there would be seven C3-P combination vessels that would provide a sailing every two weeks. On this route, APL had a distinct advantage over any competition because of its long experience and the fact that the war had not dispersed its worldwide network of agents. The Atlantic/Straits service under trade route no. 17 contemplated four C3 freighters with a sailing every four weeks. In all, twenty-four ships would have to be purchased or chartered if the company were to satisfy the commission's minimum requirements on these subsidized routes. At 1946 costs, it was estimated that these vessels would entail an investment of $52,450,000, after a 50 percent construction differential subsidy, a huge sum for a shipping line whose heavily mortgaged fleet of obsolete vessels in 1938 had a market value of less than $10 million and which reported a net loss for that year of almost $4,293,000, with a cumulative earnings deficit of $17,642,000. Yet seven years later Arthur Poole had every confidence that the company could meet the staggering sum for ships the commission demanded before it would subsidize APL's accustomed trade routes. He told the board that

> the Capital Reserve Fund, assuming settlement of taxes as tentatively offered by the Treasury Department, excluding certain contingent sources of deposits in that fund, and without making any allowance for possible transfers from the Special Reserve Fund under the Commission's policies currently under discussion, is sufficient not only to provide all ships proposed herein to be purchased, but to provide in addition an estimated

balance in reserve at December 31, 1948, of more than
$6,000,000. In addition to the moneys available from the Capital
Reserve Fund, the company has a Special Reserve Fund balance
substantially in excess of accrued subsidy recapture plus 5% of
invested capital.[5]

The optimism that Poole reflected seemed to be borne out by improved earnings and a further expansion of APL's fleet during 1947,
despite difficulties the economy was experiencing in readjusting
itself to demobilization and the dismantling of wartime controls.
APL purchased from the commission seven additional cargo ships
under the provisions of the Merchant Ship Sales Act, which set
values on all surplus vessels at 35 percent of wartime costs.[6]

But there was a sharp economic downturn in 1948 during which a
ninety-five-day strike that tied up all shipping on the West Coast
cost the company more than $4 million in direct costs and disrupted
the flow of cargo, much of which had to be directed to ports in
Canada and Mexico. The settlement's provision for substantial increases in wages for both seagoing and shore personnel raised
operating costs. Since the freight traffic and rates on APL's routes
remained static, none of these costs could be passed on to consum-
ers. In 1949 there was a lengthy strike in the ports of the Hawaiian
Islands that also adversely affected earnings. Nor was the company
successful in collecting what it regarded as its due for subsidy
allotments from the government. In 1950 the company was claiming
almost $20 million in arrears of subsidy. Yet net earnings had gradu-
ally increased to $3.8 million that year. The outbreak of the Korean
War, together with the complete closure of Chinese ports after the
collapse of the Nationalists, however, cut drastically into APL's
trans-Pacific traffic. Although military demands soon replaced most
of the lost business, net earnings for 1951 were slightly less than the
previous year.[7]

Throughout this period there had been significant changes in
management and on the board of directors. George Killion succeeded Grady as president on 12 August 1947. An amiable public-
relations expert and politician, Killion had been budget director for
California's Governor Culbert Olson in the early forties. He served
briefly as a special assistant to Ralph Davies in the Federal Petroleum
Administration, the wartime agency that controlled the nation's oil
supply. Active in the Democratic party, Killion took a leave of ab-

sence from the Petroleum Administration to help with the presidential campaign of 1944. His efforts for the party were rewarded by his appointment as treasurer of its national committee. Eminently successful as a fund-raiser, especially in California, he contributed significantly to the reelection of Harry Truman in 1948. As a reward for his service he was offered several minor diplomatic posts, which he declined. When Grady resigned as president of American President Lines, Killion recalled that Ralph Davies telephoned him and said, "Why don't you ask the President to name you head of American President Lines?"[8] Killion knew nothing about the shipping industry, but he did know the business world of California. Davies thought his flair for publicity and his experience as a reporter and in public relations would be valuable in merchandizing, an area in which Davies felt APL was deficient. And Killion's political and governmental connections were excellent, an important consideration for any subsidized shipping line.

Ralph Davies had become interested in APL as early as 1944. A shrewd businessman, he had won respect in the highly competitive and speculative oil business in California during the twenties and early thirties. As deputy petroleum administrator under Harold Ickes, the secretary of the interior, he was high in the counsels of those who were developing policies for the return of America's war-controlled economy to a peacetime environment. Though primarily if not exclusively concerned with the oil situation in the postwar world, as a Californian Davies was well aware of APL's importance to the economy of the West Coast. He also recognized that the government would dispose of its interest in APL when the war was over.

To that eventual end he had had Richard Simon, an investment banker with the San Francisco firm of J. Barth and Company, look into the affairs of APL. Simon acted promptly. He sought out William H. Thomson, who had succeeded Paul Hoover as president of the Anglo-California Bank, which still held 11,000 shares of APL preferred stock, about one-third of those shares outstanding, and 25,000 shares of Class A common stock, about 10 percent of that issue. Thomson confirmed the fact that the Fleishhacker estate owned about 15,000 shares of Class A common, which were for sale, and he knew of other smaller blocks of stock that could be purchased. Simon reported Thomson as saying that "Grady, at the time the Maritime Commission asked for bids (or rather proposals), at-

The old and the new. George Killion, president of American President Lines, 1948–66 *(left),* and R. Stanley Dollar, president of Dollar Steamship Lines, 1929–38 *(right)* examine a model of the *President Coolidge* [I]. A portrait of Robert Dollar looks down from the wall behind them. (APL Archives.)

George Killion *(left)* and Ralph K. Davies, chairman of the board of American President Lines, 1952–71. (APL Archives.)

tempted to sign up a lot of stockholders to accept relatively the same price for their Class A stock as the Maritime might accept; but the Anglo-California Bank turned him down because the Maritime Commission might accept a price for political reasons which would not be acceptable to stockholders of the Anglo-California Bank for business reasons."[9]

Simon sent along to Davies a careful analysis by a securities expert of "a friendly house for our confidential files, which had been interested in APL stock for trading purposes." After studying the analysis Davies came to the conclusion that APL would be a good risk for the investment of venture capital. What he found particularly attractive was the fact that APL had currently some $17 million in cash and claims for the purchase of ships after the war. He agreed with the analyst who had written that

> a contingency reserve of $5,200,000 seems generous indeed and should eventually prove to be in part additional equity for the company's stock. The book value of the preferred of almost $500 per share (giving effect to a $15,500,000 settlement of the company's claims) will largely represent cash until a fleet is purchased after the war.[10]

From 1944 until 1952, Davies purchased blocks of stock in his own name and in the name of J. Barth and Company. He became the principal minority stockholder, with about 11 percent of Class A common stock, or 28,892 shares, in his own name. Barth and Company held 41,245 shares of Class A common.[11]

When Davies asked Killion to consider the presidency of APL, he recalled that "the idea intrigued me—from waterfront reporter in San Diego as a cub reporter to president of the longest shipping line in the world. I went to Washington, told the President that I would like to be head of American President Lines and he appointed me to the job."[12] Davies had known Killion since 1940. At the time Davies was head of sales for Standard Oil of California and the youngest vice president in that company's history. A remarkably able merchandising specialist, he had developed the famous Chevron trademark and had been largely responsible for Standard's phenomenal success in retailing gasoline not just in California but throughout the nation.

A trim, reserved person with steady gray eyes, Davies had first gone to Washington in 1933 to work out petroleum-industry codes for the NRA. Harold Ickes, always looking for able people with business experience, became acquainted with Davies. Later, after Davies had been edged out of the presidency of Standard in an executive-suite power play, he asked Davies to come to Washington and take charge of the newly created petroleum division in the National Defense Advisory Commission. The president had declared a national emergency, and a rearmament program of which oil was an essential aspect was underway. As petroleum coordinator, Ickes was nominally in charge of the division, but the secretary had so many other responsibilities that Davies was in reality the chief executive. After Pearl Harbor, the government scrapped the Advisory Commission and created the Office of War Mobilization in its place with Donald Nelson, a former Sears Roebuck executive, in charge.

Because of its critical importance and because of Ickes's influence with Roosevelt, coordination and control of the nation's petroleum resources were placed under a separate organization, the Petroleum Administration for War. Ickes maintained his position and role as administrator, but he delegated actual management of the agency to Davies. As such he became one of the more powerful individuals in Washington and indeed in the entire Allied war effort, although except for those in the oil industry, high administration officials, and senior Allied army and navy officers, few knew of his importance.

Hard-working, hard-driving, and competent, Davies shunned publicity. During the war there was no feature story on Davies in *Time* or *Look* or *Life*, and few news stories that emanated from Petroleum Administration described Davies's work. With the loyal support of Chandler Ide, his tall, spare, equally competent, and equally reticent assistant whom he brought with him from Standard, the two men managed with a minimum of friction to deal with hundreds of highly independent oilmen, from the Texas wildcatters who owned a dozen wells to huge international combines like Standard of New Jersey or their own Standard of California. By government edict the powers of the administration embraced every aspect of the oil industry—production, refining, natural gas, pipelines, marketing, even construction targets for seagoing tankers and their control in times of emergency.

Davies's management of the War Petroleum Administration earned a grudging admiration from his fellow oilmen. But more important it alerted the nation's banking communities and highly placed members of the Roosevelt administration to the fact that he was a businessman who could be trusted with just about any job, however complex, however urgent. It was in order, therefore, that the APL situation should have been brought to Davies's attention when in early 1944 the Roosevelt administration began to plan for reconversion of war industries to a peacetime economy. High on the list were government-owned property, plant and equipment, including of course, the government-owned shipping line, APL.

Shortly after V-J day, the Petroleum Administration was dismantled. Again a loser in a power struggle at Standard of California, Davies could not return to his old position. By now he had made a considerable investment in APL, but the time was not right for any move in that direction. R. Stanley Dollar had launched a suit seeking to regain control of the line. And while APL was tied up in litigation, the government was not inclined to liquidate what it considered to be its property. Nor was Davies by nature an impulsive man. He was "single-minded and tenacious once a decision was taken," as Chandler Ide described him, but "an exasperating corollary of this decisive aspect of Ralph's character was his unwillingness to make up his mind or give up possible options when decisions could be avoided or deferred."[13]

Davies kept in close touch with the APL situation while he cast about for other industries that seemed to have an investment potential. Chief among these were the exploration and production of oil outside of the United States. Through his contacts and the respect he enjoyed in the oil and banking community, in 1947 he managed to form a corporation of eleven individuals and independent oil companies to challenge the big oil companies that had hitherto maintained a monopoly on overseas exploration, especially in the Middle East.[14] The company, American Independent Oil, became a major interest of Ralph Davies for the next fifteen years until he finally sold out at a very large capital gain.

Although deeply involved in the difficulties of launching a new corporation that would be venturing into what had been and still was forbidden territory, Davies sensed a change in the affairs of APL when Henry Grady resigned the presidency in 1947. The Dollar litigation up to this point seemed to be favoring the government. APL itself was in flourishing condition.[15] If Davies were ever to take over the line, he wanted someone to head it who had the right connections, who was shrewd enough to keep management stable, and who would be responsive to his ideas. Davies kept his options open, but he was not ready to make a commitment. Killion seemed to meet perfectly the qualifications he wanted in a manager of a potential property that was still in government hands.

Killion made few changes in executive management during his first year as president. E. Russell Lutz remained as executive vice president and a member of the board. He rewarded M. J. Buckley's years of valuable service as head of the APL's freight department by making him a senior vice president with broad responsibilities to develop new business. W. Kenneth Varcoe, whose service with the freight department went back to 1924, was selected to fill Buckley's place. Another time-tested Dollar and APL veteran, Thomas J. Cokely, the operations manager, became a vice president but his responsibilities remained the same. Two new directors were named to replace vacancies on the board, Edward Hillman Heller, a San Francisco broker and investment banker, and Leroy Mallory Edwards of Los Angeles, general manager of Pacific Lighting Corporation.[16]

Killion himself relied heavily on H. Boyce Luckett, a young traffic specialist who had been with the Washington office of the Dollar Line and APL and was a naval officer during the war. He returned to Washington at the war's end, where he served briefly in the War Shipping Administration on loan from APL that included work for Thomas Cuffe in the freight department of APL's eastern territory based in Washington, D.C.[17] When Cuffe resigned to form his own shipping company and the eastern territory was abolished as a separate division, Luckett was moved to the West Coast to become Grady's executive assistant. Luckett's practical experience and Washington connections with the technical and operating people in the Defense Department and the Maritime Commission made him an ideal choice as a key staff man.[18]

From the beginning Killion did not get along with E. Russell Lutz. The two men held different views of how APL should be run. Lutz, the sometime member of the Maritime Commission's legal department, had functioned well with Grady during the war when there had been no need to consider merchandising as an important factor in the business or to calculate the demands of the civilian market as it affected ship design and operation. Killion may not have been a shipping expert, but he listened to the younger men in the organization, especially when it came to modifications in the design of new vessels under consideration that would enhance passenger accommodations or provide better access, stowage, and space for specialized cargoes. Quite probably Ralph Davies was consulted about Lutz, whose separation might have rocked the boat. In any event, the departure of Lutz created a vacancy on the board. Killion saw to it that Ralph Davies was elected to replace him.[19]

Killion's prime motive, of course, was innovation that would make points in advertising and other aspects of sales promotion. But he did not neglect efficiency in operations, both as a service to APL's markets and as a matter of internal cost reduction. Early on Killion brought in Sheridan Gorman as a budget director with broad responsibility for controlling costs. Gorman devised and put into practice a program that required captains of APL vessels to follow insofar as possible an operations budget made up before each voyage and to report any discrepancies at its termination. Though this policy was a worthwhile reform and would be continued, Gorman's effort to engraft what in effect were government cost-accounting practices on both the financial and operations departments of the company and Killion's support of this policy inevitably caused friction within management.

Gorman's tenure was short, and as time went on, Killion took less interest in reforming procedures and devoted himself more and more to sales, public relations, and government relations, an area in which his services were most valuable to the company. Warner Gardner, APL's astute Washington counsel and a close observer of Killion, said that he was "preeminent in his dealings with the Congress and with the Maritime Administration here in Washington. At no time before or after has APL been better represented in Washington."[20]

But Killion's overall management was successful only to a limited extent. The line's net worth increased from $23 million in 1948 to $35 million in 1952; yet throughout this period its revenues declined from $60 million in 1947 when Killion took over to $49 million in 1950. Apart from any shortcomings Killion may have had as chief executive, there were three reasons for this downturn. First and foremost was the reappearance of foreign competition following the readjustment to a peacetime economy. Second, APL's most important market, China, disappeared with the Communist triumph on the mainland. Third, government failed to reimburse APL for its subsidized routes from 31 December 1946 to the end of 1952. At that date there was a balance in favor of APL on its subsidy account of $24 million after making provision for $6 million of "recapture" money to be paid the government on profits over 10 percent. A lesser factor in reducing revenues was the devaluation of the British pound in 1949, which contributed to a reduction in the volume of freight carried by all American-flag vessels.

The Korean War, which began in the summer of 1951, reversed some of these negative trends. Military cargo and troop movements to the Far East took up much of the slack in APL's operations. W. K. Varcoe, APL's freight chief, admitted that "we were bailed out by the military in 1950 and 1951."[21]

However, management showed considerable ingenuity in finding and developing new markets. In particular the unsubsidized route from the East Coast of the United States through the Panama Canal to Hong Kong, the Philippines, Indonesia, Singapore, and Malaya contributed significant revenues. American machinery and other high unit-value manufactured products were in much demand throughout Southeast Asia to rebuild war-ravaged economies. Traditional exports from this region—tin, rubber, and mahogany—enjoyed a thriving market in the United States. But the competition was intense on the Atlantic/Straits route.

In its efforts to wring every possible dollar out of the round-the-world service, management even departed from its traditional specialization in high unit-value cargo and carried such bulk commodities as coal, iron ore, and grain from the United States to Japan, while moving bulk raw materials from Southeast and East Asian ports westward to Europe. These so-called tramp cargoes may have accounted for 10 to 12 percent of the round-the-world freight revenues. But remedies were temporary at best. One of the problems management targeted was the comparative lack of refrigerated and liquid cargo space in those APL vessels that had been built for wartime service. Varcoe told a *Wall Street Journal* reporter in the fall of 1952 that

> reefer cargoes have just been handed over to the foreign flags. Before the war all our ships had refrigeration facilities. Now only half of them do. I wish we had twice the reefer capacity and better designed bulk liquid space tailored to the demands of the market. Also we don't even have the space to handle all the cotton we're offered for shipment.

Yet APL was a valuable property and once the Dollar suit was settled, it had ample resources—some $17 million in its construction fund—to build new ships that would better conform with the post-war markets. Once the arrears in subsidy payments were collected and a subsidy granted on the Atlantic/Straits route, which was probable, APL's potential earning capacity seemed excellent. At least Ralph Davies thought so. The Dollars thought so too, and so did Global Marine (representing the Matson Line and the Murchisons of Texas), who had recently purchased R. J. Reynolds's controlling shares in American Mail.[22]

Meanwhile the slow progress of the Dollar litigation through the courts had taken a turn that was adverse to the government. By 1950 the points at issue were clearly laid out. If the government could not be sued without its consent, could Emory Land—chairman of the Maritime Commission, which received the stock at the time of the "transfer"—and by implication any of his successors be considered unlawfully in possession of the stock? If that was the case, the United States would be free to assert its claim for title. The second point at issue was whether the Dollar interests had relinquished all title to the stock in APL when it was transferred to the government; or was the stock merely pledged as collateral for the debts owed? If the latter definition held, then the commission should have returned the stock to its rightful owners at the war's end because by then all debts had been paid off.

R. Stanley Dollar believed that title had been transferred, and in fact he and Lorber and the executors of his brother Harold's estate had all taken losses on the stock in their income tax returns. But counsel for the Dollar interests established that the reorganization agreement had not been absolutely clear and specific on this point. As Warner Gardner described the drafting of the government attorneys, "the work was done with stupefying incompetence."[23] On various appeals the Dollar legal team also succeeded in enjoining Secretary of Commerce Charles Sawyer, to whom the Maritime Commission now reported, to deliver the stock to the Dollars. President Truman now stepped in and ordered Sawyer to hold the stock on behalf of the United States. "All appropriate action," wrote Truman, "should be taken to assert and maintain the government's rights as owner of this stock."[24] Sawyer succeeded in winning a delay, but on appeal the Dollars won a judgment against Admiral

Land, still the defendant in the case, though long since retired from the commission. He was ordered to deliver the stock or be held in contempt of court. Sawyer appealed to the Supreme Court, but as it had in the past, the Court denied a writ of *certiorari,* in effect letting stand the decision of the appeals court.

Faced with the complete disruption of his plan, Davies decided on several moves. He engaged Warner Gardner, a partner in the Washington law firm of Shea and Gardner, to represent the minority stockholders. Gardner—urbane, cultivated, able—was one of those rare persons who blended an intimate knowledge of corporation law with the probing intellect of the incisive advocate. But more than these personal qualities, Gardner had spent much of his professional life operating in the highest circles of government. As a young lawyer just out of Columbia Law School, he had clerked for Supreme Court Justice Harlan Fiske Stone. Then, in the solicitor general's office, he served under three men, two of whom later became distinguished justices of the Supreme Court—Stanley Reed and Robert Jackson—and Francis Biddle, who served as attorney general under Roosevelt and Truman. Gardner was successively solicitor for the Labor and Interior Departments, and after serving in army intelligence during the war, became assistant secretary of interior, a position he had recently left to go into private practice when Davies approached him. If anyone could retrieve APL from the Dollars, Gardner was the man. Davies showed keen judgment in selecting him to represent the minority interests, yet according to Gardner, the prospects did not seem favorable at the time.

The day after he agreed to represent the minority interests, Gardner went over to the Justice Department, where he had many friends, and learned that it had received an order from the appeals court in Washington directing it to turn over the stock it had in custody to the Dollar interests. After discussing strategy with members of the department, they decided to try another court, the district court in San Francisco, taking the position that "a judgment against Land did not bind the United States if the United States owned the stock and they were bringing suit to clear it." This was not a new point, but as yet it had been advanced only indirectly through Truman's order to Sawyer. At the same time Gardner prepared a statement whereby Davies and other minority stockholders could make an argument against the Dollar interests as *amici curiae.*[25]

The statement itself was an adroit plea that the minority interests, and behind them the national security, would be injured if there were a change in management at this time. In particular the *amici curiae* declared that such a change would return the largest shipping line on the West Coast, which up to now had been well managed, to a group who had been proven to have been, if not incompetent, of doubtful probity. Gardner's brief complemented Admiral Cochrane's (Land's successor as chairman of the new Maritime Board) savage indictment of the Dollar interests in an affidavit that was presented to the Ninth Circuit Court of Appeals in San Francisco. Chief Judge Harris of this court accepted the government's contention and issued an order in effect staying the injunction of the Washington appellate court.

While these legal maneuvers were taking place, Davies had been lining up support for a possible takeover, depending, of course, on a favorable outcome of the case. All along he had sensed a compromise and wanted to be prepared for that eventuality. Just after the annual meeting of APL in early 1951, directors Leroy Edwards, Edward Heller, and Frank J. O'Connor retired from the board.[26] As required by its charter, Killion had to gain approval from the Maritime Commission for any nominee to the board. He consulted Ralph Davies, who had already anticipated this action. Davies recommended that Gustav Epstein, senior partner of Barth and Company, a minority stockholder, and Samuel B. Mosher, president and chief executive officer of Signal Oil, be elected directors. Killion submitted these names to Admiral Cochrane, who accepted them for the board. Accordingly they were elected to the APL board at its regular meeting on 19 March 1951.[27]

Davies had known Mosher for years, their relationship going back to the late twenties when Davies was a vice president and sales director for Standard Oil of California and heir apparent to the presidency of that organization. Mosher was head of Signal Oil, then a struggling independent oil company in Southern California. The two men had very different personalities. Davies, a self-made man whose formal education had ended with high school, was undemonstrative, almost taciturn, cold and even ruthless if crossed or betrayed, but was astonishingly well read and a clear, forceful articulator of written or verbal ideas. Though he had few close friends, he was intensely loyal to them. Mosher, from an upstate New York family, had moved to California when he was young and attended the University of California, Berkeley, before becoming an army officer in World War I. He was as outgoing and gregarious in his personal life and in his business relationships as Davies was reticent. Garth Young, an executive of Signal Oil who knew them both well, said, "two more opposite men never lived. Sam was the 'open-door' operator, a truly independent oil man, while Ralph was the 'closed-door' type. Sam was fond of saying you could always find Ralph in his 'mahogany foxhole viewing the world in general, and engineers in particular.' "[28]

Davies had helped Mosher develop important oil properties in Huntington Beach and had taken most of Signal's output in refined products and crude for Standard to the mutual advantage of both companies. During the war Davies had Mosher appointed a member of the Petroleum Industry War Council, an advisory group that met monthly in Washington. After the war, Davies brought Mosher and Signal into the consortium of eleven independent oil companies that made up American Independent Oil Company.[29] Now as a member of APL's board of directors, Davies was involving Mosher, whose personal assets in Signal were substantial, not just in the speculative possibilities of the company's stock, but in the long-term future of the shipping business. Like Davies, this hard-driving oilman clung to a romantic vision of the sea and ships.

With interest but no commitment from Signal Oil, and with the success of Warner Gardner's strategy in countering the Washington appeals court order, Davies felt he was making some progress. George Killion, on the other hand, was faced with two conflicting orders. On the advice of APL's outside counsel, Arthur B. Dunne, Killion did not deliver the stock while Dunne and Warner Gardner appealed to the Supreme Court.[30]

But then came a distinct setback for Davies. Mario Giannini, president of the Bank of America, got in touch with Killion. Giannini, whose bank was heavily involved in the San Francisco business community, was concerned about the apparent never-ending litigation. The uncertainty about APL's future was creating apprehension, he felt, among all those businesses that dealt with the line. Giannini sounded out Killion on the possibility of a compromise between the government and the Dollar interests. Killion, whose position placed him in the middle of the antagonists, saw merit in a compromise solution, but did not think Dollar would go for it. "I'll bring Stanley Dollar around," said the banker confidently.[31]

Sometime later Killion was a guest at a luncheon meeting that

Giannini had arranged where Stanley Dollar was also present. Over the coffee and the cognac, Giannini suggested a formula whereby the government would put up APL for bid and divide evenly the proceeds of the sale with the Dollar interests. Dollar listened carefully but made no comment, which Killion took to be a positive sign that at least he would be willing to consider such a proposal. On the strength of this rather tenuous evidence of intent, Killion flew to Washington and presented the plan to President Truman, who likewise made no commitment but did not discourage Killion. The irrepressible Killion again took silence for approval and urged the compromise on Attorney General McGranery, who had just succeeded J. Howard McGrath in this office and had inherited the government's defense against the Dollars. McGranery, who was already partial to the Dollars' case, was quite willing to settle on the terms that Killion presented. All that remained was for Killion to persuade R. Stanley Dollar to agree and for McGranery to bring Secretary of Commerce Sawyer around for the government, a formidable undertaking. Yet Killion and the attorney general proved equal to the task. Dollar came to Washington and he and Sawyer made the deal, doubtless with the consent of President Truman.[32]

Neither Ralph.Davies nor his counsel Warner Gardner was aware of these negotiations. The first time they heard about them was in the form of an announcement in early October from the Maritime Commission that bids would be accepted for the purchase of a controlling interest in APL with a minimum bid set for $14 million. The Riggs National Bank in Washington, which was holding the stock, would announce the winning bid on 29 October 1952. Undeterred, Davies moved ahead with his plans. "He went at it," recalled Warner Gardner, "the way he did most things. He first decided what he could afford to pay. What he would be willing to pay for it. And he bid that. He didn't worry about whether he could get it at a lower price or not. Which I might say was his general approach to any investment. . . ."[33]

On the day appointed, the boardroom of Riggs Bank was crowded with reporters who had been attracted by the news that one of the nation's largest shipping lines was about to be sold. It was known that three groups had made bids. Which would be the highest? Would it be the Dollars, former owners of APL? Would it be Matson Navigation Company? Or would it be a newly formed organization about which little was known, APL Associates, headed by Ralph

Davies, who again was not familiar to most of the reporters present? The president of Riggs Bank quieted the throng and announced to the curious crowd that the Dollars had entered a minimum bid of $14 million and that Matson's bid at $16,426,000 was also unacceptable. APL Associates had the winning bid of $18,360,000 and were therefore accorded the ownership of the controlling 113,206 Class A shares and 2,100,000 Class B shares. The reporters crowded around Davies and Gardner and Killion, who was also present. Would Mr. Davies make any comments? The quiet, unobtrusive man obliged and read from a prepared statement.

> I have long hoped to see this line back in responsible private hands. Its trade and passenger routes are world-encircling and its potentialities for development and expansion enormous. As a Californian, I am particularly aware of the significance of this vitally important Company as a West Coast enterprise. It is our plan to strengthen and go forward with APL's present progressive management. The Company has uncommonly fine personnel. We look with high hope and confidence to the lines' future.

Then he was asked whether Killion would remain as president. "We certainly hope so," he replied.[34]

One of the longest corporate suits in history was over, and Davies had accomplished an objective he had planned and worked for over an eight-year span. But as Warner Gardner remarked, "So he got it, then he had the most uncomfortable month."

The fact of the matter was that Davies had not lined up all his backers. His big break came when Signal agreed to put up half of the amount. By then Davies had formed APL Associates. He himself had risked most of his personal fortune, perhaps one quarter of the bid amount, the remainder he secured from the investment bankers, Carl M. Loeb Rhoades, the Bank of America, and several dozen individuals, friends, or associates like J. Howard Marshall, executive vice president of Signal, or Chandler Ide, who had become indispensable to Davies as a confidant, assistant, and perhaps his closest personal friend.[35]

By the end of the month, Davies had not only disposed of the one million shares at which he had capitalized APL Associates, Inc., at the price required to settle the account with the Dollars and the government, but he secured a controlling interest in the new company. Davies became chairman of the board of APL, which was now a subsidiary of APL Associates, Inc. After the financial arrangements were worked out, Davies surveyed his shipping line and prepared for what he hoped would be a prosperous future, though he was realistic enough to know that there would be difficult times too.

NOTES

1. Dollar v. Land, transcript, folder 29 (microfilm).
2. *Pacific Marine Review,* January 1948, 42–60; ibid., June 1948, 45–57. American President Lines, Ltd., Annual Report 1946, p. 1; ibid., 1947, p. 2; ibid., 1948, p. 2.
3. American President Lines, Ltd., Annual Report 1946, p. 2; Sailing Schedule, Passenger Schedule, Trans-Pacific Service, No. 5, issued July 1948, APL Archives.
4. These ships were the *President Harding, President Fillmore* [II], *President Buchanan* [III], *President Garfield* [III], and *President Taylor* [II].
5. "Minutes, Special Meeting of the Board of Directors of American President Lines, Ltd." 18 July 1946, APL Corporate Files.
6. American President Lines, Ltd., Annual Reports 1946 and 1947, APL Archives.
7. Ibid., 1951.
8. Chandler Ide in *Ralph K. Davies As We Knew Him* (San Francisco: Privately printed, 1976), 98.
9. Richard Simon to Ralph Davies, 25 July 1944, APL Archives.
10. Richard Simon to Ralph Davies, 26 July 1944, APL Archives.
11. Prospectus, American President Lines, Ltd., 7 October 1952, APL Corporate Files.
12. Killion in *Ralph Davies,* 98.
13. Ide in *Ralph Davies,* 16.
14. Ibid., 18.
15. American President Lines, Ltd., Annual Report 1948, APL Archives.
16. APL *Globe Trotter,* 1948, APL Archives.
17. Ibid., H. B. Luckett, "Oral History Transcript," 16, APL Archives.
18. Warner Gardner, "Oral History Transcript," 35, 36, APL Archives.
19. Ibid.; American President Lines, Ltd., Annual Report 1947, 1948, APL Archives.
20. Gardner, "Oral History Transcript," 28. Subsidy arrears were finally collected in full. See W. Brandt Brooksby to Chandler Ide, 31 July 1984, APL Archives.
21. *The Wall Street Journal,* 27 October 1952.
22. Ibid., 29 October 1965.
23. Gardner, "Oral History Transcript," 20, APL Archives.
24. Harry S. Truman to Charles Sawyer, 20 November 1950, in Dollar v. Land, transcript, California Historical Society.
25. Gardner, "Oral History Transcript," 21, APL Archives.
26. Dollar v. Land, transcript, testimony of George Killion; Gardner, "Oral History Transcript," 21, 22, APL Archives.
27. Dollar v. Land, transcript, testimony of George Killion, APL Archives.
28. Garth Young, in *Ralph Davies,* 68.

29. Chandler Ide to author, 11 November 1983.

30. George Killion, affidavit, Dollar v. Land, transcript, APL Archives.

31. Ibid.

32. Frank J. Taylor, "He's a Sucker for Nasty Jobs," *Saturday Evening Post*, 28 November 1953.

33. Gardner, "Oral History Transcript," 23, 24, APL Archives.

34. *Los Angeles Times*, 29 October 1952; *The Wall Street Journal*, 29 October 1952; George Killion to All American President Lines Staff, "New Company Ownership," 29 October 1952, APL Archives.

35. Gardner, "Oral History Transcript," 24, APL Archives.

9
GROWTH

Ralph Davies had a shipping line, one of the largest and heir to one of the oldest in the nation. He had originally thought of it as an investment, and a sound investment it was, though by no means a spectacular one. Tradition-bound, its destiny in large measure controlled by government policy, American President Lines was a part of an industry that was especially vulnerable to labor strife. Subsidized but still highly sensitive to international competition, much of its earnings fluctuated with the course of world trade and was subject to governmental recapture or paid into reserve funds earmarked for replacement of its fleet.

APL was a far cry from the highly independent, wheeling and dealing, risk-taking oil industry in which Ralph Davies had spent all of his adult life. In fact, he was still deeply involved in American Independent Oil, which was even then drilling dry holes in Kuwait, where it had concessions in what had been considered a prime oil-bearing region. But unknown to most of his friends and associates, Ralph Davies had a romantic attachment to ships and oceans and far-distant lands that went back to his boyhood in Cherrydale, Virginia. This image had been reinforced during his adolescent years in the dusty, dry, little farm community of Sanger, California, near Fresno, where the family moved when he was twelve years old.[1] After putting in a full day at the Standard Oil offices in San Francisco, Davies as a young man frequently found relaxation in prowling along the Embarcadero watching the freighters and the passenger vessels docking or putting out to sea. And it was the human element of the shipping business that claimed his major interest, the passengers boarding and debarking, the mounds of luggage, the excitement of travel. Yet ironically, Davies would never be a passenger in one of his own ships, nor would he ever be personally involved in the day-to-day administration of APL. That was not his style.

Neither Chandler Ide nor Warner Gardner, both astute observers, rated him as an outstanding administrator during his years at the helm of APL. Gardner thought his talents were probably more on the personal side than in the machinery and operation of the business. "He was a good administrator," said Gardner, "in the sense that he knew what he wanted and he demanded it of his subordinates. But below that level, I think he had no interest in how they accomplished what he asked them to do." Ide found him at times decisive and at other times unwilling to make up his mind if action "could be avoided or deferred. . . . Many decisions with respect to organization or policy were left in limbo—sometimes for years."[2] But Davies did not shrink from responsibility when his small group of investors took over APL.

As a venture capitalist, Davies could have let Killion run the company, keeping an eye only on revenues and financing as it affected the value of his stock. But his interest and his pride, strong traits with Davies, were deeply engaged in APL. He may have been a venture capitalist, but he was no rentier. Rather, he was a builder and he meant to make APL the largest and most efficient shipping line in the nation if at all possible, just as he was determined to make American Independent Oil one of the giants in the oil industry. Paradoxically, he failed to meet his goal with American Independent (though he came close with Natomas), despite his expertise as an oilman, and came closest to the success he had mapped out with APL, in spite of his failings and inadequacies as a shipping man. In this enterprise Davies had a good deal of luck, but at least in the early years of his tenure he was responsible for positive policies of growth that strengthened the organization.

Davies signaled his intent to take an active part in the management of APL by becoming chairman of the board, a position that had been vacant since the death of McAdoo in 1941. Though he never accepted the title of chief executive officer out of deference to the feelings of Killion and his successors, there was never any doubt that he was in charge. Davies took over the company just after the settlement of a long and costly strike that had reduced revenues on all routes but had been particularly disruptive to schedules on the new, unsubsidized Atlantic/Straits service. A sharp increase in military cargoes to Korea could not balance losses in commercial operations that reduced gross income by 7.7 percent of what it had been the previous year.

While the Maritime Administration gave with one hand, it withheld with the other. It ended years of uncertainty by making permanent subsidies on voyages to and from the East Coast and California, the round-the-world route, and the trans-Pacific run. The administration also indicated that it would take favorable action on subsidies that had accrued and not been paid since 1946. But at the same time, the Maritime Administration awarded subsidies to APL's competitors—the new Pacific Far East Line and the United States Lines—on APL's trans-Pacific route no. 29. APL protested, of course, and was challenging the legality of this decision in the courts when APL Associates gained control of the line.[3]

During his first year as chairman, Davies made few changes in personnel and none of any significance among the top management group. George T. Paine, a retired regular navy commodore, who had been acting as executive vice president, was returned to his former position as vice president of engineering, where he devoted himself to representing the interests of the line in the design and construction of new vessels. Davies did bring in two key men, one in operations, the other in legal matters. Captain T. C. Conwell, a highly experienced merchant marine skipper who had managed a tanker fleet for one of Davies's ventures, was made an assistant vice president of operations, working with then vice president of operations, Captain O. W. Pearson, an expert in stevedoring and terminal activities. At Warner Gardner's suggestion, Davies created a legal department and appointed Harvard Law School graduate Peter Teige as counsel for the company. Teige's first major task was to work on subsidy matters with Gardner and Noah Brinson, a retired army colonel whom Killion had hired to be APL's chief Washington representative.

Brinson, whose Southern birth and upbringing had given him what has been described as a kind of "corn-pone sense of humor," was very effective with certain key Congressmen, particularly Herbert Bonner, chairman of the House Maritime and Fisheries Committee.[4] Gardner's experience in Washington had been with the executive branch of government, and he acted as APL's principal representative to the Maritime Board and the Maritime Administration.

In 1951 Congress placed the regulation of American-registered and foreign-registered shipping under an independent agency, the Federal Maritime Commission. The FMC would administer provisions of the Shipping Act of 1916 and deal with rates and rules in a manner similar to that of the Interstate Commerce Commission, which regulated railroads and trucking companies in domestic interstate commerce. At the same time, Congress created the Maritime Administration (MARAD) as part of the Department of Commerce. Together with the Maritime Subsidy Board, also an integral part of the reorganizational program, MARAD took over from the old commission functions that related to award and administration of operating and construction differential subsidy contracts, ship design, and other activities related to national security as set forth in provisions of the Merchant Marine Act of 1936.

Gardner represented APL before both the board and MARAD when either agency held hearings. Brinson, Killion, and Gardner made an effective team in Washington and were quite probably the strongest and ablest of any representatives for the nation's shipping lines.

There was great need for such a vigorous program. The collection of subsidy accruals was indispensable if the company was to improve its cash position. Equally important was the award of a subsidy contract for the Atlantic/Straits route. Experience had indicated that this route would be a profitable one but only if voyages were subsidized. During 1952, four company-owned freighters and two chartered vessels from East Coast ports to Southeast Asia sailed with good cargoes in both directions, but APL still lost over $800,000. A corollary of the subsidy program and of relations with MARAD was the replacement of aging vessels either through new construction or the purchase of government-owned vessels and their conversion to meet the demands of APL's markets. Along with that concern was the expansion of its business by securing additional voyages on routes where the company deemed the traffic would bear it.

By 1952, two of APL's round-the-world liners, the *President Polk* and *President Monroe,* were eleven and twelve years old respectively. Their statutory life was almost half over. Of more immediate importance was the fact that the passenger waiting list for the round-the-world service had grown to more than three hundred and freight bookings, despite mounting competition, were also backlogged. After the end of World War II, three passenger/cargo vessels for the

The *President* that never was. The U.S.S. *Barrett* in San Francisco Bay. With two sisterships, she was built in 1952 as the *President Jackson* [III], but was acquired by the navy as a transport during construction and was never returned to APL. (Courtesy U.S. Naval Photographic Center.)

round-the-world service, the *Presidents Adams, Hayes,* and *Jackson,* were ordered from the New York Shipbuilding Corporation of Camden, New Jersey. They were ships of 14,000 gross tons, 533 feet 9 inches in length, with speeds of 19 knots, accommodations for 218 passengers, and cargo capacity for 570,000 cubic feet. Because of the Korean War, however, they were acquired by the navy while on the stocks and completed as transports. Thus APL never succeeded in reequipping its round-the-world service. On the trans-Pacific route, however, third-class passengers, mainly Chinese, numbered only one-fifth of what they had been before the closure of mainland China's ports. The two big passenger liners, the *President Cleveland* and *President Wilson,* currently under charter, had far too much third-class space, compared with their first-class accommodations. Expensive reconversion or replacement was indicated. Like

APL's round-the-world service, first-class passenger traffic on the Pacific run was increasing proportionately, while third class was declining.[5] All of the freighter fleet was from six to nine years old.

Since these ships had been built the government had developed the Mariner class, a new design in hull and propulsion that made for faster, more efficient vessels. There was an immediate need for eight new vessels, and, in the long range, perhaps a dozen more. Indeed, APL's engineering department was already hard at work revising MARAD's Mariner plans when APL Associates took over the line. Throughout 1953, APL planned for a replacement and growth program that envisaged eighteen to twenty new vessels over a ten-year period. This ambitious program, which was later substantially modified, would require a capital investment of an estimated $100 million, 20 percent of which would be drawn from the company's reserve funds and bank loans and another 20 percent from sale or trade-ins to MARAD of the vessels replaced. The remainder would be financed through long-term mortgages held by the government. APL's plans as approved by its board, and including an application for subsidy on its Atlantic/Straits service designated trade route no. 17, were presented to the Maritime Board during the spring of 1954. There followed lengthy hearings and negotiations that culminated in a decision of the board and MARAD on 30 December 1954.

The government granted a subsidy for the Atlantic/Straits route, specifying that twelve to sixteen voyages be made each year and that the *Presidents Harrison, Van Buren, Johnson, Jefferson,* and *Harding* be assigned to that run. All of these vessels except the *President Harding* were 8,000-ton C3s. The *President Harding* was a Victory ship of slightly less tonnage. APL would replace these ships with four or five cargo vessels "superior to the C3s by 1 July 1962." On the round-the-world service, the government's replacement schedule called for four new combination vessels by 1 January 1960. These ships would operate with the four Mariners APL already had in its fleet. Two of the company's round-the-world fleet of eight C3s and Victory ships, the *President Arthur,* and the *President Garfield,* both built in 1945, were to be sold or traded in.

By January 1962 APL agreed to contract with a United States shipyard for four or five new vessels on its trans-Pacific cargo service and by 1965 to replace the *President Cleveland* and *President Wilson,* which would then be very near the end of their statutory lives.[6] There were, of course, modifications to these guidelines.[7] Changes

APL owned nine C3-class ships similar to the *President Johnson* [II] shown here. She was in the company's service from 1949 to 1968. (APL Archives.)

in naval architecture and marine engineering and radical changes in cargo-handling procedures and in markets would reduce the number of new vessels required while increasing their speed and cargo-lifting capacity. But at the time the company had committed itself to a huge capital investment. As the program evolved over the years it demanded equally large expenditures of time by APL executives, especially on the part of Davies, Killion, Paine, and Teige in San Francisco, as well as Brinson and Gardner in Washington, D.C. Each ship purchased and sold required separate negotiations that involved hearings. Negotiations for the construction differential subsidy on a new vessel were the most burdensome. Since subsidies had to be approved by congressional appropriation each year, there was a constant budget problem. Shipping lines had to compete with each other before the Bureau of the Budget, congressional finance committees, as well as with MARAD and the Maritime Board for the use of funds appropriated for construction differential subsidies.

Hull and engine design and the design of all the hundreds of subsystems and components that went into a vessel were all changing rapidly as advances were being made in naval architecture and marine engineering. MARAD's policy was to stipulate everything on a given design, from the hull down to coffee-makers in the crew's galley. Any changes from this pattern required a case to be made before the appropriate department of MARAD and, if approval were given, negotiation with the suppliers—whether the shipyard that was constructing the vessel or the company that manufactured the coffee-maker. As Peter Teige put it, "There was a constant battle about disallowing subsidy. You can't get subsidy for this part of the ship or that feature. If you put that on, it is a frill. There was a constant battle going on, which always seemed to be unnecessary because in a very real sense, the company was spending its own money."[8]

Negotiating for operating subsidies was also difficult and sometimes frustrating. APL, like other lines, had to justify its rates to the board on the basis of wages, repairs, and other costs. These outlays required careful comparisons of operating costs with competing foreign carriers on specific trade routes. Establishing comparative costs of competitors so that the operating-differential subsidy could be set demanded almost constant monitoring and collection of data, which then had to be carefully analyzed for inflation because the higher a competitor made his operating costs, the less subsidy would be paid to APL and the better the competitor's edge. Arthur Poole became something of an expert in ferreting out and calculating as accurately as possible the true costs bolstered by enough hard evidence to convince the board. But Poole needed a full-time staff for these justifications, and when they failed to convince the board, litigation would ensue. The indispensable Gardner was most effective in such actions, almost always winning his case.[9]

Vexations like these had become a fact of life at APL and other shipping lines ever since the government had involved itself with the merchant marine. By no means did they deter Davies's plans for growth; nor did the vast sums required for the building program concern him, despite the fact that APL's financial picture seemed to have flattened out for the past five years. Always on the lookout for a profitable investment, Davies found one that dovetailed nicely with APL's operations.

In the summer of 1954 a controlling block of stock in American

Mail Line, or AML, came up for sale. A group of Texan en-
trepreneurs headed by the Murchisons had purchased R. J. Reynolds's stock in the shipping line in June 1951. The Murchison group
was willing to dispose of its holdings, 500,000 shares of common
stock, for $10 a share, or $5 million. Davies cleared the purchase
with the Maritime Board and the antitrust division of the Justice
Department, and he secured a loan from the Bank of America for the
principal sum. The deal was made, and in June 1954 APL owned 53
percent of AML's oustanding shares. From July through September,
APL acquired smaller lots so that, by October 27, its holdings had
risen to 80 percent. Though Davies was willing to obligate APL for a
sum equal to well over a third of its capital and special reserve funds,
the risk was not as obvious as it appeared, provided one had faith in
the economic potential of shipping and the West. Davies was
nothing if not a believer. The acquisition of AML united under single
ownership a majority of the ocean trade from California, Washington, and Oregon.[10] Powerful competitors remained, but the APL-
AML combination operated from a position of strength.

Like APL, AML had emerged from the war with its debts paid off.
Its fleet of eight C2s and C3s all purchased from the War Shipping
Administration, was complete by 1947, with the exception of the
Ocean Mail, which would go into service during the spring of 1948.[11]
Although the company had a cash surplus of over $4 million in 1946,
AML management decided to improve its financial position by issuing 49,602 shares of stock at $20 a share. All of these shares were
taken up by original stockholders, and except for Reynolds, all were
residents of the Seattle-Tacoma-Portland area. Reynolds remained
the majority stockholder with 76,454 shares.[12] Besides acquiring its
new peacetime fleet and providing ample funds for financing its
purchase, AML applied to MARAD and the Maritime Board for an
extension of its subsidized trade route to the Orient, which would
permit voyages between the Pacific Northwest and additional ports
in the Far East. The agencies approved of this change. AML's revenue picture from 1947 through 1954 generally followed the pattern of
other lines operating from the West Coast. Like APL, its earnings in
1948 and again in 1952 were reduced by lengthy waterfront strikes,
although military demands for the Korean War bolstered its revenues. But AML consistently over the years had earned a higher rate
of profit than APL, even though its export trade—mainly lumber
and grain from the Pacific Northwest—tended to be bulk cargo of

lower unit-value than what APL carried. Return cargoes were mixed with such low unit-value items as burlap to more expensive commodities like raw silk, canned goods, and tin.[13]

The reason why AML, about one-third the size of APL, year after year turned in a higher profit than APL seems to defy the principle of economy of scale and emphasizes other factors like community support, geographic position (Seattle-Tacoma-Portland were about one thousand miles closer to Asian ports on a great circle course than San Francisco or Los Angeles), and management. AML had concentrated on freighters, leaving to other lines the passenger business, which had much higher operating costs. Where APL had four trade routes, AML had only one and as a result was less subject to fluctuations in world trade. A. R. Lintner, AML's president, explained why the company's performance during 1953 was relatively stable despite sharp increases in labor costs and downward pressure on rates. "Our trade route," he wrote, "having never participated more than nominally in any 'boom' exchange of merchandise or rehabilitation materials, has been less affected than many others in the general letdown which has taken place in world exchange."[14]

Lintner could have mentioned that AML also had the benefit of a small, tightly knit management group that had had long experience in the shipping industry and that had maintained close ties with the business communities of the region. Not the least responsible for AML's success, so long as the industry hewed to proven modes of operation and utilized traditional methods of cargo handling and control, was the presence at its helm of Lintner himself. Short, wiry, a peppery sort of person with a lock of hair falling over his forehead, Lintner had come up the hard way in the industry and knew every aspect of shipping thoroughly. His connections with the business communities AML served were not only of long standing but were kept on a good footing. Similarly Lintner's service with the War Shipping Administration had gained him valuable friends in Washington, and he maintained excellent relations with members and staff personnel of the Maritime Board and MARAD.[15]

Though Lintner cultivated a brusque attitude and a no-nonsense approach to management, he was actually a rather insecure man who found it hard to make major decisions that involved matters even slightly outside of traditional experience. His greatest strength, a fanatical devotion to AML, was also a signal weakness after his company became a part of a larger organization.[16]

When he acquired control of AML, Ralph Davies had wanted to coordinate as many of its functions as were practical with those of APL in the interest of eliminating duplication in personnel and resources. It seemed obvious that the sharing of facilities, purchasing, and insurance costs would allow major savings for both companies. Thus he established a coordinating committee to investigate and recommend joint policies and practices. Lintner set himself steadfastly against cooperation. And even though Davies knew what was going on, he tolerated this independence so long as AML's balance sheets at each year's end showed a decent profit. Compared to APL, AML would indeed present a better profit picture over the long term, though both companies would have benefited from closer coordination.

Unknown to Davies, and even to the sharp-eyed Arthur Poole, who became a member of AML's board along with George Killion, one of Lintner's strategies to gain and maintain business in the Far East was to give rebates to favored shippers through its agents. Lintner, an old shipping expert saw nothing wrong in this policy. The practice was forbidden by law to American-flag carriers, but it was extensively utilized by foreign shipping lines that competed with AML. At APL, Killion had his weaknesses as a shipping executive, but he did not engage in rebating as a company policy.[17]

Whatever the ethical limitations and the innate conservatism of his policies, Lintner had run AML (sometimes with one hand, as during the war) with commendable efficiency. Despite problems of morale that arose within the company because of knowledge that a majority interest in the company might change hands and possibly policy at any given time, Lintner represented profitable stability. Neither Reynolds nor the Murchisons interfered with his management.

Davies followed their hands-off policy, though it was quite apparent from the beginning of his acquisition of AML that he viewed the company as more than a temporary investment, that eventually he meant to weld APL and AML together into a single organization. The coordinating committee was a move in that direction. The election of George Killion and Arthur Poole to AML's board of directors and Lintner's election to APL's board was another. Otherwise, for the next six years AML pursued an independent course, punctuated by occasional attempts to promote coordination.

Before APL and APL Associates made further investments in shipping, Davies himself ran into difficulties with the form of his organization. He was the largest shareowner in APL Associates, and together with the four other large shareowners, including the investment house of Carl M. Loeb Rhoades and Company, which had been one of Davies's original backers in the venture, he owned more than 50 percent of the outstanding stock. According to the Internal Revenue Code, when five or fewer individuals own a controlling interest in a corporation it is classified as a personal holding company and its earnings become subject to very heavy taxes, far beyond the normal corporate rate. APL Associates obviously fell into that category, and in fact, it had received no dividend income since its inception because of this tax feature.

Davies and the other principal shareowners were anxious to find a way for the associates to escape the status of a personal holding company. At first he sold sufficient shares in APL Associates so that he thought he had the problem solved. Associates received a substantial dividend from APL, only to find that under certain highly technical rulings of the Internal Revenue Service the problem remained. A solution was finally reached through an interpretation relating to allocation of shares agreed upon with the IRS.

In addition to this particular problem, Davies had for some time been looking for a means to convert APL Associates into a public corporation, where the stock would be broadly held and listed on the New York Stock Exchange. There were many added advantages to such diversified ownership, which would provide access to new financing and give shareowners flexibility in selling or borrowing against their stock. What he needed was a reputable, established company whose stock was traded on the big board, but whose ownership was not concentrated in any one small group. Lee Kaiser, the San Francisco stockbroker who had challenged Davies's group of minority stockholders in the closing days of the Dollar litigation, came up with the Natomas Company, which fit in nicely with his plans.[18]

Natomas was a venerable gold mining company that still operated four dredges and owned extensive real estate in Sacramento and Butte counties and a water company. Its gold fields had played out, however, in terms of the market price of gold and increasing costs of recovery. Moreover, future dredging operations were also jeopardized because of urban encroachment. Natomas was at the stage where it was beginning to pay out its capital in the form of liquidating dividends. With the agreement of Signal, which still held 47 percent of the stock in APL and participated in the same loan agreement in connection with the initial acquisition of the shares from the government, the associates developed a plan of reorganization with Natomas.

In return for all of its assets the associates received a new issue of Natomas's stock, giving it an ownership of approximately two-thirds of the company. Ralph Davies became the chairman of the board; R. G. Smith, formerly president and general manager of Natomas, became president and a board member of the reorganized company. Davies's two assistants, Chandler Ide and Raymond W. Ickes, became vice presidents and members of the Natomas board. Among other board members were APL's president, George Killion, Arthur Poole, George T. Paine, and B. I. Graves. Louis Sutter, Clyde H. Brand, Douglas McCormack and Mortimer Fleishhacker represented the old Natomas interests, a generous representation for only about one-third of the shares outstanding. But Davies had effective control of the reorganized corporation. APL Associates distributed the Natomas shares on a pro rata basis to its shareowners and then disappeared as a corporate entity, with APL and AML becoming subsidiaries of Natomas.[19]

While Ralph Davies was casting about for a corporation with a big-board listing, he was also acquiring shares of a competing line on APL's trans-Pacific route, Pacific Far East Line, whose executive offices at 111 Battery Street were several blocks away from his office in San Francisco. Pacific Far East was the creation of Tom Cuffe, who had used his contacts in Washington as APL's vice president of the Eastern division to float a new shipping line that would compete for the trans-Pacific trade.

Cuffe, a former fullback at U.C. Berkeley, was a vigorous, thickset person who radiated energy and was always ready with a practical down-to-earth answer for any question that involved the shipping industry. His bright blue eyes behind rimless glasses viewed the world with a shrewd, penetrating gaze. Generous and loyal to his associates and subordinates, he was tough and unrelenting in the pursuit of his own goals. Boyce Luckett, a retired executive vice president of APL who knew Cuffe well, described him as "a demanding boss in terms of results, hours worked, degrees of dedication . . . a very aggressive man of his time in the steamship business."[20] Cuffe's years with the freight department, first in the Dollar Line and then APL, had given him an expert's knowledge of shipping. His tenure as APL's Washington representative, which began just before the war and continued for its duration, had expanded his contacts, not just with the War Shipping Administration and the military, but with all those influential businessmen and investment bankers who flocked to Washington during the war and shared Cuffe's entrepreneurial instincts.

When he resigned from APL in 1946, Cuffe had already formed his own company, Pacific Far East Line. The climate was ripe for such a move in postwar Washington. Abundant investment capital was available, a huge surplus of government-owned vessels that could be acquired cheap or chartered under the Ship Sales Act of 1946, and plenty of military and foreign-aid cargo to be moved.[21] Cuffe seized the opportunity, lined up the capital, chartered vessels, hired the staff—many of whom he lured from APL— and commenced operations, initially without benefit of a subsidy contract in a service which competed directly with APL for the trans-Pacific trade. Later, Pacific Far East, over the protest of APL, was granted a regular twenty-year subsidy on that route.

Competition on the trans-Pacific route was already intense. Two other new U.S.-flag carriers, the States Line and Pacific Transport Line, had managed to secure operating-differential subsidy contracts in the trans-Pacific trade. With American assistance the Japanese shipping industry was being rebuilt and Japanese-flag ships, also subsidized by their government by indirect methods, were making their appearance in the Pacific trade. British, Norwegian, Greek, and other lines under the Liberian flag were in the trans-Pacific freight market, though American carriers had an edge because of their connections with the domestic railroad network and access to government-impelled cargoes. Still, the entry of Pacific Far East caused considerable concern at APL headquarters.[22]

Under Cuffe's driving will, Pacific Far East built up its fleet to seventeen vessels by 1958. Seven of these ships were of the new Mariner-class design supplemental to the C2s and Victory-type ships that had been converted to the market demands of its trade route with expanded refrigerated space, deep tanks for bulk liquid cargoes, and additional scantlings to stiffen the hulls so that they could carry more deadweight cargo. On its various services between California and Alaska, the Far East, Southeast Asian ports, the major Central Pacific Islands, and occasionally the Pacific Northwest, Pacific Far East Line (PFEL) turned in revenues of $36 million in 1958, producing a net profit of about $1 million. Net profits were low for PFEL compared to those of AML, whose gross revenues for that year were only about one-third of Pacific Far East's but whose net profits were about the same.[23] Yet over the years since its inception, Ralph Davies saw PFEL as a potential property to complete his long-range plans of dominance over the shipping industry in the western United States.

Through various brokers and banks, the companies Davies controlled had acquired a 40 percent stock interest in PFEL. Had Cuffe lived there might have been a clash between these two businessmen, but he died suddenly of a heart attack on 22 December 1959. He had never groomed a successor, and for several months the corporation was in disarray.[24] Pacific Far East's board, in an effort to put the company on a sound basis, brought in Clarence Morse as president.

Morse had seemed a good choice at the time. He had been chairman of the Maritime Board and before that an admiralty lawyer in San Francisco. Presumably he knew the shipping business and its West Coast aspects thoroughly. Davies acquiesced in the Morse appointment, but he also wanted his personal representative in the management so that he would be kept abreast of the company's financial posture and its plans. He and his two assistants, Ide and Ickes, had studied the books of PFEL and discovered major irregularities in the former management. Davies was as determined as ever to forge the strongest, largest, and, he hoped, most profitable shipping line on the West Coast under a single, unified management. He wanted PFEL straightened out and the excesses of Cuffe's one-man rule pruned back. Raymond Ickes was accordingly elected a vice president. He became executive vice president and a director the following year. Morse soon proved unable to cope with the severe management problems Cuffe had bequeathed to his successors. When he resigned on 22 February 1962 after eighteen months as chief executive, the board elected Ickes to succeed him.[25]

Raymond Ickes had been associated with Ralph Davies since 1947. A son of Davies's chief in the War Petroleum Administration, Roosevelt's redoubtable Secretary of Interior Harold Ickes, he attended the University of Chicago and had received his law degree from the same institution in 1936. He worked for the Department of Justice as an attorney in New York and in Washington. But shortly after the United States went to war against Germany, Italy, and Japan, Ickes resigned and enlisted in the Marine Corps as a private. Later he was commissioned a second lieutenant and saw combat in Guam and Iwo Jima, where he was wounded. At the war's end he joined Justice Robert Jackson's staff, participating in the Nuremberg trials. After the conclusion of the trials, Ickes returned to Chicago and went into private law practice, from which he resigned to join Ralph Davies as a vice president of American Independent Oil.

Davies was attracted to this earnest, industrious young lawyer who in some respects reminded him of his former chief, Harold Ickes. Ickes had certainly inherited his father's integrity and sensitiveness to criticism, but he did not have the immense self-assurance, uncanny political skill, and the testy disposition that gained for Harold Ickes the sobriquet of "the old curmudgeon." Though Davies came to rely on Raymond's penetrating mind not just in legal affairs but in troubleshooting situations he found himself in as a venture capitalist, he never formed the kind of close personal friendship with Ickes that he had with Chandler Ide.[26] Now that Ickes was put in charge of an independent shipping company, albeit controlled by Davies through Natomas, other qualities came to the fore. Unlike Morse, Ickes was not dismayed at the administrative tangle Cuffe had left behind. He wanted to clean house and Davies gave him a free hand.

Meanwhile the replacement program MARAD had outlined in 1954 was being implemented by APL, though not as originally planned. Study and experience dictated changes. The government accepted most of those sought after the usual hearings and negotiations. Traffic on the Atlantic/Straits route had grown more than anticipated and at a faster rate than the round-the-world service, which had to be rerouted in 1956 because of the Suez Canal closure. APL had planned to utilize four Mariners and four new combination vessels on the round-the-world service, but the estimate proved too ambitious and capital expenditures too large for the expected return. Thus two C3-Ps nearing the end of their statutory life, the *President Monroe* and the *President Polk,* were kept on the route along with one C3, the *President Pierce,* a freighter. Five Mariners—all freighters— the *Presidents Adams, Coolidge, Hayes, Jackson,* and the *Lone Star Mariner* (later renamed the *President Arthur*), made up the rest of the fleet on that service. The Mariners were all new ships from two to three years old.

On the Atlantic/Straits service APL used seven C3 freighters until they reached the end of their statutory life, which the company managed to have lengthened from twenty to twenty-five years. Yet APL did complete a significant replacement program during the middle fifties. It added eight Mariners that were modified under the company's direction to meet the market demands of the round-the-world and trans-Pacific service. Passenger traffic, especially in first-class accommodations on the trans-Pacific service, increased so rapidly that extensive modifications had to be made to the *President Wilson* and *President Cleveland* that upgraded third class to create what was advertised as "economy class."

Passenger demand continued so strongly that APL decided to put another liner on the route. The only vessel available, the *Panama*, was not quite what the company wanted. She was only 10,000 gross tons as compared with the 15,000 gross tonnage of the *Presidents Wilson* and *Cleveland*, and she was eighteen years old. The *Panama* would require extensive and therefore expensive modifications before she could go into service. But APL decided to purchase her and operate her on an interim basis. After lengthy negotiations involving not only the Maritime Board and MARAD but also her former owner, the Panama Canal Company, and the army, APL purchased the vessel for $5,704,000, along with an extension of five years to her statutory life. Renamed the *President Hoover*, she entered the trans-Pacific service in 1958. Although the company had obligated itself to about $83 million for replacement, expansion, and conversion of its fleet, it contracted for two fast freighters of a new design designated the Searacers.[27] As a down payment to the government it turned in three of its Victory ships, the *President Tyler, President Buchanan*, and *President Garfield*.

Passenger traffic on the Pacific route, which totaled 40,000 people carried in 1951, had grown to 91,510 in 1955 and one year later to the amazing figure of 110,768. In some areas of APL management the argument for committing more of the company's capital for passenger ships than previously thought prudent was intense and insistent. It was argued that the passenger business was profitable and essential if the company were to maintain its competitive edge in the Pacific passenger trade over the Japanese and the British, who were already planning to construct large passenger liners. If APL did not move in this direction it would lose what passenger business it now had and, because of a ripple effect, would lose also significant freight revenues to and from the Far East. The pro-passenger group

The *President Buchanan* [III], another C4 Mariner, off the California coast. She entered APL service in 1959. (APL Archives.)

President Hoover [II]. Built in 1939 for the Panama Railroad Steamship Co. as the *Panama*, she was purchased by APL in 1957 for the trans-Pacific passenger trade. Only about two-thirds the size of her running mates, the *Presidents Cleveland* [II] and *Wilson* [II], she was sold again in 1964. (APL Archives.)

enjoyed the wholehearted support of Ralph Davies, whose generally astute business sense seems to have been clouded by his attrac-
tion to the romance and the glamour of passenger liners.

There was, however, opposition to such heavy commitments of
company resources in what was regarded as a high-cost, low-profit
operation. For years, it was pointed out, the passenger side of APL's
revenue and, before that, Dollar Steamship revenue, had been never
more than one-third of the company's income. In addition to these
sobering statistics, opponents of further expansion of the line's passenger resources, mostly younger men like Charles Deering, chief
troubleshooter in the operations department, or Boyce Luckett, now
vice president in charge of the freight department, declared that
intercontinental jet travel would soon make the great liners, when
viewed as a means of point-to-point passenger travel on fixed
routes, as extinct as the dinosaurs. They sensed radical changes in
the ocean freight business that demanded immediate attention and
would require substantial investments of capital funds, investments
that would be inhibited by the construction and operation of new
passenger vessels. Deering and Luckett were referring to containers
for freight instead of breakbulk stowage, and the logistics that went
with them such as new terminals, gantry cranes of specialized
design, and electronic data processing.

But these contentions seemed too far-fetched in 1956 to make an
impression on Ralph Davies's romantic visions. And Davies was
backed up by Deering's chief, Captain Conwell, APL's head of operations, along with the able and persuasive J. M. Diggs, who headed
passenger traffic. The freight people soon found themselves in the
minority and in consequence reined in their criticism of company
policy.[28]

The passenger department at APL made what it calculated to be a
conservative estimate of an increase amounting to about 20,000
passengers each year over the next five years. With these numbers
seemingly based on sound evidence and enjoying Ralph Davies's
backing, Paine and the engineering department began working with
William Francis Gibbs, the famed naval architect and designer of the
large liner the *United States*. They came up with the design for a ship
of 43,000 gross tons, 908 feet long, with a speed of 26 knots and
accommodations for 1,450 passengers. The vessel, which would be
the fourth largest liner built in the United States and the largest ever
to operate from the West Coast, was to be named, appropriately
enough, the *President Washington*.

An artist's conception of the proposed 43,000-ton *President Washington*. Designs were completed in 1958 but the ship was never built. (APL Archives.)

Killion, Brinson, and Gardner began the long and tedious effort to convince the board, MARAD, and the Congress, because the *Washington* would require a special appropriation for her construction differential subsidy. APL estimated the ship would cost $73 million to build. With a 50 percent construction subsidy, the company would commit itself to $36.5 million, which, under the provisions of the Merchant Marine Act of 1936, required that it actually put up about $9 million. The government would supply the remainder on a mortgage that ran for twenty-three years at 3.5 percent interest. But because of what were assumed would be escalating labor and material costs over the three to four years of construction, APL asked Congress to waive the 50 percent limitation on construction subsidy. It signed a contract embodying these features with MARAD. Construction was scheduled to begin not later than 1 July 1957. After extensive hearings where strenuous opposition developed from competitors like Matson and other special-interest groups, a bill conforming to APL's requests passed the House Merchant Marine Committee, only to be deleted from the Appropriation Act of 1957. Finally in 1958 Congress approved the appropriation but left its implementation to the discretion of President Eisenhower. When the president made up his budget for fiscal 1958, the economy was experiencing a sharp recession. The Bureau of the Budget red-penciled the funds allotted to MARAD for the construction of the *President Washington*.

The 1958 recession also hit APL's passenger traffic. Rosy estimates of future revenues in the passenger business were trimmed back, but the passenger advocates were not deterred. APL made a formal offer to the government to acquire the former transport *General W. P. Richardson*, a ship of 18,298 gross tons, 622 feet 7 inches in length, and with a rated speed of 20 knots. After her trooping duties, she had been reconditioned for civilian passenger service and operated first to the Mediterranean as the *La Guardia*, and then from California to Hawaii as the *Leilani*. She was purchased by APL in 1961 and elaborately refitted at Seattle. The company's investment for her amounted to over $10 million. Although basically a sistership of the *President Cleveland* and *President Wilson*, the newly acquired vessel had been completed as a transport, whereas the other two ships had been designed from the bare hull upward as passenger ships. Thus it was not possible to give her arrangements that were as attractive and convenient as those of the other ships. She was renamed *President Roosevelt* and entered trans-Pacific service in 1962, carrying first-class passengers only.[29]

When the recession lifted in 1961, even Ralph Davies was convinced that the future of ocean liner traffic on the Pacific would not justify continued large capital expenditures. Grandiose plans for new construction of passenger liners were shelved, and when the *Presidents Cleveland, Wilson, Hoover,* and *Roosevelt* reached the end of their statutory lives during the sixties, intercontinental jets were rapidly supplanting passenger travel by ship not just over the Pacific but over all ocean areas. The age of the great liner extending back sixty years was fast coming to an end. Luxury ocean cruises for leisure would extend the lives of the liners, however, and Davies still clung to his cherished beliefs in the importance of the passenger business.

Largely through his insistence, accommodations for twelve passengers were included in the two cargo liners that would complete APL's ten-year construction program, the *President Lincoln* and *President Tyler*. These two ships, designated the Searacer class, were transition designs in that they were partial container vessels. Sixty percent larger than the Mariner class, the Searacers had much greater cargo capacity and higher speed, which was planned to compensate for their increased fuel consumption.

President Roosevelt [I]. Built as a transport of the same basic type as the *President Cleveland* [II] and *President Wilson* [II], she operated under three different names before purchase and conversion by APL in 1960. Sold again in 1970, she has since known two more names. (APL Archives.)

As APL was completing its ten-year building program, AML was just starting construction of new vessels to replace its aging C2s and C3s. The company, more conservative than APL in its approach to container technology, decided upon an improved Mariner design for the five ships it would build. Much greater in gross tonnage than the C3s, these vessels were faster (20 as opposed to 16.5 knots), and had more reefer capacity and improved cargo handling. Financing for AML's replacement fleet, for their Searacers, and the *President Roosevelt*, a total outlay of $46 million, was eased significantly through trade-ins and a new borrowing authority that the Maritime Board worked out under Title XI of the Merchant Marine Act of 1936. APL was permitted to issue and sell to the public 5 percent ship mortgage bonds that the government would guarantee and whose interest would be free of federal taxation. During 1959, APL alone sold $14 million worth of these ship mortgage bonds and an additional $4 million in 1962.

The decade of the sixties was one of sustained growth for APL. Eight Mariner-design freighters had replaced the C3s in its fleet. The two new semicontainer ships, *President Lincoln* and *President Tyler*, would soon join them. And two more passenger liners had been added to the trans-Pacific fleet. Through Natomas Company, Davies controlled a shipping empire, the largest in the West, of three independent lines, APL, AML, and PFEL. In all, his companies owned and operated forty-seven ships and chartered a dozen more.

Davies had realized one of his dreams and now he had to make it work. Somehow he had to have these rival organizations act together as a mutually beneficial unit without losing their sense of individual pride of accomplishment. It would have been a Herculean task even if the times were normal for the shipping industry. But they were far from that. Containerization, along with its associated equipment and unique traffic-control systems, was already bringing about radical changes in a most tradition-bound industry. Jet airliners were not only challenging but were rendering obsolete passenger travel on ocean liners, except for the recreational cruises. Millions of dollars had to be spent for the new specialized vessels, for specialized container terminals, and for the purchase or lease of the containers themselves. More important than these material items was the education and training of an entire new group of managers who needed to understand the meaning of the changes being wrought and how to capitalize on them.

NOTES_____

1. Harold C. Davies in *Ralph Davies*, 126.
2. Ibid., 16; Gardner, "Oral History Transcript," 13, APL Archives.
3. American President Lines, Ltd., Annual Report 1952, Yost Collection.
4. Peter Teige, "Oral History Transcript," 1, 7, 8, APL Archives.
5. *The Wall Street Journal*, 29 October 1952. APL purchased the *President Cleveland* and the *President Wilson* in 1954.
6. A. S. Williams, secretary, Federal Maritime Board, to American President Lines, Ltd., 31 December 1954, APL Archives.
7. For example, APL would request and the board would approve an increase in subsidized voyages in the Atlantic/Straits route from twelve through sixteen to

twenty-four through twenty-eight voyages. American President Lines, Ltd., Annual Report 1957, Yost Collection.

8. Teige, "Oral History Transcript," 9, APL Archives.

9. Ibid.

10. See consolidated balance sheet in American President Lines, Ltd., Annual Report 1953, Yost Collection.

11. The ships were the *China Mail* (C2), *Island Mail* (C2), *Ocean Mail* (C2), *American Mail, Canada Mail, India Mail, Java Mail, Oregon Mail, Washington Mail*. See Patricia E. Hartle, comp., "Ships Owned or Operated by American Mail Line, Ltd. 1940–1973," 22 October 1979, APL Archives.

12. Blythe & Co., Inc. Prospectus, 23 April 1946, APL Corporate Files.

13. American Mail Line, Ltd., Annual Report 1953, Yost Collection.

14. Ibid., Teige, "Oral History Transcript," 12, APL Archives.

15. Teige, "Oral History Transcript," 12, APL Archives.

16. Worth Fowler, "Oral History Transcript," 5, 16, 17, APL Archives.

17. Teige, "Oral History Transcript," 12, 13, APL Archives.

18. Ide, "Oral History Transcript (I)," 21–27, APL Archives.

19. Natomas Company, "Proxy statement, April 20, 1956," Natomas Company, Annual Report 1956, Chandler Ide Collection, St. Helena, Calif.

20. Boyce Luckett, "Oral History Transcript," 6, 7, APL Archives.

21. Ibid.; Teige, "Oral History Transcript," 15, 16, APL Archives.

22. Luckett, "Oral History Transcript," 17, 18, 21, 26, APL Archives.

23. Pacific Far East Line, Inc., Annual Report 1958, Ide Collection; American Mail Line, Ltd., Annual Report 1958, Yost Collection.

24. Ide, "Oral History Transcript (I)," 104, 105, APL Archives.

25. Ibid.

26. Gardner, "Oral History Transcript"; Ide, "Oral History Transcript (II)," passim, APL Archives.

27. George Killion, "Statement Before the Merchant Marine and Fisheries Committee, U.S. House of Representatives, February 4, 1958," APL Archives.

28. Luckett, "Oral History Transcript," 21, 34, 34; Charles Deering, "Oral History Transcript," 12, 13, APL Archives.

29. Ibid.

10
CONTAINERSHIPS

RALPH Davies was impressed with big, personable Worth
Fowler, who had been acting as Lintner's liaison with APL
management. Lintner had guided the destinies of AML since 1940,
but he was slowing down. His health failing, he seemed to be
having difficulty making decisions.[1] Fowler had been associated
with the shipping industry in the Northwest since his graduation
from Princeton in 1933. A native of Portland, Oregon, his father was
a leading lumberman in the area. Since the family business involved
shipping and receiving lumber, young Fowler early became interested in railroads and ships. Through his family connections he
managed to get a job as a dock checker with the States Line in
Portland. He made a trip to China as an ordinary seaman on one of
the States Line's freighters and was then assigned as a clerk to the
company's local freight office. After serving in all aspects of freight
operations, he was transferred to the Seattle office of the States Line.
There, in 1939, he met Lintner, who was then managing the line's
freight department.[2] The two men got along well. The small, tense
Lintner with his seamed face and his brusque manner contrasted
with Fowler's loose-limbed frame and his easygoing style.[3]

But there was more to Fowler than personality that brought the
two men together in a partnership that would last many years.
Behind Fowler's deceptively bland appearance was intelligence and
an understanding of the Northwest shipping industry that was quite
comprehensive. In an executive position he tended to over-
generalize, to delegate authority without adequate follow-up, and,
like Lintner, could have been better informed about the state of the
industry. But for a small, community-oriented shipping line that
followed traditional, even conventional, methods of operations,
Fowler was an ideal manager. When it came to foreseeing and

Chandler Ide, chairman of the board, Natomas Company, 1971–83; chairman of the board, American President Lines, 1971–74. (Photo courtesy of Chandler Ide.)

implementing changes that required large capital investments and new management concepts, he was slow to act.[4]

No such judgments about Fowler could have been made in 1940 when he joined Lintner as his assistant in the reorganized American Mail Line. Nor indeed could they have been made during the next quarter of a century when, as Lintner's deputy, he played a significant role in managing a profitable shipping line. There was no question in Davies's mind, nor in the mind of Chandler Ide, whom he always consulted before making an important decision, that Fowler should succeed Lintner as president of AML. Thus, when Lintner was unable to cope with the new construction program that AML had contracted with the Maritime Board, Davies and Ide eased him out of his post. He remained a director of AML and a member of the board's executive committee, however. In October 1959, Fowler was elected president of the line.

Fowler took over AML at a time when the recession of 1957 had run its course. While open-market freight rates for bulk commodities were still soft, rates in general had improved considerably. The business picture was bright enough for AML to purchase from APL the *President Arthur,* formerly the *Dartmouth Victory,* to replace the *Schuyler Otis Bland,* which had been chartered from MARAD.

Although AML was committed to replacing its aging C2 and C3 fleet, Lintner had refused to enter into any construction contracts, a delaying policy that generated considerable criticism in Washington. When the *Washington Mail* broke in half and sank during a storm in the Gulf of Alaska, fortunately without loss of life, this issue was brought to the fore.[5]

Lintner's philosophy on replacement is best set forth in his comments to AML's board on 23 May 1956, just after the loss of the *Washington Mail.* He referred to the crowded condition of American shipyards and stated that in view of the present state of naval architecture he believed it unwise for the company to begin its building program until certain experiments on hull configuration had been completed. In his opinion the most logical stopgap arrangement would be, if possible, "to charter a replacement vessel at least until such time as suitable tonnage became available for sale."[6] Grudgingly, MARAD agreed to the charter of the *Schuyler Otis Bland,* a C3, but insisted that AML provide it with guidelines on the replacement of its subsidized vessels with new construction. Lintner gave an approximate target date of 31 December 1957 for new ships to replace three C2s, the *China Mail*, the *Island Mail*, and the *Ocean Mail*. He was even more vague about the C3s, the *American Mail*, *Canada Mail*, *Bengal Mail*, and *Java Mail*, which made up the balance of AML's fleet. As he put it in an official letter to Clarence Morse, administrator of MARAD, he advocated "a deceleration of [replacement] of our . . . C3s as reasonable and practical."[7]

Despite Lintner's excessive caution, there were solid reasons for his ambiguity on new construction. The shipping industry was in flux over the advent of containerization, a system of stowing and unloading freight that promised to be far more economical and efficient than traditional methods. For years, longshoremen and ships' crews manhandled cargoes. They used shipboard and on-shore gantry cranes and forklifts to transfer freight. It was a very labor-intensive method of cargo handling. Frequent work halts due to weather conditions and dockside disputes made delivery dates and times uncertain. Damage and pilferage of goods were among the accepted risks of a tradition-bound industry that had taken for granted low profit margins.

World War II changed many of the governing concepts. For the first time in the history of moving freight by ship, army and navy specialists, most of them traffic experts from the trucking and railroad industries but also civilian engineers now in military service, began shipping mixed cargoes in palletized boxes rather than in bulk as before. They adopted these means because military urgency demanded fast delivery to ports of unloading and equally fast distribution. Their inventive methods came to the attention of the War Shipping Administration, which conducted experiments with shipborne containers. These proved so promising that the administration issued a series of reports that publicized their use for the shipping industry.[8]

Little came of this wartime innovation until trucking magnate M. P. McLean formed a shipping combine. One of his subsidiary companies, Sea-Land, utilized the World War II method of shipping by containers, but in this case he used vans that fitted his fleet of trailer trucks. Satisfied that he could develop an integrated freight-moving system where preloaded vans with easily identifiable contents and consignees were craned to waiting trailer rigs or railroad cars, McLean invested large sums in the modification of five C3s to trailer ships. He visualized these vessels as seagoing container vehicles in the way that trucks and railroad cars are simply land-traveling container vehicles. And he began to develop cranes that were specifically designed for moving containers off and on ships. To McLean the ships were links in an intermodal transportation system. The traditions and the folklore of the sea meant nothing to him. Savings in time, labor, speed, flexibility, and accuracy of the delivery system meant much.

Sea-Land prospered in part because McLean and his team of traffic experts understood the mechanics and the dynamics of containerized ships and in part because Sea-Land's principal markets were the eastern United States and Europe, where highly developed land and river transportation already existed. The profitability of McLean trailer ships promoted this novel means of moving freight in maritime circles throughout the United States and Western Europe. MARAD, which had long been interested in ship designs that would be built around the container function, pushed for the new concept.

At APL George Paine and his engineering group made the mistake of attempting to bridge the old and the new in the design of the Searacers, the next generation of cargo liners to be constructed. Some hatches of the Searacers were fitted out for containers, others conformed to traditional methods of stowage and off-loading. It was a costly error to attempt a compromise design when it was clear that the industry was in a state of such uncertainty. The Searacers, named the *President Lincoln* and the *President Tyler,* never operated efficiently. Two systems of freight carriage that were not compatible existed side by side on one vessel. They simply got in the other's way, slowing down rather than speeding up the loading and unloading process.

Charles Deering, then Conwell's assistant in APL's operations department, said:

> We all erred there by probably building containerships a little bit too early. Because what happened was that even during the course of the building, the standards were changing . . . the configuration of the boxes was never set at that time. When the ship was laid down it was proposed to have seventeen foot containers and the reason for the short length was [that]—the concept in those days was to use a bogey and not a trailer. In other words you could have a structure in the box itself so when you take the box off the ship, you just put a set of hind wheels on it, take a tractor and go away with it. The structure was in the

box. Then that started to go away as people got smarter. Then the next step was to a twenty-four foot box. And we finally wound up . . . with a twenty-foot box.[9]

But if the technology of containership design was in transition, the logistics were also largely underdeveloped. APL had made a stab in this direction when it contracted for the Searacers. It had already set up a containerization group within the operations department headed by Captain D. S. Holler, a traffic specialist. On 24 October 1958 Holler and John N. Conway, assistant vice president in freight sales, left San Francisco on the round-the-world route to inspect ports for container terminals and distribution networks. They visited twenty-six ports in sixteen countries, paying particular attention to local labor situations and the condition of highways and railroads. To some extent they studied the infrastructure of the countries they visited. Their mission was to report on whether containerships were feasible on the round-the-world service, but they also included in their trip ports in Japan, Korea, and the Philippines. In general Holler and Conway found port facilities adequate but noted problems with the rail and road networks.

In Japan, for instance, hundreds of rail and road tunnels through mountainous terrain put strict limitations on the height of the vans or containers. And Japanese highways were in no condition to handle heavy trailer rigs. None of the ports visited had container-rigged gantry cranes or the associated facilities for efficient moving of containers from ship to shore or the reverse. Holler and Conway recommended that containers be supplied with bogies or wheels so that they could be moved and loaded on truck chassis. They thought that container size should be standardized at eight feet by eight feet by seventeen feet, although in India, Italy, and France, twenty-foot containers were acceptable. In major Japanese ports like Yokohama, they noted that 90 percent of general cargo handled moved to and from ship by barge. The average barge in use could carry four eight-foot by eight-foot by seventeen-foot vans or eight vans of the same dimensions stacked two high. However, most bridge clearances over canals and waterways under which these barges had to pass would restrict the loading to one tier (four vans). Unfortunately, Holler and Conway did not go into varying labor conditions as deeply as they might have. They also minimized the problem of government regulations and restrictions.

Their report on the whole was quite optimistic. It provided valuable information and in a general way it pointed to problems ahead, particularly the necessity for a rather complete reconstruction of foreign terminal facilities before an integrated container system could be set up. The report made considerable impact on the operations, freight, and engineering departments, but not enough to commit major resources toward solving the logistics problems that surrounded containerization. In many ways it was not only imprecise, but it lacked engineering and design input. Holler and Conway were not engineers or naval architects, nor did they provide the kind of in-depth studies necessary to plan the integration of ship design with container design or the precise interaction of the new designs with terminals and land distribution.[10]

A further and at the time far more serious problem was that APL's customers had not been prepared for container shipment. John E. Espey, former vice president of freight sales and an expert on the Asian market, described a no-win situation where both customers and competitors in rate conferences maintained a consensus against container shipping:

> There was no integration. We didn't have the equipment. You were handling it along with the breakbulk operations. The *Lincoln* would come in and handle a few containers, but nearly all was breakbulk cargo. In Japan, for example, they didn't achieve any of the economy of the cargo-handling savings. And we lost a lot of space because the container hatch really blew space in that area of the ship. There wasn't a demand for containers from the shippers, for a number of reasons. One, they just had not been convinced that it was a desirable mode despite efforts to impress on them the fact that the damage and loss experience would be way down and so on. One of the biggest difficulties was that we were having real problems with the freight conferences. Freight conferences were made up of carriers that were all breakbulk operators. And this included the Japanese. They looked at the containers as something they didn't want. They weren't ready to go into container activity in any sizeable form. So they did everything they could conceivably do to disadvantage containers by not adopting the required tariff rules, to protect their own interests. . . . They had no containerships and no containers. And there we were with the *Lincoln* and *Tyler,* starting off. Rules were placed or

retained in tariffs that made the cost of shipping in a container higher than breakbulk. When it should have been the other way around. As a result, we had a helluva time selling containers because of the rate structure. Obviously, we could have pulled out of the conference, and we considered this on a number of occasions. But every time we decided against it. Then, of course, we were not geared up to it. We didn't have the conviction to commit the investment required to change over to a full container operation. So we were betwixt and between.[11]

The *President Lincoln* and *President Tyler* were expensive lessons. But at least their performances would point to new and more compatible designs in vessels and in containers themselves. They especially emphasized that capital investments were equally necessary in the logistics that wholly containerized ships required for maximum efficiency.

In this respect, AML's cautious, conservative approach to the new technology proved in the short run to be a better solution. Its entire replacement fleet of ten vessels were all tried and true Mariner designs, enlarged and modified for AML's cargoes and routes. Gross tonnage was about one-third greater than earlier Mariners. Power plants were larger and more powerful, and as a result speed was increased from 20 to 22 knots. Extensive model basin tests conducted by J. J. Henry Company, a consulting firm of naval architects, prompted AML's engineering department to have the bow flared further back on the hull line. These design changes contributed to the *Washington Mail's* speed and particularly helped to shield the deck from heavy seas, thus protecting deck cargo. Early in 1963 the *Washington Mail* broke both west-east and east-west trans-Pacific records. Together with the *Oregon Mail* and the *Canada Mail*, sisterships that were delivered in December 1963 and in March 1964, these vessels represented a capital outlay of $24 million after the construction differential subsidy. They were financed by trade-ins of the *Alaska Mail* and the *Indian Mail*, the issue of $10 million in Merchant Marine bonds, payments from AML's reserve funds, and government-held mortgages.

Even before AML received the last of the new Mariners from National Steel of San Diego, it contracted for two more Mariners. Costs had risen rapidly in American shipyards since the first three Mariners were purchased. The company now had to pay about one-third more for these ships, or some $12 million each.[12] In 1965, AML

In the foreground is the *Washington Mail* of AML, later the *President Roosevelt* [II], a C4 Mariner. Beyond her is the *American Mail*, later the *President Cleveland* [III], a C5 Mailiner. (APL Archives.)

President Harrison [III]. A C4 Master Mariner, built in 1966. This photograph shows her before conversion to a full containership in 1973. (APL Archives.)

completed its modernization program by contracting for four C5 cargo liners. A fifth was to be purchased in 1967.

While AML was replacing its fleet and committing itself to a significant capital investment of about $125 million, APL had followed up the Searacers with contracts for three Master Mariners, 20.5-knot breakbulk ships. Experience with the Searacers convinced engineering, operations, and freight executives that the industry was not ready for container vessels and certainly not for hybrids like the *Presidents Tyler* and *Lincoln*. Thus the new vessels were essentially of Mariner design and represented a return to traditional concepts, though they were faster and carried slightly more cargo than their prototype. The only concession to the changing state of the art was more automated equipment on the bridge, in the engine room, and in the operation of the cargo booms. The decision to backtrack on building containerships was not made without some challenge from executives who were concerned that APL should fully implement container technology in all of its new construction. Inevitably these arguments reached Davies, who over the years had become increasingly concerned about the management of APL and especially about the failure of the three shipping lines he controlled to coordinate their procedures more closely and bring some economies of scale to their operations.

As far back as 1959, when Natomas acquired 40 percent of the stock in PFEL and the controlling interest, Davies had set up a coordinating committee with representation from the three lines to study the problem and propose a plan of action. Out of the committee's deliberations came Consolidated Marine, Inc., an independently organized company whose stock was owned by the three lines.

Consolidated Marine had too small a staff for all the problems it had to address, and its board represented the special interests of each of the participating lines, rather than the kind of coordination and cooperation Davies had envisaged. Its most successful operation was the management of the new terminals in Los Angeles and San Francisco for the benefit of the three companies. Availability of dock space, stevedoring service, and routine maintenance facilities were improved. But in other problem areas—purchasing (a large item in operations budgets), insurance, and, later, data processing for traffic control—Consolidated Marine made only slow and halting progress in its efforts to cut through company loyalties and antagonisms.

The core of a coordinating organization had been established, and in Davies's mind this was an essential first step to a merger of the three companies. He also had been watching carefully the net earnings of AML, APL, and PFEL as a function of consolidated gross revenues. Not one year between 1962 and 1966 did APL, though twice as large as AML and PFEL combined, match the total net profit of the other two. In 1965, for instance, AML's net profit margin was 13 percent, PFEL's was 10 percent and APL's 8.2 percent.[13] For many reasons—and not the least the need for more cash—Davies decided that grave faults existed in APL's executive ranks.

Besides the heavy capital expenditures the three lines committed for new construction, Davies had made significant venture capital investments in the construction and maintenance of missile bases, land development in California and Colorado, gold mining in Peru, and oil exploration and refining. But by far the greatest investment, some $11 million, was in the construction of a new office building at Saint Mary's Square at the corner of California and Kearny streets on the edge of San Francisco's Financial District. As a long-term investment, the building proved to be a good one, but like Davies's fascination for passenger liners, it was more a matter of his personal satisfaction rather than a quest for profits that underlay his decision. The building, said Chandler Ide, "has worked out fine. But it was built basically, I think, as a matter of prestige, and, again, there's a little pride showing, perhaps Davies had always wanted an office building so by God, we build an office building. The arithmetic of the thing—you are not making much money. . . . You more or less have broken even by the time you paid your interest on your mortgage, and the company was maybe making one or two percent on its investment."[14]

In 1959, Natomas acquired the land for the building; for the design it engaged the architectural firm of Anshen and Allen. Davies had first used its services in the late 1930s, when the new and struggling partnership of William Stephen Allen and Robert Anshen had first established their business in San Francisco. Davies, then a vice president of Standard Oil of California, had decided to build a new home on a large tract of land he had purchased in the picturesque hills of the peninsula near the town of Woodside, a suburb of San

Francisco. Impressed by the young architects' proposal to build a comfortable but at the same time arresting structure utilizing wood and stone lavishly for both exterior and interior walls, Davies accepted their plans and was so well satisfied with the house that he had kept in touch with them over the years and backed one of their ventures in "stressed skin panels" for a prefabricated housing market that was expected to develop after World War II.

So Davies quite naturally turned to Anshen and Allen when he decided to construct an office building and corporation headquarters at Saint Mary's Square. He wanted a quality building with no expense spared for workmanship and materials. It must also, as Allen has described Davies's view, be "a handsome, distinctive building with a San Francisco flavor, compatible with the area, not just another anonymous high-rise. He wanted it sturdily built of durable materials with the best of equipment and maximum interior flexibility." Davies rejected the suggestion that the building be named after him. The twenty-two-story edifice that rose over Saint Mary's Square was named simply the International Building, an appropriate designation, it seemed, because it described the activities of Natomas and its subsidiary companies.[15]

Now that the International Building existed, now that APL and Natomas executives and staff had moved in, the nagging problem of APL's profitability became a matter of increasing concern to Davies as more funds were being committed to capital expenditures and most of Natomas's venture investments between 1962 and 1965 were not panning out. Consolidated Marine was not functioning as he had hoped. Merger of the three lines, an objective Davies had thought desirable for the past five years, became his most important concern.

Realizing that such a consolidation would be upsetting not just to the executives of three independent companies but to their stockholders and customers as well, Davies felt that tact and sensitivity were as important as the legal and procedural problems posed. In the past he had invariably entrusted the handling of delicate problems to Chandler Ide, who had been a vice president of Natomas since the reorganization, a member of the board for the past seven years, and on its executive committee since 1961. Again this time he asked Ide to work out an equitable formula among the various interests involved. Warner Gardner would secure the necessary permission of the Maritime Administration and clearance from the Justice Department.

As expected, there was a subtle opposition from the three component parts, as executives worried about their positions in the new merged corporation. But Natomas management reassured all of the principals involved and dampened fears and jealousies in San Francisco and Seattle. Employee morale, customer sensibility, and labor reaction, three vitally important areas, were never jeopardized. Nor did any serious problems arise from the government or from the shareowners.

At the annual meeting of Natomas shareowners in 1965, Davies announced the proposed merger, subject of course to the government's approval. Signal, the principal minority stockholder, offered no objection. But the obstacles in conforming diverse style, policies, schedules, agents, and offices throughout the world and all those hundreds of minor factors that had created distinctions between the several shipping lines were not so easily overcome. Most of these differences were trivial in themselves, but collectively they imposed a set of difficulties that taxed Ide's patience and his ability to move things ahead without disturbing the sensitive maritime community.

Davies's decision to merge the three lines, while primarily aimed at improving their overall profitability, was also prompted by his desire to improve the management of APL. In preparation for the merger, he had seen to it that Boyce Luckett was made executive vice president and a member of APL's board of directors. John Espey was accorded vice presidential status and placed in charge of the all-important freight sales division. Clay Miller, who had worked closely with Luckett, became vice president of freight traffic. In 1964 Arthur Poole retired, but he remained on the board, where his pungent analysis and his more than twenty-three years of experience as financial head of the company continued to be made available for policy guidance.

Any major change in APL's management, however, had to involve George Killion, who had been president since 1948. Davies had recognized this fact. For some time he had been dissatisfied with Killion's performance but had delayed making any decision. He considered Killion's political connections valuable for the company, and he also felt under a certain obligation to Killion for his assistance when he acquired APL. Moreover, Killion and Samuel Mosher of

Signal were close friends. It would not do to ruffle Mosher's sensibilities unduly, especially when a merger was about to take place.

But the time seemed appropriate. For the past few years Killion, a member of Metro-Goldwyn-Mayer's board of directors, was donating a considerable amount of his time and interest to the movie industry. Davies was well aware of Killion's interests in Hollywood and would not have been concerned had the profit picture of APL improved, but it did not. Nor was Killion of much assistance in combatting the factionalism that was developing in the lower echelons of management over the persistent problem of containerization, a crucial policy area where Davies felt he needed guidance. By 1966, when Killion reached retirement age of sixty-five, Davies still had not taken any action beyond ascertaining that Killion wanted to stay on. It was while Davies was pondering whether Killion should remain or be asked to retire that William Joseph Biehl, a management consultant, appeared on the scene. Biehl was an imposing figure, tall and rangy, who combined an air of self-assured confidence with a relaxed, down-to-earth style. He had been introduced to Davies by another management consultant, Kerry Atkinson, at a business function in San Francisco. Biehl had just retired from active participation in Fry Associates, a Chicago firm of which he had been the chairman, chief executive officer, and principal stockholder for the past sixteen years and which still retained him as a consultant. An ambitious, aggressive man, he was eager to develop new accounts.

Biehl's career had been one of amazing success in the difficult business of troubleshooting among organizations where management problems could not be resolved internally. Son of a feed and grain merchant, Biehl grew up among the farm communities of rural Indiana. He graduated from the University of Indiana with a degree in chemical engineering in 1937. But characteristically, he had already landed a job before graduation at a time when engineering positions were extremely scarce because of the steep economic downturn of that depression year. He stayed with the company that first employed him, Libby McNeill and Libby, a food-processing firm, until 1943, becoming eventually "the number two" production man. While at Libby, Biehl had specialized in production method and control; and he proved unusually adept at working out systems that increased labor productivity and was equally successful in establishing his reputation as a problem-solver well beyond the world of food processing.

Blocked from further advancement at Libby, Biehl left that company and joined a newly formed management consulting firm in Chicago, Fry Associates. There he added to his reputation as a production engineer by becoming a management expert in labor relations. After another stint as a food-processing executive, Biehl purchased a controlling interest in his old firm, Fry Associates, which became under his guidance a major force in the management consulting field. In 1965 he decided to relinquish executive control, to sell his stock to other members of the firm, and to be retained as a floating representative, developing and serving new accounts. On one of his scouting expeditions in California, Biehl met Davies just when he was trying to come to a decision on George Killion.

Biehl made a good impression on Davies. After several general conversations, he offered, and Biehl accepted, a consulting arrangement with APL. What Davies wanted was his opinion on whether to retain or retire George Killion, and if the latter, who in the APL organization he might recommend as a replacement. He also wanted outside advice relating to the various problems facing APL. Since Biehl knew nothing about shipping lines or about APL's management, Davies arranged for him to interview the executives, including Killion.

Biehl talked with Killion, then Arthur Poole, Peter Teige, and Boyce Luckett and others in the top management group. After only two days of interviews, Biehl reported to Davies that Killion was spending too much of his time as a director of MGM and was neglecting APL. However, he had strong support from the management of the Signal Company, which owned a significant block of shares. In addition, Killion commanded considerable loyalty from APL executives. After weighing these factors, Davies decided that Killion should retire. Next he wanted Biehl's opinion of Raymond Ickes as a replacement and, if affirmative, to sound him out on the presidency of APL.[16]

Raymond Ickes was a logical choice to succeed Killion. He had turned in an impressive performance as the president of PFEL, boosting its earnings from a mere $529,000 in 1960 on gross revenue in excess of $35 million to $4,618,000 in 1965 on gross revenues of almost $50 million. In addition, Ickes had eliminated or reduced

Raymond W. Ickes, president, American President Lines, 1966–68. (APL Archives.)

unprofitable subsidiary operations and had completed the replacement of PFEL's World War II vessels with modern Mariners. It was true that the Viet Nam buildup had been largely responsible for PFEL's improved showing because military cargo had been its major revenue producer since Cuffe formed the company in 1946. But Ickes had shown himself to be a competent executive and, in fact, was loathe to leave his relatively secure position for the problems he knew he would face as APL's new president. What tempted Ickes was the prospect of heading not just APL, but an APL that would be enlarged by its merger with AML and PFEL. After some hesitation and some hard bargaining, Ickes agreed to become president of APL. His financial officer, Leo C. Ross, succeeded him as chief executive of PFEL.

Before Ickes left PFEL, he had become an enthusiast for a novel concept that the Maritime Administration was promoting, the so-called lighter on board ship, or LASH concept. Product of a New Orleans firm of naval architects, LASH was in fact a compromise technology that would obviate the need for extensive, specially designed shoreside gantry cranes and terminal facilities for containerships. Each LASH vessel would be designed to carry fully containerized lighters that would be lifted out of the ship and towed to terminals by tug.[17]

LASH vessels were an efficient means of moving containers where there were extensive inland waterways as in the eastern United States or in Western Europe with its navigable rivers and interconnected canals. This particular means of inland transportation did not exist in Japan, Korea, Hong Kong, Taiwan, or the Philippines, the major trading areas for the shipping lines on the West Coast. Nor were the West Coast ports of the United States much better endowed with waterways that would support extensive barge traffic. The Columbia River had few tributaries and did not serve large population densities; the Sacramento and San Joaquin river system was minuscule when compared to the Mississippi or to the Great Lakes/Saint Lawrence Seaway. However, LASH would have temporarily solved the problem of introducing expensive container facilities in those East Asian and Southeast Asian ports where locally owned, strictly controlled lighters or sampans handled the freight.

Ickes and his vice president of operations, G. J. Gmelch at PFEL, found this feature attractive. They also saw in LASH a solution to the persistent port congestion problem in Viet Nam and the Philippines.[18] But more compelling for them and for APL management was pressure from MARAD to accept LASH under the 55 percent construction differential subsidy for a new round of replacement vessels. A recent ruling of MARAD had stipulated that companies could not choose their own design but must use a design that two or more companies agreed on. The W. R. Grace/Prudential Line had chosen the LASH concept and it was APL's turn to accept or reject. PFEL would be next in line. The LASH concept made sense to Grace/Prudential. Its subsidized routes to the Caribbean ports of South America had long been afflicted with port congestion and its service to the west coast of South America had to depend on lighters because of the lack of natural ports. For a time it also made sense to Ralph Davies.

Jerome Goldman, a partner in the firm that had developed LASH, was a persuasive, articulate naval architect who put on a presentation in the executive conference room at the International Building that very nearly sold APL's management on the idea. Charles Deering, APL's former operations chief, recalled that "Mr. Davies was enthralled with the LASH concept. Jerry Goldman is the God Damnedest salesman that you ever saw in you life. And he came up and put a dog-and-pony show on with slides and pictures and all the rest of it. And to a guy like Davies, it just looked magnificent."[19]

One reason for Davies's and Ickes's enthusiasm was that LASH had come along just when Sea-Land and Matson had made *containerization* a household word in the shipping industry. Matson, whose trade was mainly with the Hawaiian Islands, had developed a unique gantry crane that could load or unload five hundred twenty-foot by eight-foot by eight-foot containers in twenty-four hours. Since its freight was specialized, it could and did make the capital investments necessary to build containerships and their surrounding port systems. By 1965, when the LASH concept came to the fore, Matson had demonstrated the superior efficiency of containerization, especially in its dramatic reduction of longshoremen hours. But it was Sea-Land that really made an impression on the management of APL and its subsidiary companies. A major item in its business was trade with Southeast Asia and military cargo. As the buildup began in Viet Nam, Sea-Land, an unsubsidized but fully containerized line, bid on a major portion of the military cargo going to that part of the world. None of the APL companies had the capability to provide the service at the low bid of Sea-Land. Recalled John Espey:

> We were just helpless. I mean all of our ships were subsidized with fixed trade route commitments. There were no other ships available. To go out and buy ships out of the lay-up fleet and convert them would take too long. It would have been extremely expensive, and who knew how long the Vietnamese war was going to continue. So Sea-Land secured a tremendous container contract with MSC, basically, from Oakland out to Cam Ranh Bay. They put a crane and equipment out there. Well, they operated outbound, fully loaded, under their contract, and they came homebound empty. Containers empty. They did that for about a year. Then they signed a new contract with the government and made the logical decision that instead of coming back with the containers empty, they would start serving Japan. So they went into Kobe and into Yokohama.[20]

Once that decision was made Sea-Land did not stint on its capital investment. Without waiting for the Japanese government to modernize its port facilities, it went ahead and put in gantry cranes, chassis, and all the associated equipment needed for container handling. The Japanese, who had stalled on containerization, now were forced to move and so they moved rapidly to design and build containerships and to equip their own terminals with the new gear. "So at that point in time," said Espey, "the conference situation changed, which opened the door for us to containerize. Additionally, of course, we were ourselves gradually gearing up to convert to the container mode."[21]

But was it too little, too late? APL, AML, and PFEL were in immediate danger of losing the greater part of their business not just to Sea-Land but to Japanese, British, and other subsidized lines that were moving fast to develop container capability. LASH might be just the right design to head off competition in Asian and Southeast Asian ports. For the Indian and Mediterranean legs of the round-the-world service, the flexibility of LASH vessels seemed a balanced solution. They seemed also a practical means of transportation for underdeveloped South Asian ports, where there were inadequate terminals and transportation infrastructures for integrated ship-to-shore container service. These were the points Jerome Goldman made most forcefully in his presentation of the LASH concept to

APL and PFEL, although he neglected to mention or shunted aside its applicability to major ports on the West Coast of the United States and the fact that Sea-Land was already pioneering container terminals in Japan, Korea, and Taiwan.

Factionalism that had been brewing in management ranks over containerization and the larger issue of passenger versus freight broke out into the open over LASH. Operations, engineering, and freight traffic all made reports. The tenor of their evaluations was largely negative.[22]

Davies, backed up by Ickes, who had just become president of APL, supported LASH. Charles Deering argued that LASH not only posed serious problems for operations but he presented at the same time a rationale that demonstrated the superiority of the Matson/Sea-Land concept of containerships. Others, including Captain Conwell, Peter Teige, and Arthur Poole, who was retired but still influential as a board member, voiced their apprehensions about LASH. Chandler Ide, who had listened to the arguments on both sides, advised caution.

Davies may have been a gambler, but he always hedged his bets if possible. He knew that PFEL, next in line for the MARAD contract, would take up the LASH design. Leo Ross, who had succeeded Ickes as president of the line, and the PFEL board had already indicated a willingness to contract for two LASH vessels in their replacement program. Why not let PFEL go ahead and reserve judgment in what he had come to understand was a fast-changing technology? But Davies came to the decision slowly, and it turned out to be a "cliff-hanger." Deering recalled the feeling of relief that came to him and others of the anti-LASH contingent when the decision was made that APL would wait and see. "By God, we prevailed," said Deering. ". . . The money would go to the next guy on the line, which happened to be PFEL. So they went along with that contract, I think, blindly without really having evaluated it or studied it all."[23]

If the controversy over LASH for a time divided management, there was no such division in accepting a precedent-shattering agreement with the maritime unions. Increasing automation of shipboard operations was reducing manning. Containerization pointed to a significant cutback of longshoremen and other terminal employees. The Maritime Administration had already recognized the impact that these technological changes would have on labor. Since it paid a differential subsidy for each crewman, MARAD began pushing for reduction in crew numbers. The unions, of course, resisted, but Harry Bridges, spokesman for the West Coast longshoremen's union, indicated that he might make a deal; moreover, leaders of other maritime unions also seemed receptive. The Pacific Maritime Association, which represented the shipping lines and which handled the employers' side of union contracts, began a series of talks with the union leaders through its head, Paul St. Sure.

Up to this time, terminal activities were highly labor intensive. There had been little change in loading and unloading ships since the days of sail. Collective bargaining agreements in the 1930s and in the postwar period had actually increased the number of longshoremen hours for given jobs, much of it in costly overtime pay. Longshoremen, divided into gangs, manhandled crates that had been swung out of holds in the breakbulk ships and placed them on pallets, which were then forklifted to designated areas for shipment by train or truck. In the loading procedure, the sequence was reversed, though an added task was shoring up cargo in the holds with lumber to prevent shifting. Containers drastically reduced the work hours of stevedores. Cargo in containers was stowed in cells on shipboard and required no shoring. Gantry cranes loaded and unloaded directly to or from truck chassis or railroad cars.

Similarly, automation in the engine room and on the bridge of the new vessels eliminated many positions. APL crews on the Mariner ships numbered 58 persons, but through automation competing foreign vessels of comparable size and design were operating with crews totaling as low as 28. The engine room was a prime example. As Peter Teige put it, "All U.S. flag ships were steam turbine ships. Instead of having a lot of men down there checking temperatures and all this kind of stuff—adjusting boilers, changing speed, and all this sort of thing, many developed sensors and remote control equipment so this could be done from the bridge."[24]

Bargaining between St. Sure and the various unions was long and tough. Finally, a rough formula was worked out by which APL and other members of the Pacific Maritime Association agreed to pay large sums into the union pension funds of the various unions to compensate for the loss of jobs. Thereafter, as automation and containerization moved ahead, there were more negotiations and more payments. APL alone during the sixties and early seventies paid the unions over $5 million in compensation.[25]

The early sixties were a time of turmoil and impending change for the West Coast shipping industry. Important decisions were made that would affect significantly the future course of Natomas and its subsidiary companies. Ralph Davies was the major force behind these moves. By 1966 he felt he was on the threshold of accomplishing certain long-held goals. The most important was the merger of the three shipping lines controlled by Natomas. This consolidation, which would make APL one of the largest shipping combines in the nation, seemed about to be realized when Davies decided to shift direction. By now Biehl had become his unofficial deputy, and although remaining a consultant, he was a power in the management of APL.

NOTES

1. Fowler, "Oral History Transcript," 16–18, APL Archives.

2. Ibid.

3. Teige, "Oral History Transcript," 12, APL Archives.

4. Ide, "Oral History Transcript (II)," 6; Luckett, "Oral History Transcript," 27, 28, APL Archives.

5. For a vivid account of the loss of the *Washington Mail*, see *Life Magazine*, 26 March 1956.

6. American Mail Line, "Minutes, Regular Meeting of Board of Directors," 23 May 1956, APL Corporate Files.

7. Lintner to Clarence Morse, undated, 1956 (copy), APL Archives. Lintner was including the *Washington Mail*, which had not as yet foundered.

8. See War Shipping Administration, *Annual Report 1944* (Washington, D.C., 1945), passim; U.S. Maritime Commission, *The Post War Outlook for American Shipping, A Report Submitted by the Postwar Planning Committee, June 15, 1946* (Washington, D.C.: U.S. Government Printing Office, 1946), 86–90.

9. Charles Deering, "Oral History Transcript," 14–15, APL Archives.

10. D. S. Holler and John Conway, "Containerization, 'Round-the-World' Research Trip," APL Archives.

11. J. E. Espey, "Oral History Transcript," 38–39, APL Archives.

12. *AML Newsletter*, March 1963, Yost Collection.

13. Figures have been taken from an analysis of the balance sheets in the annual reports of APL, AML, and PFEL for the years 1958–65. Chandler Ide Collection, St. Helena, Calif.

14. Ide, "Oral History Transcript (I)," 131–32.

15. Wm. Stephen Allen in *Ralph Davies As We Knew Him*, 107–13.

16. W. J. Biehl, "Oral History Transcript," 1–9, 20–28, APL Archives.

17. Raymond Ickes, "Oral History Transcript," 20–23, APL Archives.

18. Ibid.

19. Deering, "Oral History Transcript," 26, APL Archives.

20. Espey, "Oral History Transcript," 38.

21. Ibid.
22. Teige, "Oral History Transcript," 22, 23.
23. Deering, "Oral History Transcript," 27.
24. Teige, "Oral History Transcript," 25–26.
25. Ibid., 27.

11
TRANSITION YEARS

A S APL moved into the later sixties, management's record was one of vivid contrasts. After a slow start, the company and its subsidiaries began to react vigorously to containerization. Davies had spread the risks of LASH by permitting PFEL to go ahead with the concept, but at the same time sided with those at AML and APL who were arguing for containerships that were loaded and unloaded at the pier. During 1967–68 APL took delivery of five new Seamasters, the *President Fillmore, President Grant, President Taft, President McKinley,* and *President Van Buren.* These 14,000-ton ships were all of the basic Mariner design upgraded for greater breakbulk cargo capacity and higher speed. The *President Van Buren* made the voyage from San Francisco to Yokohama at an average speed of 25.55 knots, the fastest on record. With an eye to possible conversion to full containerships, flush deck, holds, and hatches were designed for the adaption to container cells, should that become necessary.[1]

Similarly, AML had completed in November 1969 its replacement program with five Mailiner class 16,000-ton freighters.[2] These 21-knot ships, though also designed for breakbulk cargo, had on-deck container capacity of 6,352 measured tons. Designated C5s, they represented a total investment of about $80 million, 55 percent of which AML financed through its reserve funds and the issuance of merchant marine bonds.

Well before APL took delivery of the first of the Seamasters, its engineering department was working with Sharp, a firm of naval architects, to design the first of the full containerships, the Pacesetter, a ship with a capacity of 1,200 twenty-foot container equivalent.[3] *President Lincoln* and *President Tyler* were being scheduled for a conversion that would give each a 378-container capacity.

APL's decision to build the Pacesetters was not made without

President Van Buren [IV]. Originally a C4, she was converted to a full containership in 1972. In the process she was lengthened nearly a hundred feet and her tonnage was increased from 14,000 gross to 17,801. The photograph shows her making 27 knots on her trials in Puget Sound. (APL Archives.)

President Adams [V]. She was a C5 type, built for AML as the *Alaskan Mail* and renamed *President Adams* in 1978. Notice the equipment for heavy lifts just aft of the central deckhouse. (APL Archives.)

vigorous dispute within APL's management. When Ickes became president in the spring of 1966, he found plans well advanced for the construction of five more Seamasters. Ickes thought a continuation of these designs would not make economic sense. Although they would have a statutory life of twenty-five years, he was certain that they would be obsolete in less than five. "I got that stopped. It was very painful," he said. "It took a helluva lot of doing but it got done. I was probably never forgiven for it."[4] And at Ickes's insistence, backed up by the operations, engineering, and traffic departments, Pacesetters were substituted, but not before APL had worked out a joint construction project with Farrell Lines, which would take four of the new vessels.

Ickes also sought to challenge Matson's near-monopoly of the Hawaiian trade. In repeating R. Stanley Dollar's ill-fated attempt to compete for the lucrative traffic between the Islands and the West Coast, APL formed a new company, Hawaiian Lines, together with Isthmian Lines and Castle and Cooke, the huge, diversified Hawaiian-based company.[5] Even though the Maritime Commission (renamed in the Reorganization Act of 1961) approved his deal, Hawaiian Lines met a fate similar to that of Dollar's venture. Matson's opposition forced Isthmian Lines out of the new organization in 1967 and a new firm was formed in which APL owned two-thirds of the stock and Castle and Cooke, one-third.[6] But the companies involved could not agree on the new Hawaiian service. With Ickes's departure, both parties, APL and Castle and Cooke, agreed to dissolve Hawaiian Lines.[7]

Chairman Davies, however, still clung to his romantic vision of large passenger carriers. He had scaled down his plans of the late fifties, when he had pushed the company to develop the *President Washington*, first of a class of large passenger liners that was never built. APL's engineering department came up with the preliminary design for two combination vessels that would accommodate 250 passengers each.

Biehl had recognized Davies's penchant for passenger ships. Though he was aware that they remained a losing proposition unless they could be subsidized, which was unlikely, he followed a principle he had made for himself when he first became a consultant. If he perceived that Davies wanted something—a new executive or a passenger liner, an acquisition or a merger—he would accept his judgment, even encourage it, and then try to make it

Worth B. Fowler, president, American Mail Line, 1959–67; president, American President Lines, 1967–73. (APL Archives.)

work. As he had persuaded Ickes to become president of APL because he sensed accurately enough that he was Davies's choice, so now he was prepared to urge his replacement because he felt Ickes had lost Davies's confidence.

The major point was whether APL should continue with its combination ships on the trans-Pacific route after these vessels reached the end of their twenty-five-year statutory life, only three years away. Ickes and a substantial group of APL's management pointed out repeatedly that the three large combination vessels, *President Wilson*, *President Cleveland*, and *President Roosevelt*, were costing the company from six to ten million dollars a year in losses. Davies refused to listen and Biehl had his consulting firm Fry Associates make surveys that maintained the passenger business could be profitable. At Worth Fowler's suggestion, APL retained J. J. Henry, the Seattle firm of naval architects, to develop plans for the new vessels. Without consulting Ickes, Davies accepted designs for two 250-passenger combination ships.[8]

When Ickes discovered what was in process, he actively and vociferously opposed the project. "It was perfectly patent," said Ickes, "that kind of arrangement could not work. The passenger end of it would hurt the freight end of it, and the freight end of it would hurt the passenger end of it. I mean, these passengers could not count on a certain itinerary without foregoing freight. And the freight people would not book if they knew they had to sail on a certain hour on a certain date because of passengers."[9] Biehl had been making every effort to work out a means not only to make the passenger business profitable but to expand it.[10] In June 1968, with Davies's consent, he brought in a respected passenger expert, Warren Titus, who had had long experience in developing the cruise-ship idea for the British-owned P & O Line.[11]

At about the same time the LASH controversy came to a head. Davies had concluded that the LASH concept was not feasible for APL. But Ickes refused to accept his decision. On 4 July 1968, Davies asked for Ickes's resignation in a formal note that was delivered unsealed to Ickes's desk. A close relationship that went back twenty-two years was now broken irreparably. A reluctant Worth Fowler, president of AML agreed to take over APL. Robert E. Benedict, a veteran of Moore-McCormack Lines and Phelps Dodge overseas operations succeeded him.

Ickes had been a good administrator. He was a hard-working, conscientious executive who had kept abreast of the dramatic changes that were taking place in the shipping industry. But he was too outspoken, too candid in expressing his views, too much the unyielding advocate rather than the plausible, pliable executive who bent means to achieve desired ends.[12] Ickes's departure from APL, as Chandler Ide observed, began Biehl's significant involvement in the management of the line through Fowler and his other chosen executives.

Boyce Luckett and Peter Teige, on whom Ickes had relied heavily for the management of the line, and who joined him in his many protests to Davies, followed their chief out of the company. Fowler, with Davies's concurrence, abolished the position of executive vice president and downgraded the post of company counsel. Signaling the continued importance of the passenger business, Warren Titus was made a member of the board of Natomas and of APL. He did not report to APL's new president, Worth Fowler, but would go directly to Davies. Biehl accomplished this organizational anomaly by having APL create a new company, American President Lines Passenger Service, Inc.

But Biehl did not fare so well with his commitment to the merger of the three lines. When all seemed to have fallen in place, all points of disagreement among the erstwhile competitors ironed out, Matson and States Lines in the courts attacked the Maritime Commission's decision to permit the merger.[14] Meanwhile, Natomas had become deeply involved in the exploration of offshore oil fields in Indonesia. The need for capital became intense as extremely expensive rigs drilled a series of dry holes, along with some small finds, off the coasts of Java and Sumatra. When Consolidated Freightways approached Davies with an offer for Natomas's stock in PFEL, he was quick to accept. Davies drove a hard bargain, however. Natomas made a capital gain on its original investment of over $13 million and brought in $20.6 million of much-needed cash.[15]

The sale of a controlling interest in PFEL reduced considerably the anticipated gains from a merger of Natomas's shipping interests. A decision of the Federal Court of Appeals for the Ninth Circuit blocking the merger prompted Davies to cancel all merger plans. He announced his decision on 20 January 1969.

With the collapse of his merger plans, Davies, again encouraged by Biehl, took a renewed interest in Consolidated Marine, which had made but slow and fitful progress in coordinating the activities of the three lines. Consolidated Marine had been most successful in terminal management at Los Angeles and San Francisco and in data processing, least successful in joint scheduling and purchasing. Even in terminal management, deep rifts had appeared as PFEL began planning for new facilities in both ports to accommodate its LASH vessels.[16] In data processing, though Consolidated Marine had begun implementing a general ledger and accounting system for APL and was about to install a container inventory control system that could accommodate APL and PFEL, the latter company had insisted on developing and utilizing its own data processing system for internal and external procedures. Despite Worth Fowler's influence with AML (he remained chairman of its board), that company had devised its own inventory control system in conjunction with the Port of Seattle Authority and its management generally opposed any coordination as an article of faith.

Beginning in the new year of 1970, Davies and Biehl began attending board meetings of Consolidated Marine. After listening to the independent views of board members representing the lines, Davies concluded that joint purchasing should be scrapped. He was distressed by the wide diversity of opinions on data processing and terminal operations that were freely expressed. APL complained that it was bearing "too much of the heavy fixed-cost burden" because of PFEL's low participation in programming and computer activity. Ross, the president of PFEL, admitted that his company was utilizing outside programming contractors. But he justified this policy by declaring that PFEL required programs designed for its particular needs. PFEL, he said, was developing a freight documentation system that was not compatible with APL's. PFEL, of course, was now an independent company. At this point Davies interjected with a request that Fowler and Ross report within thirty days on whether joint data processing should be continued. Their report was negative and crippled Consolidated Marine's joint computer program. Well before this decision, AML, APL, and PFEL had gone their separate ways in purchasing and in husbanding of their vessels and indeed in all terminal activities.[17] Hugh H. Howard, head of Consolidated Marine, summed up its dilemma succinctly when he said that "too much control was retained in San Francisco and Seattle and too little delegated to CMI management." By the end of 1970, Consolidated Marine had virtually ceased to function.[18]

Biehl's and Davies's efforts to coordinate the management of APL and AML fell victim to the entrenched vested interests of the two lines. Their plans to revitalize the passenger business failed also. After six months at APL, Warren Titus had analyzed the report of Biehl's firm that APL's passenger business could be profitable and found that its data base was invalid. Among other factors, the report had failed to consider the impact of catch-up clauses in union contracts, which increased operating costs on the three large combination vessels at a far faster rate than could be compensated by the differential subsidy. Nor were the *Presidents Cleveland, Roosevelt*, and *Wilson*, now nearing the end of their twenty-five-year statutory lives, able to offer accommodations equal to the newer competing cruise ships. The *President Roosevelt* never overcame the limitations on accommodations imposed by her original troop-transport design, and while the two other ships did not suffer from this defect, they were becoming less competitive each year. Moreover, their subsidized route from San Francisco to Honolulu, Yokohama, Hong Kong, and Manila, with repeat calls only at Hong Kong, Yokohama, and Honolulu on the return voyage and with eight days at sea between Honolulu and Yokohama, was not the sort of varied ocean travel with short intervals between ports that cruise passengers preferred. Still there were possibilities that APL could participate in the burgeoning cruise ship market if it had ships better designed for that trade, and if it could get more flexibility in its subsidized routes. As it was, the *President Roosevelt* was placed on the round-the-world schedule twice a year beginning in 1966 and after she was sold in 1970 round-the-world cruises were made occasionally by the other *President* ships. By that time, the trans-Pacific subsidized voyages were varied with the addition of new ports such as Keelung. In addition the *President Cleveland* and *President Wilson* made occasional cruises to Alaska, Mexico, the Mediterranean, Scandinavia, and round the Pacific.[19]

As Titus saw it, there had to be first a new market strategy that emphasized first-class travel and took scheduling away from freight movement and fixed routing. Second, the three old ships should be sold. As replacements, there were two passenger liners available on the East Coast that were suitable for cruises, the *Brasil* and the *Argentina*. Each vessel had fine accommodations for 550 passengers in first class, but little or no cargo capacity. These two vessels would be interim carriers in Titus's plan, while negotiations were undertaken with the Maritime Commission and MARAD for the construction and the subsidy of two passenger liners designed specifically for the cruise trade.

Politically it was difficult to arrange for subsidies on what were regarded as luxury voyages. MARAD had permitted a few cruises outside of the subsidized route 29 for the *President* liners. But chances seemed slim that APL could get government financing and subsidy for its cruise ships. A new merchant marine bill was before Congress that would provide from six to seven billion dollars for a new construction and subsidy program. But no such legislation was expected for at least a year.[20]

Acquisition of the *Brasil* and *Argentina* from Moore-McCormack as interim vessels, however, was absolutely crucial for APL's passenger service. Unfortunately, APL ran into a roadblock when it began negotiations to purchase the liners. The maritime unions were divided on a regional basis. East Coast ships were staffed by crews belonging to East Coast unions and the same applied to the West Coast. East Coast unions would only permit the *Brasil* and *Argentina* to sail with its own crew members and on their unions' contracts. But West Coast maritime unions would not permit these ships to operate on the contracts of eastern unions. On these jurisdictional rocks, APL's plans for entering the cruise ship trade foundered. Warren Titus has explained the labor situation in this fashion:

> We could not get any major concessions from the deck and engine side. The Masters, Mates and Pilots and the MFOW (Marine Firemen, Oilers and Watertenders Union) were very, you know, inflexible, both with officers and the segment of the SUP (Sailors' Union of the Pacific). The marine cooks and stewards were prepared to ease up on their work rules and do certain things that would have given us greater flexibility. And I must say that they were very interested in saving jobs. They were receptive to ideas, but we never got to the point of writing a contract. So it was a combination of the jurisdictional problem, plus the high labor costs which we were not able to overcome. So we could never put phase one together. . . . Meanwhile, I spent a considerable amount of time in Washington while all this was going on in '69, trying to get support for a new subsidy program for new ships. It was right at a time when it was just an impossible situation. 1969 was not the year.[21]

Titus had several long talks with Davies about the whole spectrum of passenger business for APL. With the *Brasil* and the *Argentina* out of the picture, he presented hard evidence that the old combination liners could not work out as cruise ships, even with new merchandising strategies and more flexible itineraries that MARAD accepted within the subsidy structure. Labor costs were far outstripping operational subsidy payments. These costs, combined with other fixed charges on the *President* liners, were too high for the number of passengers that could be carried in first-class accommodations. Titus backed up his conferences with detailed reports that removed any illusion about the profitability or even the possibility of APL operating subsidized cruise ships under the American flag. Without government support in the construction and the operation of new vessels for this particular service, a continuation of the passenger business was not possible financially for APL. Davies accepted the inevitable. As Titus put it:

> That was my understanding. He recognized finally that there was not a profit to be made in those ships, and there was not an opportunity in the present political climate to get a subsidy program for new ships. We had to give up the *Brasil* and *Argentina* because that seemed to be an insurmountable objection. So what was the alternative? I gave him my projection which showed how much money he would lose. And, also, you had the fact that they had reached the end of their statutory life. Or they were reaching it. So he would not be able to get subsidy for an extended period. As far as I was concerned, when I left the company, the decision had been taken, at his level, that they would get out of the passenger business and concentrate their efforts on the cargo side which was the right decision to take.[22]

Titus left the company to return to the cruise business and become the head of the highly successful Royal Viking Lines.

To manage the passenger steamers until they were phased out of service, John A. Traina, Jr., was transferred from his post as sales manager to that of general manager of passenger operations in July 1970. Although his task was basically one of winding up a service that the top management had decided to abandon, he carried on an aggressive advertising campaign with the result that revenues from the passenger ships increased somewhat. The *President Cleveland* reached her statutory retirement age late in 1972, and the *President Wilson* completed her last voyage, a round-the-world cruise, in April 1973. This brought to an end the trans-Pacific passengership service that had been carried on by the American President Lines and its predecessors without interruption except during World War I and World War II since 1867.[23]

Throughout this difficult period, while Davies was trying desperately to cope with the cyclical fortunes of shipping lines, made more difficult by the advent of new technologies, and while he was venturing millions of dollars of Natomas's capital in risky oil ventures, his health was slowly deteriorating. In 1966, a routine physical examination detected early lung cancer. After surgery he seemed to bounce back, but Chandler Ide, his closest associate, recognized that he did not have his former energy and ability to penetrate to the fundamentals of any complex problem. There was no doubt that Biehl's ascendency in APL affairs was due largely to Davies's physical condition, which sapped his vitality and in turn gradually made him more dependent on his subordinates.

Davies had always confided in Ide and had shared with him all aspects of corporate policy. In 1966, when R. G. Smith retired as president of Natomas, Davies had Ide elected in his place. He had been a member of its board since 1956 and a member of the board's executive committee when Davies formed it in 1961. Ide was the only person in the corporation who knew of Davies's illness, and he was concerned about Biehl's increasing influence in decision-making, especially in areas such as the passenger business, where his advice seemed to be clearly moving APL and hence Natomas in what Ide regarded as the wrong direction. There was a lowering of morale throughout APL's and Natomas's management structure during this period.

In part to counteract the drift and confusion in company affairs, in part also to position Natomas for its future in oil and gas exploration and production, Ide convinced Davies that Natomas needed a first-rate financial expert. On 1 March 1970, at the suggestion of Biehl's management firm, they brought in Bruce Seaton, a specialist in international currency matters, as vice president of finance.

Born in Philadelphia, Seaton had graduated from UCLA in 1948 with a major in business administration. After a year of graduate work, he joined the public accounting firm of John F. Forbes and Company. While there he earned his CPA certificate. Tall and trim, Seaton's direct manner obscured a fine sense of humor and a sensitive understanding of human foibles. Professionally he was an expert in the oil business, having spent thirteen years with Douglas Oil and the past four years with Occidental. He had been assistant treasurer of Occidental, but in actuality was the head of that giant firm's foreign and domestic treasury functions at a time when its sales rose from $30 million in 1966 to $2 billion in 1970.[24] Both men liked Seaton's solid grasp of financial complexities and his keen insights into organizational behavior and function. They realized that any executive from Occidental's financial department would have had under Armand Hammer, its gifted but unconventional head, a broad and creative experience in international oil investments. And, as they hoped, Seaton would bring a sense of strength

Norman Scott, president, American President Lines, 1973–77. (APL Archives.)

and stability to Natomas's affairs. The following year, on Seaton's recommendation, Davies selected W. Brandt Brooksby, another able financial specialist, to be comptroller. At the same time Seaton was elected to the Natomas board of directors.[25]

Meanwhile, as Natomas's oil explorations in Southeast Asia began to pay off, profits from shipping started on a long decline that was particularly evident in APL's operations. Lengthy, expensive strikes of longshoremen and unlicensed shipboard personnel disrupted schedules. When the strikes were settled, operating costs rose without compensating increases in rates or in volume of freight. At the same time AML and APL were beginning to invest heavily in containerships, and in conversion of their breakbulk fleet to container carriers. They were of course purchasing containers, acquiring expensive electronic data systems for the control of traffic, and they were also purchasing huge gantry cranes that were especially designed to load and unload containers. Although port cities like

Seattle, Tacoma, San Francisco, and Los Angeles underwrote most of the costs of new terminal facilities, APL and AML were obligated to shoulder a part of the burden in discharge fees. In overseas ports like Manila, APL bore a larger portion of the capital costs for conversion to container facilities than it did in the port cities of the United States. Eventually most of these extraordinary outlays flattened out. The savings on turnaround time and labor costs were substantial. Vessels increased significantly in size and speed, thus permitting a reduction in the fleet and a subsequent decrease in fixed charges. But in this period of transition, earnings of the two lines continued to shrink. In 1970, Natomas received only $77,280 in dividends from its shipping interests, compared with $1,371,244 in 1969, which had certainly not been a banner year for APL.[26] Despite these negative results, a basis for sustained growth had been laid with the conversion of five Mariner vessels to containerships and the reduction of unprofitable services.

In 1970 Davies had Biehl search for a shipping man who would be a Natomas executive but responsible for overseeing the operation of APL and AML. Biehl came up with an attractive, knowledgeable person who had made a name for himself with Matson—Norman Scott. A U.S. Naval Academy graduate, Scott had been involved in Matson's container program but had recently found himself blocked from further development of the new technology as Matson began to cut back its operations. Though his responsibilities were not specifically set forth, Scott accepted the new post of Natomas's vice president of transportation and became a member of its board of directors.[27]

The year 1970 marked Davies's last major management move, the Scott appointment, and also his complete acceptance of containerization. APL contracted for the conversion of five Seamasters to full container capacity. AML began conversion of three C4s that would give each vessel a cargo capacity equivalent to 892 twenty-foot containers. As if to highlight the necessity for a rapid changeover, the longshoremen went out on strike during the early summer of 1971 in what was to be the longest strike in the history of maritime labor on the West Coast.

By now Ralph Davies was critically ill, but he continued to work as long as he was physically able. He had also in these last days of his life realized how much he had let affairs of APL and Natomas slip away. And for the first time he recognized how disruptive this indirect management had been—not just among top executives, but extending down through the three organizations. Two weeks before he died, he confided to Ide that he had been mistaken in some of the major personnel and policy changes he had made over the past five years. Ide was one of the executors of his will and his successor.[28]

Ralph Davies died on 19 September 1971, ten days after his 74th birthday. With his death a distinct phase in APL's history came to an end.

NOTES

1. Ingalls Shipbuilding Company of Pascagoula, Mississippi, built all of these vessels.

2. These ships were named the *Alaskan Mail, American Mail, Hong Kong Mail, Indian Mail, Korean Mail*. See Hartle, "Ships Owned or Operated by American Mail Line Ltd."

3. American President Lines, Ltd., Annual Report 1968, APL Archives.

4. Ickes, "Oral History Transcript," 16, APL Archives.

5. Natomas Company, Annual Report 1966, Ide Collection.

6. Ibid., 1967.

7. Ibid., 1968.

8. Natomas Company, Company Annual Report 1968, Ide Collection.

9. Ickes, "Oral History Transcript," 18, 30, APL Archives.

10. Biehl, "Oral History Transcript," 31, 33, APL Archives.

11. Warren Titus, "Oral History Transcript," 4, 5, APL Archives.

12. Ickes, "Oral History Transcript," 26, 27, APL Archives.

13. Ide, "Oral History Transcript (II)," 1, 2, APL Archives.

14. Fowler to all American Mail Line Employees, memorandum, 15 January 1968, copy, in Yost Collection; *Seattle Times*, 21 January 1969; *Marine Digest*, 25 January 1969.

15. Natomas Company, Annual Report 1969, Ide Collection.

16. An analysis of terminal revenue for the first six months of 1970 disclosed that APL provided 69.4 percent, PFEL 23.9 percent, and other lines that used the facilities 6.7 percent. Consolidated Marine, "Minutes of Regular Meeting of Board of Directors," 27 May 1970, APL Corporate Files.

17. Ibid.

18. Ibid., 21 April 1971.

19. American President Lines, Ltd., Annual Report 1966, p. 5; 1970, p. 4, Yost Collection; APL Passenger Cruise Schedules, 1969, 1971, 1972. The *President Hoover* [II] had been sold in 1964.

20. Jeff O'Neill, "Greatest Peacetime Merchant Shipbuilding Program Ready for Launching," *Navy Magazine* (November 1970): 18–22.

21. Titus, "Oral History Transcript," 11, APL Archives.

22. Ibid., 28.

23. American President Lines, Ltd., Annual Report 1970, 1973, Yost Collection.

24. Bruce Seaton, "Oral History Transcript," 1, 2, APL Archives.

25. Ide, "Oral History Transcript (II)," pp. 1, 4, 8–10; (I), 10, 11, APL Archives.

26. Natomas Company, Annual Reports 1966–70, Ide Collection.

27. Biehl, "Oral History Transcript," 42; Norman Scott, "Oral History Transcript," 6–15, 17, 18, APL Archives.

28. Ide, "Oral History Transcript (II)," 1, APL Archives.

12
FULL CIRCLE

At a special meeting of the board of directors in December 1971, Chandler Ide was elected president and chief executive officer of Natomas Company. Shortly after, APL's board made him chairman. Within two months or so William J. Biehl resigned from APL's and Natomas's boards.

Ide was in charge of a business organization that controlled assets of approximately $168 million and employed about four thousand people.[1] Brilliant prospects for the company seemed indicated on the one hand, but on the other, there were difficulties and uncertainties that could dim a lustrous future. Much depended on Ide. For years he had worked in the shadow of Ralph Davies. He was sixty-two years old. Could he grasp the reins securely and manage the sprawling company? More than that, could he repair the damage to internal order and external relationships that had confused policies and hampered operations during the years of Davies's illness?

Ide was scarcely the popular image of the big-business man, much less the expansive, risk-taking entrepreneur that has come to be associated with the aggressive independent oil companies. Six feet tall, with graying hair and regular features, he was reserved in public, although a good conversationalist in small gatherings among people he knew. Moreover, he could be surprisingly open and decisive should the situation warrant it. Judicious, a gifted administrator, he was at his best resolving conflicts among strong-minded ambitious individuals, usually finding a course that all could agree upon. His knowledge of the oil industry was comprehensive, his understanding of the shipping industry less so. But Ide was a rapid learner. With his well-developed capacity for mastering complex data and putting it together in understandable form so that a clear mode of action could be projected, he soon schooled himself in the problems and possibilities of APL and AML.

Born in Mount Vernon, New York, in 1909, Ide was the second son of a Congregational minister. When he was seven years old, his father accepted a parish in Redlands, California, and moved the family west. It was natural that Ide and his brothers would all attend Pomona College in nearby Claremont, a private, liberal arts college that ministers of the Congregational Church had founded in 1887.

Ide graduated in 1930, just as the Depression was carrying the economy down in a deep spiral. Jobs for new college graduates were virtually unobtainable. He did manage to secure a position teaching in a private school, however, and while there became interested in educational products, textbooks, relief maps and other teaching aids. Sensing a possible market, Ide left teaching and started a business in developing a variety of teaching aids. He was able to sustain himself in this business for three years. But in 1934 he married and decided he could never support a wife and family on the income from his various ventures. Though job prospects everywhere in California were bleak, they looked best in San Francisco. In 1935, Ide pulled up stakes, moved to the Bay Area and began making the rounds of prospective employers. Among other companies, he applied at Standard Oil of California. There the personnel officer asked if he could type. Yes, Ide replied. Could he take dictation? Unfortunately no. "You'd have to be able to do that," said the personnel officer, "and then there would be an opening for you."

For the next six weeks Ide studied Gregg shorthand, then returned and took a typing and dictation test that he passed easily. He was hired as relief secretary who would be made available to any of the departments on a need basis. As such, Ide learned a good deal about the operations of Standard.

In the course of his secretarial stints he worked for Ralph Davies, who liked his manner and was impressed by his ability. When Davies's secretary was transferred to another department, Ide replaced him. From then until Davies's death in 1971, Ide was first his secretary, then his assistant, and finally his associate or rather junior partner in the government during the war and in his various ventures afterwards. No person shared Davies's confidence as Ide did.

Davies was a difficult man to work with and an even harder person with whom to share a confidential relationship, but the calm, somewhat diffident Ide with his scholarly inclinations was just the kind of person Davies felt he could trust. Ide repaid Davies with complete loyalty, industry, and strong powers of analysis and judg-

President Jefferson [III]. A C6 Pacesetter, she was built in 1973 as a full containership. The photograph shows her in Hong Kong Harbor. (APL Archives.)

ment. In the formation of American Independent Oil, in the creation of APL Associates, the Natomas reorganization, the purchase of a controlling interest in AML and PFEL, the attempted merger of the three lines, the sale of PFEL, and the decision to risk millions of dollars in the as-yet unexplored Indonesian oil fields, Ide was not only consulted but played an important role in every decision. Among those few who understood his unique qualities—in effect, Davies's dependence upon him—there were no qualms about his ability to manage Natomas. Warner Gardner, for one, and Ralph Davies himself in the last months of his life bore testimony to this fact.

After straightening out the lines of authority at Natomas, Ide put Seaton on the board of APL and made him a member of the executive committee of the Natomas board. Another of Ide's early decisions was to remove all passenger accommodations that had been designed into the Pacesetters at Davies's insistence. He also made it plain that APL would get out of the large-scale passenger business when the *President Cleveland* and the *President Wilson* reached the end of their statutory lives. The phasing-out of the passenger business stemmed some of the losses APL was incurring. But its economic condition remained stagnant or declined, while profits from the Indonesian oil venture rose dramatically.

By early 1973, APL and AML had completed their container conversion programs. Five Seamaster types and three Master Mariner types were cut in half and a midbody section added. In the case of the Seamasters, their hulls were lengthened 191 feet and their capacity boosted from 250 twenty-foot equivalent containers to 1,066. Similarly, their tonnage was increased by 3,803 gross tons. The smaller Master Mariners were lengthened 104 feet, gross tonnage increased by 6,407 tons, and container capacity expanded to 792 twenty-foot equivalents.[2] But because of the shipyard delays APL had not received its new Pacesetters, wholly containerized ships.

Labor problems had been a major contributor to the decline in profits and, though the lengthy longshoremen's strike was settled during the first quarter of 1972, negotiations foundered between the Pacific Maritime Association, bargaining agent for the West Coast shipping companies, and the International Organization of Masters, Mates, and Pilots. A forty-two-day strike followed that tied up half of APL's and AML's fleets. Operations that were coming back to normal after the longshoremen's strike were again disrupted and business was lost to competing foreign lines that were not affected. Despite the precedent-setting formula negotiated with longshoremen and the unlicensed personnel in 1966, there were painful and difficult times before all the various unions agreed to the reductions in personnel that increasing automation on the ships themselves and containerization imposed.

Losses caused by the interruption of service and the enforced idleness of capital equipment accelerated the rapid pace toward containerization. In 1971, 58 percent of all freight carried in APL vessels between California ports and Japan, Korea, and Singapore went by way of containers, a striking increase of 35 percent in two years. APL planners were projecting that 95 percent of all cargoes would be containerized in another five years.[3] This equipment, which by 1972 had cost some $25 million, would, it was estimated,

President Tyler [IV]. Built as a LASH-type ship for Pacific Far East Lines as the *Japan Bear* in 1972, she was converted to a full containership in 1978 and renamed *President Tyler* the next year. She is shown here in the Oakland Estuary approaching the APL Middle Harbor Terminal. (APL Archives.)

require another $42 million before the program was completed. These outlays did not consider investments that AML was making in containers, about $20 million more. There was no construction subsidy for containers. Such substantial capital expenditures for their purchase or lease had to come entirely from the company's funds.[4] Yet as the numbers of containers multiplied, there were ever-increasing capital investments in larger, faster ships, in redesigned and reequipped terminal facilities, the purchase and staffing of elaborate electronic data systems to handle documentation, and tracking of the containers themselves (even the goods they held if less than container lot), and finally the need to have much greater acreage in terminal facilities for parking containers that awaited loading or shipment.[5]

The need for a new terminal and sufficient acreage in San Francisco had become an urgent matter for APL management as early as 1969. Across San Francisco Bay in Oakland, Ben Nutter, the driving, imaginative manager of that city's new Port Commission, for some time had been touting its benefits as a container port for APL's new fleet. And Oakland had much to recommend itself as APL's home port.

Oakland was a terminus of all the major east-west and north-south railroad systems—the Santa Fe, the Western Pacific, and the Southern Pacific. The Southern Pacific was the only railroad line that served San Francisco directly, and much of the cargo landed at the port of San Francisco had to be barged across to Oakland for shipment north and east, an added cost in time, labor, and money. Land area around Oakland's harbor was flat and comparatively cheap, while land area surrounding San Francisco's waterfront was restricted, hilly, and expensive by comparison.

These facts and figures made an impression favorable to Oakland on some of APL's and Natomas's executives like Norman Scott, Bruce Seaton, and Chandler Ide. But Davies, usually so receptive to practical considerations, resisted Nutter's blandishments. When Cyril Magnin and the new mayor of San Francisco, Joseph Alioto, promised to construct a multimillion-dollar terminal with sufficient acreage for containers at Pier 94, Davies rejected any thought of a move to Oakland.

San Francisco had been the home port of APL and all its predecessor companies extending back to 1849. It had been Davies's home, his place of business, and he associated his fondest memories with the city. Not only did he take great pride in San Francisco's natural beauty, its cultural activities and amenities, but Natomas's ownership of the International Building in the Financial District gave him a financial stake in its continuing growth and prosperity. Magnin, the department store magnate and a social leader in San Francisco, was a good friend of the Davies family. He was also president of the San Francisco Port Commission. His arguments in favor of San Francisco as the coming port on the West Coast for containerships easily persuaded Davies and his wife, Louise, who, like her husband, was proud of the city.

When Ide became the head of Natomas, he may have had some doubts about San Francisco as opposed to Oakland as APL's home port, but Magnin and Alioto presented him with the plans for a multimillion-dollar facility and an agreement on behalf of the city to have construction completed in three years. Reluctantly, Ide and Fowler signed for APL at a brief ceremony in the mayor's office at the city hall. "And then," as Ide described it, "absolutely nothing happened; the city never performed, they never did make the engineering studies."[6]

After almost a year of procrastination on the part of San Francisco, the city of Oakland made what it termed its last proposal. The city had the land available, it had the funds to build the terminal, but if APL did not agree to accept its offer, Nutter indicated that the facility and the acreage would go to another line. Norman Scott, who had just taken over as president of APL, argued forcefully to Ide that the move be made. Others of the company's management made similar pleas. Though sympathetic to their arguments, Ide knew he would come under great pressure from the San Francisco advocates, influential businessmen, the city government, and Louise Davies.

But APL was facing a heavy loss, its first since 1939, and the savings were so obvious in Oakland's favor that he had little choice. "At that point," Ide said, "I decided, well, we will go to Oakland, because the future of APL is at stake here. The city of San Francisco had treated us shabbily, they had not made good on one, on any single one, of the undertakings that they entered into with this agreement."[7] After the decision, as Ide had expected, he had some uncomfortable moments while criticism rained down upon him. The boards of the two companies and their managements were solidly behind him, however, and he never wavered. "Anyway, we made the move," he said, "I think it was good, a very sound move."[8]

Ide had hardly settled himself in his new position of authority when, despite the reforms initiated in the management structure of APL and its operations, the company posted net losses of $10,093,519.[9] Efforts to identify the problem areas and to correct them were already underway when Ide decided that Fowler, with all of his shipping experience, was not measuring up to the new demands of containerization. A thoroughly likeable person and a good manager of the small, tightly knit operation of AML, Fowler had found it difficult to adjust to the far greater pressures and responsibilities of APL. Then too, the management problem that existed at APL when Fowler took over had undermined his confidence in himself. He found himself circumvented and frequently isolated from top authority. It was an exceedingly frustrating experience that Fowler bore with good grace.

Ide understood that situation well and resolved that Fowler be given complete authority at APL. But Fowler was not able to move

The APL Middle Harbor Terminal in Oakland, California. Two ships are shown alongside. The nearness to the yards of three transcontinental railroads is notable. (APL Archives.)

fast enough in coping with the problems that had accumulated over the past five years and at the same time to grapple successfully with the technological changes that were reshaping the company.[10] Unquestionably Natomas shareowners would look askance at the losses that were accruing quarter after quarter in 1973; a change in the top management of APL was indicated. Fowler resigned in April 1973. Norman Scott, the pleasant, experienced and perceptive shipping specialist in the Natomas organization, seemed an ideal choice. He replaced Fowler on 1 May 1973.[11]

Scott moved rapidly to make important policy changes. He pushed hard and successfully for the move of APL from San Francisco to Oakland. With the help of Warner Gardner and the strong

Bruce Seaton, president, American President Lines, 1977– ; president and chief executive officer, American President Companies, 1983– , and chairman of the board, 1984– . (APL Archives.)

support of Ide, he worked out a merger of AML into APL. As Scott explained it, "The economies of scale were such that that little company was going to get eaten alive. That plus APL was going to be better than the sum of the two components. And if they remained as individuals, one of them was going to go down the drain."[12]

Robert E. Benedict, AML's president, joined the Everett Steamship Company, which had acted as agents for AML in the Far East. Ide had insisted that Benedict, who had done a good job as president of AML, be offered the post of executive vice president of APL. But he found too many imponderables in a situation where it seemed obvious that Scott was not the type of executive who would delegate authority.[13]

Scott also tackled the problem of the round-the-world service, which was incurring heavy losses. Since the closure of the Suez Canal in 1967, the vessels no longer called at Mediterranean ports and sailed thousands of extra miles around the Cape of Good Hope to the east coast of the United States. He assigned Henry Kozlowski, a Polish-born, Scottish-educated naval architect whom he had known at Matson and who had done some troubleshooting for Natomas before he joined APL, to the task of analyzing all APL services and coming up with a recommendation.

With respect to the round-the-world services while the Suez Canal remained closed, Kozlowski worked out an ingenious solution that restructured the service in such a way that a completely containerized service operated out of the same ports as formerly but eliminated the need for six vessels on the route. He accomplished this feat by having two vessels assigned as feeders or bridges between Indonesian ports, Malaysia, Sri Lanka, India, and Pakistan by relaying containers to the Atlantic/Straits service in Singapore. The profitless thousands of miles of steaming from Pakistan around the Cape of Good Hope were eliminated, while at the same time the round-the-world coverage was continued with improved service.[14]

The results of the reforms Ide and Scott initiated very soon registered themselves on the balance sheets of APL. These moves, together with the delivery of the four Pacesetters well over a year beyond their contract delivery date, brought in a net profit for the year 1974 of $10,835,000. But profits of 4.8 percent of gross revenues were far too low, considering the huge investment in capital equipment of some $254,216,000 over the years.[15] Management at Natomas was pleased that Scott had for the time being reversed the losing trend. Ide was not satisfied with such low profit margins, however, and Seaton, who was keeping a careful watch on financial performance, wondered whether the capital tied up in APL might not be better employed elsewhere, especially in the oil business. Moreover the restriction MARAD placed upon its assets and its profitability meant that funds paid out in the form of dividends to Natomas were strictly controlled.

Since Scott seemed to be pulling the company together, Ide turned his attention to Natomas. He was approaching his sixty-fifth birthday and was anxious to be relieved of some of the responsibilities that had evolved over thirty years of high-pressure work with the restless, frequently difficult Davies, and now the crushing burden of the Natomas Company. As he remarked, "I did not have the ambition like some people perhaps do, to die in my tracks. I figured that, come the end of a reasonable period of time, somebody else should have a chance. So I wanted to get everything neatened up and put it in competent hands."[16]

Ide felt that there were some defects in Natomas's top management. And given his inclinations at the time, he preferred to bring in as chief executive officer a person whose experience had been entirely outside of Natomas, but who knew the oil business and who had the particular leadership qualities he thought essential for the company. Seaton recommended his former superior at Douglas Oil and Occidental, Dorman Commons.

Commons had recently resigned from Occidental and set up an independent consulting company, but he was available. Ide talked with him and was impressed by his pleasant manner and wide range of interests. Commons was a native Californian who had grown up in a Central Valley farming community. A Stanford graduate and, like Seaton, an accountant by profession, Commons had devoted his spare time to community activities while he rose to positions of leadership at Douglas and Occidental. Ide was completely frank with Commons about his desire to play a less active role in Natomas. He also sketched out his understanding of the problems besetting the company despite its rising profit margins. The two men agreed that Commons should join Natomas as a full-time consultant for a year before any decision was made. However,

Dorman L. Commons, chairman of the board, American President Lines, 1973–83; president, Natomas Company, 1974–83. (Photo courtesy of Dorman L. Commons.)

Ide had him elected to the Natomas board of directors and made a member of its executive committee.[17]

Commons went to Indonesia and came back with the report that at the price of oil at the then-current level of $3.65 a barrel, the small Natomas fields were "marginal operations at best." The world price of oil would have to go up by a dollar a barrel, or about 35 percent, before he thought the economics of the fields would be substantially profitable. A few months after Commons's return in December 1973 after the second Suez crisis, oil prices had advanced to $10.00 a barrel and were increasing in value by almost a dollar a month.

What was good news for Natomas was distinctly bad news for APL. The reopening of the Suez Canal in the spring of 1973 brought about another restructuring of APL's round-the-world service with the usual initial problems in APL's operations. The skyrocketing price of fuel oil, too, dealt a heavy blow to the company's profitability.

Commons had been analyzing APL's profile. Even without the instability of the Middle East and its impact on APL's operations, he viewed the line as a dubious economic enterprise. As he explained:

> APL had been in and out of profits. . . . The total profits over that ten year period, as I recall, were something like $30–35 million—$3 million, $4 million a year average. And I didn't know anything about the transportation business, and it was subsidized to the tune of between $35–$50 million a year, and I didn't particularly like that kind of an operation. So I wasn't particularly intrigued by the shipping side.[18]

At the end of his consulting year, Commons decided to remain with Natomas. In general he found good management strength in the company. He knew that he could rely on Seaton and W. Brandt Brooksby, Natomas's controller. He got along well with Ide, whom he respected as a man of integrity and of liberal sentiments that resembled his own. He was particularly taken with his grasp of Natomas's many and varied interests. As for Ide, he found in Commons an energetic, broad-minded executive with penetrating insights about financial matters, easy in his personal relationships but with an air of command. Commenting on Commons many years later, Ide said:

> The chemistry was good. Put it that way. I liked his style and I liked his ideas and his experienced views on the various problems that we had. And so, the following year I put him in as president and chief executive officer. And it left me in the role as chairman of the board. And I have never regretted it. It is very difficult, on the basis of just having lunch or dinner, or meeting a person a few times, but here I had about a year to work with

him and to talk to him about the direction that he thought the company ought to go to prosper.[19]

Commons reshuffled the top management of Natomas's Indonesian subsidiary IIAPCO, and in line with his plans to improve Natomas's stake in domestic energy resources, he initiated a new program of acquisition and development.

None of these events affected APL for the time being. Norman Scott remained president and chief executive officer of the company and a member of Natomas's executive committee. But the renewed emphasis on expanding Natomas's energy investments, besides creating an insistent demand for new capital, pointed up the essential incompatibility of the shipping component in a company increasingly devoted to energy resources.

Yet APL seemed to be operating better than it had for some years. Scott's reforms had helped, particularly the merger with AML, but in effect the configuration of the company had been set when he took over. Scott gave full credit to Davies for pushing the company into containerization, though the Fowler-Biehl interlude of mixed management had been unable to position the company so as to take full advantage of the efficiencies containerships brought to its operations. Scott saw his mission as bringing in experienced people, in his case from Matson; Les Harlander in operations, Henry Kozlowski in planning, and later Gordon Bart in marketing. Scott described what his new management team sought to accomplish:

> First the scheduling of the ships, the layout of the terminals, the control of equipment, the dissemination of traffic information, the coordination of marketing and traffic. Even the definition of what traffic means. . . . What we did was basically try to set up an operations entity which was responsible for the ships and traffic, which was operating the shore equipment, the containers and the chassis; and the marketing people who priced it and sold it all. And each of these three guys reported to me. And we had a pretty good organization going. These people had all cut their teeth with Matson. All of them had been involved with the Hawaiian trade. All of them had had some exposure in some depth to this venture into the foreign trade of the Far East.[20]

With the fleet largely containerized and port facilities on its routes equipped to handle the ships, Scott, Harlander, and Kozlowski concentrated on improving the company's electronic data capability for expediting the movement of cargo over national boundaries—that is, computerizing the complex documentation required for the export and import of goods and the tracking of ships and containers. Scott made a clean sweep of the existing systems department and arranged for Ross Perrot's Electronic Data Systems Company (EDS) to develop the software, which turned out to be a wise decision. EDS was making considerable progress in this vitally important area when the Suez Canal reopened in 1975.

Although the international trade situation was in a state of flux, Scott began repositioning APL's fleet so that elements would again sail through the Red Sea, the Suez Canal, and call at Mediterranean ports enroute to the East Coast of the United States. He was motivated partly by anticipated profits, partly by a desire to extract maximum potential from the new containerships. But the heavy expenses of rescheduling, marketing, and lost cargo space while the ships were being rerouted could not be justified by the available cargo market of the round-the-world service, even with the substantial savings from containerized transportation.

Competition was far more intense than it had been before 1967, and rate cutting and rebating—especially in the Mediterranean—were widespread.[21] Net losses of $2,608,000 were incurred for 1975 and dividends that had supplied almost $2 million in cash to Natomas for the previous year were cut to $90,000. Scott sensed that Commons and other board members were in a mood to dispose of APL if a fair price could be obtained.

Under the impression that he had the authority, early in 1975 Scott approached Signal, which still owned 47 percent of APL's stock and worked out an understanding whereby Signal would make an offer for Natomas's 53 percent of the company's stock. While Commons was pondering the Signal offer and another bid for APL from Joseph Alioto, Brooksby, Natomas's controller, was also studying the possible sale. He came to the conclusion that neither offer should be accepted until it was definitively established whether the controlling interest in APL should be sold and, if so, whether the price offered was adequate. He convinced Commons that nothing should be done until an outside evaluation of APL's worth was made. Thus Commons was not prepared to accept the Signal buyout offer when Scott presented it, and the deal fell through.[22] In fact, Signal suddenly lost all interest in purchasing the line, but indicated that it would be happy to sell its shares to Natomas, or if Natomas could find a customer, it would also join in the sale of its shares. Seaton, who had long been critical of the profitability of APL and shipping lines in general, urged that Natomas dispose of the company. Commons agreed with him.[23] But how he might arrange a sale was another matter. Despite Scott's proposal and Alioto's bid, which was also rejected, APL was not that salable, as Commons soon discovered.

After two years of watching APL's operating results swing drastically from modest profit to sharp losses, Commons had finally decided that something had to be done and concluded that an analysis should be made of APL. He began by having an in-house corporate development group make a study in depth. "Okay," he said, "Let's lay out a program here to really study it, not just the company but the whole industry. Let's understand the context in which it operates, let's understand how it stands in relation to that context, how it is in relation to its competitors, and what we ought to do." As a result of the study, Commons found that

> There had been no long range planning. . . . Most of the port facilities were on either public ports or short-term leases or whatever. They had just not thought in terms of this as a long-term on-going business. . . . Originally they had made some good decisions to convert from bulk-type operations to containerized operations, and they paid the price. They were leasing most of their equipment, not owning it, which, in retrospect, was not a good decision. . . . But they were simply not competitive. Their organization was poor. . . .[24]

He initiated a search for a competent consulting firm, and after interviewing a number of qualified consultants, he selected the Boston company, Temple, Barker and Sloane, which specialized in the management problems of the shipping industry. At the same time, he authorized a tax study by Arthur Andersen & Company in case Natomas should liquidate APL, and a third study by the legal firm of Lillick, McHose & Charles of the government's position, including the legal aspects if liquidation or sale were decided upon.[25]

Commons phoned Scott and informed him of the studies. He wanted the full cooperation of Scott's staff and assurance that he would make whatever changes were recommended and seemed appropriate. Scott assigned Kozlowski as APL's liaison with Temple,

Barker and Sloane.[26] He was responsible for many of its recommendations.

Following a year of intensive analysis, the three investigating groups in mid-1977 made reports that in some respects surprised Commons, Ide, and others of Natomas's top management. The tax consequences of sale or liquidation would be most costly and complex because they involved reserve funds on which taxes had been deferred for years, employee pension funds to which the company had contributed and had received tax credits, and other problems associated with the special relationship APL maintained with the government. A subsidized line, by law APL could be sold only to another American company. As expected, financial reporting and control were not as accurate or as systematic as they should have been, but Arthur Andersen's evaluation reported signs of improvement.

The surprising feature was that the Temple, Barker and Sloane report demonstrated that APL could be highly profitable if it divested itself of services that were losing money—the reinstituted round-the-world and the Atlantic/Straits routes—and concentrated on its trans-Pacific service. Temple, Barker and Sloane produced an array of figures that indicated rapid growth of ocean trade in the Pacific Basin, especially between the United States and Japan, South Korea, Taiwan, Malaysia, and the archipelagoes of Southeast Asia. It noted that with the exception of the ships of the Searacer class, the *President Lincoln* and *President Tyler,* APL had a modern, containerized fleet as advanced and efficient as any shipping line in the world. It had, in addition, a well-respected name, especially in the Far East. APL's management, however, could not seem to engage in the kind of planning and control that the advanced equipment and rapidly changing world markets warranted. The report identified five problem areas: (1) vessel utilization; (2) cargo handling expenses; (3) cargo equipment cost and overhead; (4) unprofitable routes; and (5) unprofitable fleet elements.

During 1974, a profitable year, APL's fleet sailed at only 58.2 percent of capacity. In 1976, another year of profitable returns, utilization had climbed to 73.8 percent. Sea-Land's performance on the same route during the same years had been 93.15 percent and 93.55 percent, respectively. U.S. Lines, another competitor, had even higher levels of utilization. Had the APL fleet used cargo capacity as effectively as its competitors, the report estimated, gross revenue would have been increased by well over $90 million in 1974 and over $70 million in 1976. Indeed, 7.4 percent of APL's container inventory in 1976 remained idle, while repositioning costs for empty containers increased sharply, some 76.7 percent between 1974 ($845,000) and 1976 ($6 million). The rise in overhead was due to inadequate tracking and positioning of containers relative to market demands.[27] The cost of procuring containers through short-term leasing as dictated by extravagant market forecasts was much too high when compared with the container inventory of other carriers. An excess of containers resulted in a loss estimated at $1.7 million in 1976.

Besides these shortcomings in management, the round-the-world service, which Scott reintroduced in 1975, had piled up heavy losses. Even more costly was the Atlantic/Straits service over and above subsidies. APL management had finally recognized that the Atlantic/Straits service should be terminated. After securing the requisite permission from MARAD, Scott discontinued it during the first half of 1976. But the round-the-world service was still operating when the report was made. Both of these unprofitable services should have been eliminated before they had cost the company over $20 million since 1973.

Finally, the report pointed out the extremely high cost of operating the Searacers, compared to other containerships in APL's fleet. It made no recommendation for action in this regard, but the implication was clearly in favor of disposing of these vessels even before their statutory life was up.[28] By eliminating the round-the-world service and some unprofitable feeder operations, three Master Mariners and the two Searacers could be sold for approximately $28.7 million.[29] The remainder of the fleet, which contained its most efficient ships, could then be deployed on what Temple, Barker and Sloane predicted would be the dynamically expanding markets of East Asia and Southeast Asia. In making forecasts of these markets, the report drew up a high and a moderate market growth scenario for 1978, assuming that the changes it recommended in equipment use and control were all made. The high-growth scenario estimated $24.4 million in operating profit before taxes, a full 56 percent more than APL's operating profits in 1976, its best year since 1967, and a year when it reported extraordinary gains from nonoperating items of $6.8 million. Even on a moderate growth prediction, profits were estimated at $19.5 million on revenues of $222.7 million, a significant increase. On the basis of the report Commons concluded that APL could be quite profitable if good management were instituted, together with the elimination of nonproductive routes, the sale of surplus ships, and concentration of all resources on the trans-Pacific service.

During this period, APL suffered its only loss of a ship since World War II. The *President Grant*, a Seamaster class vessel that had been built by Ingalls at Pascagoula in 1967 and converted to a full containership in 1972 at Los Angeles, went aground during impaired visibility at the entrance to the harbor of Keelung, Taiwan, on 1 September 1976. With severe bottom damage, the ship floated free, but salvage operations were unsuccessful when she broached and became impaled on another reef. There was no loss of life, but fewer than half of the sixty-six containers aboard were taken off by the salvage tug that came to her aid. At the end of September the company announced that it had abandoned efforts to refloat the ship and was proceeding with salvage operations. Insurance proceeds exceeded the depreciated book value of the ship and costs incurred, and the gain on her loss amounted to $4,450,000.

APL reported a net profit of $13,742,000 for 1976. More than half of the profits, however, were the result of two extraordinary items, the insurance settlement for the loss of the *President Grant* and penalties that Litton Shipyard paid for its failure to meet contract deadlines on the delivery of the Pacesetters. Thus the actual operations performance of APL seemed to bear out certain conclusions of the Temple, Barker and Sloane report that reflected on management.[30]

Scott resigned on 8 July 1977, putting Commons in a quandary about his replacement. He had instituted a search and had found that it was difficult to find someone with the requisite ability and experience to run APL. The fact that APL had had three chief executives in less than ten years, each one averaging a tenure of about three years, did not make the position especially attractive for an ambitious man of talent. Then too, Natomas was an energy company and prospective candidates could not help but speculate about its intentions regarding APL, which was, after all, not in its major field of interest. Commons also found that "the industry was not over-run with talent." As he explained, the shipping field had declined measurably over the years, a victim of wavering government policy and the declining position of the United States in world trade. "Good people had just not gravitated to it," he said, a statement that may have applied to APL, considering its checkered record, though not to such prosperous enterprises as Sea-Land.[31]

In any event, Commons could not find anyone that he considered had the potential to pull APL together. Then he turned to his own executive group, and after considering various possibilities, decided upon Bruce Seaton. Seaton had been on the board of APL for five years. As chief of Natomas's financial operations, he was thoroughly familiar with the profit-and-loss picture of APL and had formed an impression of management's shortcomings before the Temple, Barker and Sloane study. Though Seaton had spent most of his career specializing in financial matters, he had a flair for administration policy and procedure that Commons had admired during the many years they had been associated together. Clearly Seaton had executive qualities and a leadership presence, which, though an indefinable quality, was nevertheless recognizable to all who dealt with him. He also had an orderly, precise mind, developed over the years in sorting out complex and sometimes confusing financial information and formulating it into a cohesive policy. At fifty-two, he was in his prime as an executive: articulate, vigorous, ambitious, and not bashful about accepting responsibility.

Seaton had been the most forceful of the Natomas executives in his criticism of APL, the most persistent advocate of divestiture. Thus when Commons said, "Bruce, I want you to go over and temporarily run APL," he agreed, but he sought and received assurances that he could come back to the energy side of the business if he so desired. Seaton went over to 1950 Franklin Street, Oakland, APL's executive offices, in August 1977 and took charge as president and chief operating officer. Commons remained as chairman of the board and chief executive officer, but he gave Seaton free rein.[32]

Seaton's arrival was the signal for a change in policy. He found Henry Kozlowski and Gordon Bart completely overburdened with responsibilities. They had been left running a business that was inadequately staffed. For example, every branch office had its own directors of traffic, marketing, and operations, each of whom communicated directly to Bart or Kozlowski in Oakland. Scott had developed a highly and indeed overcentralized operation.[33]

Seaton recognized that he had much to learn about the shipping business, but he knew enough to be shocked at the management structure at APL. "It was obvious," he said, "as soon as you looked at it. You had 20–25,000 pieces of equipment . . . you have to keep track of it . . . and computerization was in a very rudimentary stage."

He discovered also that there was an acute shortage of skilled managerial personnel to operate a large shipping firm that was faced with what he perceived to be a technological revolution. Under Scott's management policy, key personnel had either been discharged or had not been replaced when they left the company.[34]

One of Seaton's first moves was to ease Kozlowski's and Bart's responsibilities. Kozlowski was managing traffic, planning, and operations. Bart's marketing department had no geographical divisions. A staff of twenty-five in Oakland controlled directly all the regions in the world that APL served. Dorman Commons managed to hire away from Sea-Land one of its top operations executives, William B. Hubbard, who had been general manager of Sea-Land's containership service to Viet Nam, including the building at Cam Ranh Bay of the largest container terminal in the entire world. Hubbard came in as senior vice president of operations. Then Seaton decentralized Bart's marketing department along regional lines and assigned T. J. Rhein and S. F. Schmidt as regional vice presidents for North America and South Asia, respectively. Rhein, an attractive younger member of the APL organization, had been with the firm since 1967 and had acquitted himself well in cost analysis before becoming a marketing specialist.

For the important area of Japan, Korea, Taiwan, the Philippines, and Hong Kong, Seaton chose J. Hayashi, who was born and raised in Japan and whose father had been associated with APL in Kobe since the prewar years. When he was eighteen years old, Hayashi came to the United States to study agriculture and business first at Cal State-Fresno and then at Armstrong College in Berkeley. Though he could only speak a few words of English when he arrived in California, he became fluent in the language within two years. In January 1964 he joined APL as a translator for Japanese passengers on the trans-Pacific route. Hayashi was later promoted to purser and made several voyages in the *President Roosevelt* when she was used as a cruise ship. He also made six round-the-world voyages. With his pleasant personality and by now thorough knowledge of shipboard freight and passenger procedures, Hayashi was given his first shore job selling freight space in northern California. He was particularly effective with Japanese customers both in the United States and abroad. Japan at the time was experiencing very rapid economic growth and was becoming increasingly important to APL as a market for American commodities such as cotton, pulp, raw hides, high unit-value nonferrous scrap metal, scrap paper, and refrigerated fruits and vegetables. In 1972 Hayashi was placed in charge of sales for southern California.

When Scott and Ide merged APL with AML, Hayashi was sent to Japan. His mission was to consolidate APL's and AML's agencies in the Far East. In line with his centralizing policy, Scott decided to create an agency company, headquartered in Japan, that would combine the services of Everett Steamship Company and APL's branch offices. All the details of establishing and staffing this new company under Japanese law were left up to Hayashi.

In the short period of five months, Hayashi had overcome all local opposition and bureaucratic obstacles and had created a smoothly functioning organization called APL-Everett Agencies, Ltd. with 125 employees operating out of Tokyo, Yokohama, Kobe, and Osaka. Robert Benedict, who had gone to Everett from AML after the merger with APL, became head of the new agency company as well as continuing with Everett. Hayashi stayed on directing its financial operations. When Benedict left Everett and the agency company, Hayashi took advantage of his departure to point out to APL's management what he considered were the weaknesses in the agency concept. Management was impressed. It authorized dissolution of the agency and a return to the branch mode of marketing along lines Hayashi suggested.

From the beginning APL had a built-in conflict of interest with APL-Everett Agencies. But its greatest weakness was that it could not effectively capitalize on APL's name and goodwill, which meant much to its Asian customers. Hayashi liquidated the company with the same expertise he had shown in forming it. Scott made him head of the branch with the title director of sales for Japan and Korea. The Everett connection was now broken and direct identification with APL reinstated.

Marketing for North Asia, however, was still controlled directly from Oakland with little functional autonomy permitted at the regional level. When Seaton took over he reversed that policy. He promoted Hayashi to vice president and gave him wide latitude in developing sales. Hayashi overcame initial prejudice and in fact was able to make some major changes such as moving APL's Asian headquarters office from Japan to Hong Kong, where overhead was less and where communications with Southeast Asian markets and West Asia are better. Hayashi soon was brought back to the United States as a senior vice president in charge of all corporate functions and then executive vice president and chief operating officer of APL.

Besides adding more executives to APL's marketing effort and dividing it up into regions that had a large measure of local control, Seaton strengthened management capability in other aspects of APL's overall structure. He brought in Richard L. Tavrow as vice president, general counsel, and secretary of the company to replace J. Donald Kenny; he also promoted Charles Deering to chief of vessel operations under Hubbard, whom he encouraged to build up management strength in operations. But Seaton had not been on board six months when near-disaster struck.

The winter of 1977 had unfortunate consequences for all domestic transportation in the United States. Massive blizzards swept over most of the nation, closing major highways and interrupting rail services. Strikes in the Northeast and Middle West complicated further a difficult situation. Temporarily the entire transportation system of the United States east of the Rockies was shut down. APL had thousands of containers on the railroads but no control over their ultimate destination or in fact their routing, once they had been delivered to the appropriate carriers.

By this time, the company was developing an electronic data system for traffic control. At great cost and many painful steps, and over a three-year period, the complex documentation required by foreign governments and agencies of the American government for the import and the export of goods was being computerized. The lengthy bills of lading that had been the responsibility of hundreds of employees on ship and shore, and had been processed manually, were now about to be handled by a fraction of the personnel, at a fraction of the time, and with far higher accuracy than formerly. Strides had been made not just in the electronic tracking of equipment, but also in utilizing bills of lading data to identify the particular cargo carried in a particular container, its routing, its destination and its consignee. It was to be a comprehensive traffic control system, but it had a major weakness: its software was being designed specifically for ocean transportation. And, like all highly computerized systems, it was vulnerable to breakdown should any of its major components fail to function in programmed sequence.

What APL management had failed to do was extend its traffic control within the confines of the United States. In fact, the company had but one executive in the management group who specialized in land transportation. APL had not become a truly intermodal transportation company that interacted completely with the land link of the network, the railroads and the trucks. After its ships discharged their containers onto railroad cars or truck chassis at West Coast terminals, the company's complete surveillance ended. It was now the responsibility of the railroads and the trucking companies to deliver the containers to their destination. The information APL and other shipping companies sent along with their containers was not compatible with the waybills and other documentation used by domestic transportation companies. Railroads, in particular, were not comfortable with the form and content of the instructions the shipping industry supplied. When the domestic transportation networks were running smoothly, containers routed through their traffic systems arrived at their destinations, though not always at the dates and times the shipping lines specified. But when blizzards and strikes slowed and finally shut down large segments of the nation's ground transportation, the railroads lost control of the containers. William B. Hubbard, APL's new operations head, said,

> Most of them [the railroads] didn't know what they were doing with a lot of the paperwork dealing with international traffic. Then as their ramps began to clog [and they] couldn't get them plowed open, they started moving cars around, trying to find ramps that were clear in order to free up equipment because the whole world of containers was beginning to show up in the New York area and nothing was leaving. Moving the cars only made things worse as the railroads didn't move the documents with the containers and the U.S. Customs would not allow cargo to be handled without proper documentation.

Commons, Seaton, Hubbard and Donald Orris, APL's director of intermodal operations, flew east and had an emergency meeting with the president of the Conrail System and his chief operating officials. It became obvious to them that the railroads would not change their traffic control to suit the requirements of the shipping industry. The only conclusion possible was that APL had to extend in some way its own procedure for tracking its containers to the domestic carriers. The company had to become intermodal in every sense of the word. As Hubbard explained it, "We began to evolve then into a strategy of self-destiny. We talked about it at first but then steadily we began to make it a policy that we had to control our own fate and our own destiny to the greatest possible extent."[35]

Seaton mobilized APL's specialists in cargo-handling operations, intermodal systems, and terminals and flew them east. After three months of crisis management, they cleaned up the confusion and enormous container jam in the greater New York area. A hard but necessary lesson had been learned. Never again, if APL's management could help it, would such a situation develop. Seaton directed Hubbard to bring domestic transport specialists into APL. He recruited heavily from the industry, concentrating on acquaintances whom he knew had capability and at Seaton's insistence were to be resilient in their thinking and ambitious for the quick recognition that APL was willing to accord them, but seasoned in their respective fields. It had been a taxing period for the new president, but he welcomed the challenge.

The new operations management team began to show favorable results almost at once. APL worked out a method of time-chartering trains with the railroads, the APL Linertrains that ran on predetermined schedules. Having suffered from a car shortage during prosperous years, it leased its own cars so as always to have equipment available. The company also acquired its own ramps at key transport centers. At Seaton's decision, APL's electronic tracking and documentation system was expanded throughout the United States and into Asia. Eventually its highly sophisticated computer facility would be able to direct less than container lots directly to customers.

Once it had become an overland carrier, APL's operations group developed various economies in the system. Most of its traffic was to industrial and population centers in the Northeast, Midwest, Southeast, and Middle Atlantic regions of the country. This flow of trade meant that thousands of containers would be returned empty. Equipment that had cost millions of dollars was being utilized up to a maximum of about 50 percent of capacity, not counting the charges for handling and returning the empties.

Loading containers on chassis to an APL Linertrain in Los Angeles, 1980. (APL Archives.)

APL's intermodal department worked out a tripartite agreement with the large shipping forwarder Transway, whereby it undertook to secure container freight from the highly industrialized regions of the country for consumption in the Southwestern and Western United States, the area of rapid population growth known as the Sunbelt. Of course, this method had to be sold to both Transway and the railroads, which had been shipping freight on piggyback trailers. But forwarders like Transway had been in the same predicament as APL, though for them it had been even costlier since they had to get their trailers back. By guaranteeing the return of thousands of high unit-value, filled containers, APL managed to secure rate reductions and very nearly complete utilization of its containers and rental earnings for the use of its equipment.

A company that had never earned more than $12 million a year in net profits was now averaging $45 million a year under Seaton's leadership. As he himself has described it, "In a period of three years, we went from the worst intermodal operator in the country to the best." It took, however, a total commitment from Seaton who communicated his energy, air of decision, and special sense of mission to the entire organization. "I felt very productive," he said, "because I was totally concentrated in turning the thing around. . . . it wasn't the type of thing that in my constitution led to worries or anything like that. It was just a challenge."[36]

In part because Seaton needed a top executive to oversee the additional expenses incurred for the computers and software that these moves entailed, and in part because he needed a deputy to handle the mounting administrative and financial concerns of the company, he persuaded Commons to let him bring to APL W. Brandt Brooksby, Natomas's capable comptroller. One of Brooksby's first missions was to analyze the monitoring and control functions of APL's data processing systems and make recommendations. Brooksby became a senior vice president and a member of the board of APL. Like Seaton he also remained a member of Natomas's executive group.[37] Within a year or so Brooksby had mastered the complex data processing systems, identified their weaknesses and reorganized their management to utilize them efficiently and effectively.

The development of a complete intermodal system monitored by electronic data equipment brought about significant economies in operations and raised utilization of containerships to near 100 percent outbound and from 80 to 90 percent inbound. Although ocean freight rates in the Pacific declined some 30 percent between 1976 and 1981, APL was able to make substantial profits, in part because its management was paying proper attention to the size and design of its replacement vessels and to the terminals that would accommodate them. Seaton had quickly grasped the central problem that beset not only APL but much of the shipping industry.

As he saw it, the industry had not faced up to the full implications of containerization and the appropriate logistics that this implied. Companies like Sea-Land, Maersk, and Matson had begun to respond in the late sixties to the unique demands of containerization. Sea-Land in particular had recognized that a technological revolution was sweeping the industry. APL, too, had begun to identify some of its fundamental aspects. In the early seventies Norman Scott had started to develop procedures that were consistent with rapid technical changes. But, unfortunately, APL was still weighed down by custom and tradition. Even its most forward-looking managers were unable to comprehend integrated transportation systems in their fullest aspect.

Seaton recognized this weakness in the company and devoted himself initially to overcoming what he perceived to be a built-in inertia. His solution was marked by a fundamental change that defined logistics as a specific managerial function requiring senior management specialists who could develop a depth and breadth of capability in this area throughout the organization. To that end he began recruiting a new management group of transportation specialists both inside and outside of the shipping business. At the same time he pushed hard for the further development of highly sophisticated electronic data systems that he felt were essential if his company were to compete successfully. Though capital expenditures rose rapidly, so did earnings as the strengthened management group under Seaton's direction began to understand and implement the powerful tools at their disposal. Seaton insisted that managers be not only experts in their own specific areas, but flexible enough to switch jobs as a means of broadening experience with a minimum of adjustment.

A carefully orchestrated decentralization became the guiding policy with maximum responsibilities assigned to individual managers. In retrospect Seaton admitted that adoption of the new order had been difficult. But he thought that the shipping industry had done "a lot better job in adjusting to change than the steel industry or the automobile industry or the chemical industry in adapting to new technology and foreign competition."[38]

While APL was beginning to realize the full potential of intermodal transportation, it was replacing its older vessels with big, fast containerships, the C8 class. APL had purchased from a bankrupt PFEL its three 26,000-ton LASH ships, which had been converted to container vessels at bargain prices and without the usual financial assistance from the government. Minor structural changes were made at the Bethlehem shipyard in San Francisco that brought their cargo capacity up to 1,856 twenty-foot equivalent containers.[39]

At the same time that the landbridge service across the North

American continent was being developed and perfected, operations of the company's ships in the Pacific were the subject of careful consideration. The money-losing round-the-world service had been abandoned in 1977. Containerships from Oakland, Los Angeles, and Seattle made the crossing to Yokohama on twelve-day schedules. They served directly ports in Japan, South Korea, Taiwan, as well as Hong Kong. Some proceeded further west to Singapore, Colombo, and ports in India and Pakistan. Company ships were assigned to the "Singapore Swing," which was a service operating out of Singapore that carried containers brought there from the United States to Indonesia, Malaysia, Sri Lanka, India, Pakistan, and on to Arabian Gulf ports. In addition to using APL ships for services, "feeder" connections were offered to Australia and to other ports around the northern rim of the Indian Ocean in vessels of other owners with whom firm arrangements for connections had been made.

Acquisition of the converted LASH vessels was just the first round in the replacement of smaller containerships with faster, larger vessels that could also be more fuel-efficient, now that the OPEC-dictated price of fuel oil had risen to over $30 a barrel in the fall of 1980. APL's engineering department was already working on a new design, the C9, for a 50,000-ton (displacement) containership that would be propelled not by fuel-extravagant steam turbine power plants but by fuel-efficient diesel engines. However, arguments that developed over the design within the engineering department became so heated that Seaton decided he needed outside counsel.

Les Harlander seemed a logical choice to resolve the impasse. He had directed the company's containership fleet conversion programs and initiated the preliminary design for new ships when he headed APL's operations department under Norman Scott. He had other qualifications as well. Perhaps more than any naval architect in the nation, Harlander was responsible for the original containership design, and the design and development of gantry container cranes. And he was available, living in semi-retirement at nearby Richmond, California, where he was managing his own boatyard and engaging in engineering consulting work. Seaton drove out to Richmond in June 1978 and explained the situation in APL's engineering and planning. Would Harlander be willing to join APL as a consultant and head the program? Harlander agreed and put together a team consisting of among others, Eugene K. Pentimonti, director of engineering, and Charles Deering, vice president, marine operations.

Harlander quickly managed to settle all the outstanding disputes. Contract plans and detailed specifications were prepared; shipyard bids had been solicited when Dorman Commons became concerned at the huge capital investments that would be necessary, some $150 million for a three-ship program after the government-subsidized construction differential. Even though favorable financing was available through government-guaranteed merchant marine bonds and mortgages, the down payment was considerable and the interest charges would represent a drain upon earnings over future years.

Commons decided that it would be a far better investment for APL to convert to full containerships the C5s it had taken over from AML when the two lines merged than to contract for new ones. He stopped all engineering work and all the implementation of the contracting for the construction of the C9s and directed Harlander and his team to develop bid specifications for the C5s to be converted. But MARAD refused to accept the converted ships for subsidized operation. Thus Commons had to reverse himself and approve the original concept. Though they had lost valuable time and had to meet a strict deadline set by MARAD, Harlander and his team had their plans and specifications ready. They were able to negotiate both a construction contract with a shipyard and a favorable construction differential subsidy [CDS] rate with MARAD in time.

Probably the most challenging aspect of the design and construction program was to introduce a 42,300 H.P. slow-speed diesel propulsion plant in lieu of steam turbine propulsion called for in the plans and specifications. Because of the rapid increases in the price of fuel at the time, which was making fuel-efficient diesel propulsion very attractive, APL had negotiated into the contract a provision that permitted it to change from steam to diesel propulsion one month after contract signing. No marine diesel engines of this size and capacity had ever been built in the United States. While large diesel engines had been manufactured in Europe and Japan under license for years, steam-turbine power plants had been standard marine equipment in the United States. But in order to qualify for subsidy, at least part of the power plant had to be manufactured in the United States, in this case under license from a European company. MARAD would not approve of any foreign licensing agreements until it saw and approved a detailed manufacturing plan that identified the facilities to be used and specified the engine components and the percentages to be manufactured by the American company.

The Harlander team had one month after entering contract to complete cost studies using Natomas's best forecasts of future fuel prices, compare diesel versus steam power plant performances, analyze each of the three European diesel engines proposed for the C9s, and prepare preliminary plans and specifications to assist the shipyard in developing a fixed price for a cost change while also working with the yard on the steam plant development in case the diesel option did not prove economically feasible. They chose a design developed by Sulzer, a large Swiss concern. Allis-Chalmers, the American company they selected, entered into a licensing agreement to build the unit. MARAD approved the plans for the Sulzer/Allis-Chalmers engines. But there were two more obstacles. APL engineering and marine operations department had to prepare the cost estimates and the operating data necessary for an economic feasibility study to be made by the planning department and by Temple, Barker and Sloane that would justify an additional $10 million the diesel engines would cost over conventional steam turbines. "We did everything we could to get our arms around this total diesel propulsion project" said Harlander. There were many additional questions to be resolved besides the economic ones. Harlander has summarized them: "How do we corner all the bases of concern within APL? Crew manning, union agreements, training programs and new shoreside maintenance programs had to be developed by Charlie Deering. How do you do all these things? Well, you have to at least delineate them enough so you can cost them out and see what you are getting into."

Seaton set up a new vessel coordinating committee, which he chaired. Pentimonti and Harlander would identify the problems not just in the power plant but in the overall construction program and if necessary Seaton would see to it that they were referred to the appropriate departments for action. In this way all aspects of the program were coordinated and implemented to the satisfaction of APL management. MARAD followed suit, approving the hull, the power plant and all the hundreds of subsystems and components that went into the vessels, though not without lengthy negotiations.[40] Contracts were awarded in 1978 to Avondale Shipyards of New Orleans for three C9s, the *President Lincoln*, the *President Washington*, and the *President Monroe*.

The decision to go ahead with the C9s immediately focused atten-

President Lincoln [III]. One of the three diesel-powered containerships built for APL in 1982–83. She is 860 feet long and measures 40,627 gross tons. Here she is shown proceeding to sea from San Francisco on her maiden voyage. (APL Archives.)

In 1984, APL introduced precedent-breaking lightweight rail equipment—cars capable of carrying containers stacked two high. These company-owned trains now crisscross North America, connecting with vessel calls on the West Coast, and carrying both international and domestic cargo.

tion on the facilities necessary to support these huge ships, each of which would have a capacity of 2,500 twenty-foot equivalent containers. Terminals claimed first attention, and Hubbard headed the company's program to enlarge and equip them. He negotiated the agreement APL made with the Port of Seattle and by 1983, the company had the largest and finest port facility in the Northwest. The Oakland terminal was already equipped to handle the anticipated increase in containers. But the Los Angeles expansion required some tough negotiations with the city's harbor department before agreement was reached. Los Angeles had property available that was too large for one operation but not large enough for two busy container terminals.

While discussing the problem with Ernest L. "Roy" Perry, director of the Port of Los Angeles, Hubbard came up with the idea that APL take over the total facility and become the manager, securing tenants and leasing them space as well as other terminal facilities. Hubbard said:

> Roy, why don't we take the piece of real estate that you have? You want to move the greatest number of boxes through L.A. that you can. And as an operator, I am interested in a very efficient terminal with one gate and one administration building. Piers that we can share. One maintenance facility that we can share; and we will become the terminal operator, and will jointly try to find other tenants, but we will manage to maximize the "throughput" in that facility instead of developing it into three facilities that are all basically inefficient. We will rationalize it.

Perry was convinced and eventually APL became what is known in the industry as the "anchor tenant" of the 115-acre facility in San Pedro, the Port of Los Angeles. The terminal itself would be capable of accommodating 5,000 twenty-, forty- or forty-five foot containers. "If all goes right and we get the tonnage that we think is built into the formula," said Hubbard, "we will run a beautiful, big facility at zero cost." His prediction was overly optimistic. But overhead was being reduced when Seaton and Tom Bradley, the mayor of Los Angeles, dedicated the terminal on 24 May 1984.[41]

By then, Hubbard negotiated the "anchor tenant" status with the Port of Seattle and actively sought and secured subtenants in APL's newly enlarged container port facilities at Yokohama and Kobe, at

At Los Angeles Harbor, APL opened a new container terminal in 1984. This view looks eastward. Under the three cranes in the distance is one of the C9 ships. The terminal is the largest on the Pacific Coast with a capacity of 5,000 containers. In the foreground is the freight building, where goods are stuffed or broken out for less-than-containerload customers. (APL Archives.)

Hong Kong, Busan, Korea, Kaohsiung, Taiwan, and Manila. Through all these negotiations, Hubbard had the assistance of Ben Nutter as a consultant. Nutter was the man most responsible for making Oakland one of the leading container ports on the West Coast. He had just retired as director of the Port of Oakland.

With rare foresight APL decided that Kaohsiung would be its major port facility in the Far East. Midway between Japan and the South Asian ports, it was well located geographically for relay operations. Hubbard was hard pressed at first in making the case for expansion at Kaohsiung as APL was only making 20,000 moves a year at the time. In 1983, APL was making 200,000 moves through its

Kaohsiung terminal. When the facilities development program was completed, including a new port at Dutch Harbor, Alaska, and a terminal at Chicago for its intermodal business, APL had invested $600 million in new ships, terminals, electronic data processing equipment, containers, chassis, and railroad ramps.

Drawing on his experience with Sea-Land, Hubbard recommended to Seaton that APL organize its own stevedoring service that would not only provide the company with its longshoremen, crane operators, and the like, but might eventually sell its services to other lines. Seaton agreed and set up Eagle Marine, a separate company, "to make it," in Hubbard's words, "a little more palatable to some of the competitors that we would be serving some day." Eagle Marine in the latest reorganization is now responsible for terminal operations on the U.S. West Coast.[42]

Once Commons had made the decision for APL to contract for the C9s, he looked upon the company as a sound investment, albeit small, compared to Natomas's oil business. As such he concluded that it would be wise to buy out Signal's share of APL stock and those held by all minority stockholders with a new issue of approximately 1,688,000 shares of Natomas stock. Forrest Shumway, Signal's chairman and chief executive officer, agreed to the deal, which was consummated on 30 June 1979.

Net profits of APL rose to $59.2 million in 1979 and continued near that high point for the next three years. The new containerships, *President Washington*, *President Lincoln*, and *President Monroe*, were delivered and deployed during 1982 and 1983. They were soon followed by two more large and fast containerships, the *President F. D. Roosevelt* and *President Eisenhower*, that had been acquired from another company and modified to APL's specifications.

APL's experience with costly delays on the delivery of the C9s, running one year beyond their contract date, had furnished telling arguments for building ships abroad. High cost overruns on the C9s had convinced MARAD that American shipyards could not compete with foreign yards even after increased construction differential subsidies. After the Reagan administration removed construction differential subsidies from its 1981 budget and induced Congress to follow suit, it became only a matter of time, while this policy prevailed, before American President Lines would go abroad for new construction. When APL learned that the Lykes Lines, one of its major competitors, had received permission from MARAD to have a

A gantry crane loading containers aboard the *President Lincoln* (III). (APL Archives.)

President Eisenhower [II]. She and her sistership, the *President F. D. Roosevelt*, joined the fleet in 1984. They were the first APL ships built outside the United States, having been constructed in Japan in 1980. (APL Archives.)

number of its new ships built in foreign shipyards, it sought equal treatment, which was granted. Within carefully prescribed limits, subsidized lines like APL were permitted to purchase ships abroad.

Meanwhile the future for Natomas seemed as secure as any business could be that was involved in two sensitive international operations, oil exploration and production, and ocean transportation. Despite some unfortunate investments in domestic oil and coal resources, Dorman Commons was satisfied that he had made the right decisions for Natomas and APL over the long term. As for APL, major credit for its achievement must go to Seaton, who had quickly grasped the essential aspects of the changing shipping industry. In specific terms he had designed an organizational structure along geographic lines. APL's market areas were North America, North Asia, and South Asia. Within each of these geographic divisions, he created market areas of regional responsibility.

The shipping industry, he had early recognized, also required generalists rather than specialists in top management positions. APL executives should be able to run a terminal, deal with customers, manage complex logistics, and have some expertise in financial matters and operations that would affect the entire corporation.

With these personal characteristics in mind, he began the difficult and delicate task of finding and tempting the many managers who would staff his new organization. He offered those who met his criteria an opportunity to take on major responsibility and share in the rewards of what he was now convinced would be a dynamically expanding company. But he warned potential managers that they would be involved in all facets of APL's business. They would be concerned not just with ships or with the ocean link, but with railroads and all other aspects of land transportation, including ultimate delivery to customers. As Seaton remarked, "In that way we attracted a lot of bright people into the company who were from good jobs elsewhere in the industry."[43]

When he had completed this phase of APL's management reconstruction, Seaton had in place a team that met his exacting standards of performance. He had in fact positioned the company to take full advantage of the great efficiencies that resulted from a wholly integrated sea and land transportation system.

In the fall of 1983, Chandler Ide retired after eight years as president and ten years as chairman of the board of Natomas. And soon thereafter the company sold at a very substantial gain Ralph Davies's monument, the International Building.

This deal had scarcely been concluded when Natomas was faced with a hostile takeover by the large Texas company, Diamond Shamrock Corp. Natomas had been preparing to counteract such a move for years, ever since its oil exploration and production in Indonesia had become profitable. It had a prominent New York law firm and two investment banking firms watching Wall Street moves. It had also lined up a $1 billion credit line to defend its interests should that become necessary.

The financial community had watched Natomas's spectacular rise in oil and gas revenues, but had never understood its real estate operations or its ownership of APL. Its stock, therefore, had been consistently undervalued, a cause of concern to Commons, because its low price-earning ratio made it especially attractive for acquisition. Yet when rumors of a Diamond Shamrock tender reached San Francisco, Commons at first refused to believe them. After they had indeed proven true, he had several options, but all of them, he felt, after careful consideration, would come close to bankrupting the company.

As it turned out, Diamond Shamrock was willing to bargain and had no interest in APL or the real estate properties. An agreement was reached whereby APL and Natomas's real estate would be spun off to be formed into a separate, independent company. The tender was also increased sufficiently so that Commons, considering the costly alternatives of opposition, thought it represented a fair offer for the oil, gas, and coal business. On 1 September 1983 the deal was completed. APL retained its name, but its parent organization became American President Companies. Seaton was elected its president and chief executive officer, and it began again to do business on its own.[44]

The shipping line had come full circle, returning to what it had been prior to 1956, again pursuing its own destiny as it had done before. The way had been tortuous since William Aspinwall decided to speculate on the future of California at the close of the Mexican War. The cast of characters had been large and interesting, men ranging from New York merchants to Wall Street speculators, railroad magnates, timber barons, and oilmen. At times in its colorful history APL came close to disappearing as a transportation company and a factor in the economic growth of the West. But APL survived and eventually prospered to become one of the strongest and best-managed shipping companies flying the American flag. Its future, insofar as any company's future can be assessed in a perilous world, has never been brighter.

NOTES

1. Twenty-two hundred in APL, five hundred in AML, the balance in Natomas and other subsidiary companies; "Container Financing Package," 7 March 1972, APL Archives.

2. Ide, "Oral History Transcript (I)" 3, 4; W. G. MacDonald and D. V. Reardon, "Past and Present President ships of the American President Lines, Ltd., and Predecessor Companies," APL Archives, passim; *Gangway,* March/April 1972, p. 2.

3. "Container Financing Package," 7 March 1972, APL Archives.

4. Ibid.

5. Ibid.

6. Ide, "Oral History Transcript (I)," 126, 127; (II), 13, APL Archives.

7. Ibid.; Dorman Commons, "Oral History Transcript," 10, APL Archives.

8. Ide, "Oral History Transcript (II)," 13, 14, APL Archives.

9. American President Lines, Ltd., Annual Report 1973, Ide Collection.

10. Les Harlander, "Oral History Transcript," 24, APL Archives.

11. Natomas Company, Annual Report 1973, Ide Collection.

12. Scott, "Oral History Transcript," 41, APL Archives.

13. Ibid., 42.

14. Henry Kozlowski, "Oral History Transcript," 6, 7, APL Archives. American President Lines, Ltd., Annual Report 1973.

15. American President Lines, Ltd., Annual Report 1974, Ide Collection.

16. Ide, "Oral History Transcript (II)," 8, 9, APL Archives.

17. Natomas Company, Annual Report 1973, Ide Collection.

18. Commons, "Oral History Transcripts (II)," 4, 5, APL Archives.

19. Ide, "Oral History Transcripts (II)," 8, 9, APL Archives.

20. Scott, "Oral History Transcript," 29, APL Archives.

21. Ibid.; Temple, Barker and Sloane, "Strategic Evaluation of American President Lines II," 22–28, APL Corporate Files.

22. Scott, "Oral History Transcript," 38, 39, APL Archives; John Niven, "Notes on Interview with W. Brandt Brooksby," 12 July 1984, Claremont, Calif.

23. Commons, "Oral History Transcript," 11, 12; Ide, "Oral History Transcript (II)," 6, 7, 16, APL Archives.

24. Commons, "Oral History Transcript," 6, 7, APL Archives.

25. Ibid.

26. Ibid.

27. Temple, Barker and Sloane, "Strategic Evaluation of American President Lines," 3–72, 17, APL Corporate Files.

28. Ibid., 27.

29. Ibid., 14.

30. APL News Release, 28 September 1976, APL Archives; *Seattle Post-Intel-*

ligencer, 10, 16, 17 September 1976; APL, "Notes to Consolidated Financial Statements," 31 December 1977, APL Archives.

31. Commons, "Oral History Transcript," 9, APL Archives.

32. Seaton, "Oral History Transcript," 1–7; Commons, "Oral History Transcript," 9–11; Natomas Company, Annual Report 1977, APL Archives.

33. T. J. Rhein, "Oral History Transcript," 28, APL Archives.

34. Seaton, "Oral History Transcript," 8, APL Archives.

35. W. B. Hubbard, "Oral History Transcript," 9, 10, APL Archives.

36. Seaton, "Oral History Transcript," 7, 11, APL Archives.

37. American President Lines, Ltd., Annual Report 1980, Yost Collection; Natomas Company, Annual Report 1980, Ide Collection; W. Brandt Brooksby, "Oral History Transcript," 22–28, APL Archives.

38. Seaton, "Oral History Transcript," 14, 15, APL Archives.

39. The ships were renamed the *President Grant, President Hoover,* and *President Tyler.* American President Lines, Ltd., Annual Report 1978, Yost Collection; MacDonald and Reardon, "Past and Present President Ships of the American President Line, Ltd., and Predecessor Companies."

40. Harlander, "Oral History Transcript," 40–46, APL Archives.

41. Hubbard, "Oral History Transcript," 26–27, APL Archives. American President Lines, News Release, 24, 25 May 1984, Yost Collection.

42. Hubbard, "Oral History Transcript," 32, 33, APL Archives.

43. Seaton, "Oral History Transcript," 16, 17, APL Archives.

44. Commons, "Oral History Transcript," 15–23, APL Archives.

APPENDIX A
SHIPS OF THE AMERICAN PRESIDENT LINES

This list is based largely on a compilation prepared by W. G. MacDonald and Captain D. V. Reardon, who had long careers in the service of the American President Lines. The dimensions given for ships are in order: length overall, beam and depth from keel to main deck.

Abbreviations and Symbols

APL	American President Lines
C. F. Bale	Capacity of cargo space in cubic feet measured to the inside of cargo battens, to tank top ceiling, and to underside of beams.
TEU	Twenty-foot equivalent
USAT	U.S. Army Transport

President Adams [I] ("502")
502 type, built 1921, Camden, N.J., by New York Shipbuilding Corp.
522'8" × 62' × 42', 10,496 gross tons.
Reciprocating steam engines, 14 knots.
Cargo: 445,800 cu. ft.; passengers: 153.
Ex-*Centennial State*. Renamed *President Adams* [I] 1922. Purchased by Dollar Steamship Lines from U.S. Shipping Board 1923. Transferred to APL 1938. Renamed *President Grant* [II] 1940. Grounded on Uluma Reef off New Guinea 26 February 1944. Declared a total loss 17 June 1944.

President Adams [II] (C3)
C3-P type, built 1941, Newport News, Va., by Newport News Shipbuilding and Drydock Co.
491'10" × 69'6" × 42'6", 9,260 gross tons.
Steam turbine, 16½ knots.
Cargo: 512,353 cu. ft.; passengers: 96, as planned for commercial operation by APL.
Acquired by U.S. Navy before delivery to APL. Renamed U.S.S. *President Adams* (APA 19). Decommissioned after World War II. In reserve merchant fleet, Suisun Bay, Calif., 15 December 1958. Sold to National Metals for scrapping, February 1973.

President Adams [III] (P2-S1-DN3)
V-2000 type, built 1952, Camden, N.J., by New York Shipbuilding Corp.
533'9" × 73' × 49', 14,000 gross tons. APL design.
Steam turbine, 19 knots.
Cargo: 570,000 cu. ft.; passengers: 228.
Acquired by U.S. Navy during construction, completed to Navy specifica-
   tions. Renamed U.S.S. *Geiger* (AP 197). After layup in Suisun Bay, Calif.,
   loaned to Massachusetts Maritime Academy in 1980 and renamed *Bay
   State*.

President Adams [IV] (C4-S-1h)
Mariner type, built 1953, Newport News, Va., by Newport News Ship-
   building and Drydock Co.
563' 7¾" × 76' × 44'6", 9,277 gross tons.
Steam turbine, 20 knots.
Cargo: 758,779 cu. ft.; passengers: 12.
Ex-*Palmetto Mariner*. Renamed *President Adams* [IV] 6 July 1956. Sold for
   scrap 25 January 1974. Broken up at Kaohsiung, Taiwan, 1974.

President Adams [V] (C5-S-75a)
C5 type, built 1968, Newport News, Va., by Newport News
   Shipbuilding and Drydock Co. (Hull No. 587).
605' × 82' × 46', 15,949 gross tons.
Steam turbine, 24,000-shaft horsepower, 20.8 knots.
Cargo: 1,082,207 C.F. Bale; 332 TEU containers, passengers: 12.
Ex-*Alaskan Mail*, American Mail Line. Renamed *President Adams* [V] 11 April
   1978.

President Arthur [I] (VC2-S-AP3)
Victory type, built 1945, Portland, Oreg., by Oregon Shipbuilding Corp.
455'3" × 62' × 38', 7,643 gross tons.
Steam turbine, 16½ knots.
Cargo: 483,309 cu. ft.; passengers: 4.
Ex-*Dartmouth Victory*. Renamed *President Arthur* 14 February 1951.
Renamed *Dartmouth Victory* 30 April 1959. Sold to American Mail Line 19
   September 1959. Renamed *Alaska Mail*. Turned in on new construction at
   Portland, 26 February 1965. Sold to Dwyer Steamship Co. and renamed
   Choctan Victory. Believed to have been scrapped 1968.

President Arthur [II] (C4-S-1p)
Mariner type, built 1952, Pascagoula, Miss., by Ingalls Shipbuilding Corp.
563' 7¾" × 76' × 44'6", 9,171 gross tons.
Steam turbine, 20 knots.
Cargo: 780,923 cu. ft.; passengers: 12.
Ex-*Lone Star Mariner*. Renamed *President Arthur* 1 July 1959.
Sold to American Export Lines 10 September 1974. Renamed *Export Democ-
   racy*. Transferred to Maritime Administration in 1978, and renamed *Lone
   Star Mariner*. In laid-up fleet in James River, Va., 1 December 1983.

President Buchanan [I] ("502")
See *President Monroe* [I]

President Buchanan [II] (VC2-S-AP3)
Victory type, built 1945, Portland, Oreg., by Oregon Shipbuilding Corp.
455' 3" × 62' × 38', 7,652 gross tons.
Steam turbine, 16½ knots.
Cargo: 483,309 cu. ft.; passengers: 4.
Ex-*Skidmore Victory.* Renamed *President Buchanan* 5 February 1948.
Traded in to Maritime Administration 28 February 1958. Renamed *Skidmore
    Victory* 23 May 1958. Renamed *Range Tracker.* Sold to American Ship
    Dismantlers, Portland, Oreg., 10 July 1970, for scrapping.

President Buchanan [III] (C4-S-1p)
Mariner type, built 1952, Chester, Pa., by Sun Shipbuilding and Dry Dock
    Co.
563' 7¾" × 76' × 44' 6", 9,171 gross tons.
Steam turbine, 20 knots.
Cargo: 768,949 cu. ft.; passengers: 12.
Ex-*Hoosier Mariner.* Renamed *President Buchanan* 1 May 1959.
Sold to Waterman Steamship Co. 30 August 1974. Renamed *Carter Braxton.*
    Transferred to Maritime Administration 1978. Renamed *Hoosier Mariner*
    and laid up. In reserve fleet at Beaumont, Texas, 1 December 1983.

President Cleveland [I] ("535")
535 type, built 1921, Newport News, Va., by Newport News Shipbuilding
    and Drydock Co.
535' × 72' × 41', 14,124 gross tons.
Steam turbine, 17½ knots.
Cargo: 479,105 cu. ft.; passengers: 934.
Ex-*Golden State.* Renamed *President Cleveland* 3 June 1922. Sold by U.S.
    Shipping Board to Dollar Steamship Lines 1925. Transferred to APL 1938.
    Sold to U.S. Navy and renamed U.S.S. *Tasker H. Bliss* (AP 42) in July 1941.
    Sunk by German submarine 12 November 1942 during invasion of North
    Africa.

President Cleveland [II] (P2-SE2-R3)
P2 type, built 1947, Alameda, Calif., by Bethlehem Shipbuilding Corp.
610' × 75' 6" × 43' 6", 15,437 gross tons.
Steam turbine, 20 knots.
Cargo: 193,984 cu. ft.; passengers: 330 first class, 220 economy class.
Sold to Oceanic Cruise Development (C. Y. Tung Group) 9 February 1973.
    Renamed *Oriental President.* Scrapped at Kaohsiung, Taiwan, 1974.

President Cleveland [III] (C5-S-75a)
C5 type, built 1969, Newport News, Va., by Newport News Shipbuilding
    and Drydock Co. (Hull 591).
605' × 82' × 46', 15,949 gross tons.

Steam turbine, 24,000-shaft horsepower, 20.8 knots.
Cargo: 1,082,207 C.F. Bale, 332 TEU containers; passengers: 12.
Ex-*American Mail*, American Mail Line. Transferred to APL and renamed *President Cleveland* 2 May 1978.

President Coolidge [I]
Built 1931, Newport News, Va., by Newport News Shipbuilding and Drydock Co.
654'3" × 81' × 52', 21,936 gross tons.
Steam turbo-electric, 32,000-shaft horsepower, 20 knots.
Cargo: 608,850 cu. ft.; passengers: 845.
Built for Dollar Steamship Lines, transferred to APL in 1938. Sank 26 October 1942 after striking a U.S. mine at entrance to harbor at Espiritu Santo. Of some 5,440 troops and crew aboard, two lives were known lost.

President Coolidge [II] (C4-S-1h)
Mariner type, built 1954, Newport News, Va., by Newport News Shipbuilding and Drydock Co.
563' 7¾" × 76' × 44'6", 9,271 gross tons.
Steam turbine, 20 knots.
Cargo: 734,773 cu. ft.; passengers: 12.
Ex-*Cracker State Mariner*. Renamed *President Coolidge* 25 April 1956.
Sold to American Export Lines, 21 September 1974. Renamed *Export Defender*. Transferred to Maritime Administration 1978. Renamed *Cracker State Mariner*. Laid up in James River, Va., reserve fleet.

President Eisenhower [I] (C6-S-1x)
C4 type, built 1962, San Pedro, Calif., by Todd Shipyards Corporation (Hull 79) (C4-S-1s).
563'7" × 76' × 44'8", 12,436 gross tons.
Steam turbine, 19,250-shaft horsepower, 20 knots.
Cargo: breakbulk; passengers: 12.
Ex-*Philippine Mail*. American Mail Line.
Converted to containership by Bethlehem Steel Co., San Francisco, 1972. Lengthened to 667'11", gross tonnage increased to 16,518. Shaft horsepower increased to 22,000, speed 20 knots.
Cargo: 1,108 TEU containers.
Renamed *President Eisenhower* 16 October 1975. Traded to Maritime Administration 25 October 1982 and chartered back to APL. Trade-in canceled, vessel sold to Delta Lines, 7 September 1983, and renamed *Santa Paula*.

President Eisenhower [II] (C9-M-F148a)
Built 1980, Kure, Japan, by Ishikawajima Harima Heavy Industries (Hull No. 2689).
758'9" × 105'8" × 62'4", 35,553 gross tons.
Lengthened, 1981, at Yokohama, Japan, by Ishikawajima Harima Heavy Industries to 853'9".

40,200-brake horsepower Sulzer 12-cyl. diesel, 22.5 knots.
Cargo: 2,522 TEU containers.
Ex-*Neptune Jade,* Neptune Orient Lines, Singapore flag.
Acquired by APL 18 June 1984. Modified and converted to U.S. flag require-
    ments by Ishikawajima Harima Heavy Industries, Yokohama, Japan.
    Cargo: 2,600 TEU containers, 36,859 gross tons.
Renamed *President Eisenhower* 30 August 1984.

President F. D. Roosevelt (C9-M-F148a)
Built 1980, Kure, Japan, by Ishikawajima Harima Heavy Industries (Hull
    No. 2690).
758'9" × 105'8" × 62'4", 35,553 gross tons.
Lengthened 1981 at Yokohama, Japan, by Ishikawajima Harima Heavy
    Industries to 853'9", 35,553 gross tons.
40,200 brake horsepower Sulzer 12-cyl. diesel, 22.5 knots.
Cargo: 2,522 TEU containers.
Ex-*Neptune Garnet,* Neptune Orient Lines, Singapore flag.
Acquired by APL 22 July 1984. Modified and converted to U.S. flag require-
    ments by Tacoma Boat Works, Tacoma, Wash.
Cargo: 2,600 TEU containers, 36,859 gross tons.
Renamed *President F. D. Roosevelt* December 1984.

President Fillmore [I]
Built 1904, Camden, N.J. by New York Shipbuilding Corp.
615' 8" × 65' × 51' 3", 15,455 gross tons.
Reciprocating steam engines, 14½ knots.
Cargo: 559,000 cu. ft.; passengers: 260.
Ex-*Mongolia.* Renamed *President Fillmore* 1930. Transferred from Dollar
    Steamship Lines to APL 1938. Sold 1940. Renamed *Panamanian.* Broken
    up for scrap in Shanghai 1947.

President Fillmore [II] ("502")
See *President Van Buren* [I]

President Fillmore [III] (VC2-S-AP3)
Victory type, built 1944, Portland, Oreg., by Oregon Shipbuilding Corp.
455'3" × 62' × 38', 7,646 gross tons.
Steam turbine, 16½ knots.
Cargo: 483,309 cu. ft.; passengers: 4.
Ex-*Rutland Victory.* Renamed *President Fillmore* 13 February 1948.
Sold to Explorer Ships, Inc., 22 June 1962. Renamed *Smith Victory* 1962.
    Renamed *U.S. Victory* 1965. Renamed *Oriental Arrow* (Liberian flag) 1969.
    Renamed *Oriental Ace* 1972. Lost at sea on voyage from Seattle to Kobe 13
    February 1976.

President Fillmore [IV] (C3)
See *President Harrison* [II]

President Fillmore [V] (C6-S-69c)
Seamaster type, built 1968, Pascagoula, Miss., by Ingalls Shipbuilding
    Corp. (C4-S-69a).
573' 10¹⁵⁄₁₆" × 82' × 45'6", 14,000 gross tons.
Steam turbine, 23 knots.
Cargo: 845,020 cu. ft.; passengers: 12.
Converted to containership by Todd Shipyards Corp., San Pedro, Calif., in
    1972. Lengthened to 664', 17,801 gross tons.
Cargo: 1,094 TEU containers.

President Garfield [I] ("502")
502 type, built 1921, Camden, N.J. by New York Shipbuilding Corp.
522'8" × 62' × 42', 10,496 gross tons.
Reciprocating steam engines, 14 knots.
Cargo: 445,800 cu. ft.; passengers 149.
Ex-*Blue Hen State*. Renamed *President Garfield* 1922. Purchased from U.S.
    Shipping Board by Dollar Steamship Lines 1923. Transferred to APL 1938.
    Renamed *President Madison* 1940. Sold to U.S. Navy and renamed U.S.S.
    Kenmore (AP 62). Converted to hospital ship and renamed U.S.S. *Refuge*
    (AH 11). Transferred to War Shipping Administration 1946. Renamed
    President Madison. Sold for scrapping 2 February 1948.

President Garfield [II] (C3)
C3-P type, built 1941, Newport News, Va., by Newport News Shipbuilding
    and Drydock Co.
491'10" × 69'6" × 42'6", 9,260 gross tons.
Steam turbine, 16½ knots.
Cargo: 512,353 cu. ft.; passengers: 96.
Renamed U.S.S. *Thomas Jefferson* (AP 60), later (APA 30). Laid up in U.S.
    Navy reserve fleet at Hunter's Point Navy Yard, San Francisco, about
    1955. Transferred to Maritime Administration's merchant reserve fleet,
    Suisun Bay, Calif. about 1958. Sold to Zidell Exploration, Portland, Oreg.,
    1 March 1973 for scrapping.

President Garfield [III] (VC2-S-AP3)
Victory type, built 1945, Portland, Oreg., by Oregon Shipbuilding Corp.
455'3" × 62' × 38', 7,659 gross tons.
Steam turbine, 16½ knots.
Cargo: 483,309 cu. ft.; passengers: 2.
Ex-*Willamette Victory*. Renamed *President Garfield* 19 January 1951. Renamed
    Willamette Victory 28 February 1958. Traded to Maritime Administration 2
    April 1958. Sold 26 June 1973 to Grain Storage Co., Washington, D.C., for
    nontransportation use.

President Garfield [IV] (C4-S-lp)
Mariner type, built 1952, Pascagoula, Miss., by Ingalls Shipbuilding Corp.
563' 7¾" × 76' × 44'6", 9,177 gross tons.
Steam turbine, 20 knots.

Cargo: 768,439 cu. ft.; passengers: 12.

Ex-*Magnolia Mariner.* Renamed *President Garfield* 6 March 1959. Sold to Waterman Steamship Co. 2 October 1974. Renamed *Samuel Chase.* Transferred to Maritime Administration 1978. Scrapped in Taiwan 1980.

President Grant [I] ("535")
535 type, built 1921, Sparrows Point, Md., by Bethlehem Shipbuilding Co.
535' × 72' × 41', 14,124 gross tons.
Steam turbine, 17½ knots.
Cargo: 452,000 cu ft.; passengers: 873.
Ex-*Pine Tree State.* Renamed *President Grant* 1922. Renamed U.S.S. *Harris* (APA 8) 1940. Renamed *President Grant* 1946. Sold for scrapping 20 July 1948.

President Grant [II] ("502")
See *President Adams* [I]

President Grant [III] (C3-S-A4)
C3 type, built 1945, San Francisco, Calif., by Western Pipe and Steel Co.
491'7" × 69'6" × 42'6", 7,924 gross tons.
Steam turbine, 16½ knots
Cargo: 548,981 cu. ft.; passengers: 12.
Ex-*Sea Beaver.* Renamed *President Grant* 8 August 1945. Renamed *President Hoover* [III] 26 September 1967. Sold to Excelsior Marine Corp., 27 October 1972. Renamed *Hoover.* Sold for scrapping at Kaohsiung, Taiwan, 1973.

President Grant [IV] (C6-S-69c)
Seamaster type, built 1967, Pascagoula, Miss., by Ingalls Shipbuilding Corp. (C4-S-69a).
573'10^{15}⁄₁₆" × 82' × 45'6", 14,000 gross tons.
Steam turbine, 23 knots.
Cargo: 845,020 cu. ft.; passengers: 12.
Converted to containership by Todd Shipyards, San Pedro, Calif., 1972. Lengthened to 664', 17,801 gross tons. Cargo: 1,066 TEU containers.
Stranded on 1 September 1976, and lost 9 September 1976 at Keelung, Taiwan.

President Grant [V] (C8-S-81e)
LASH type, built 1971, New Orleans, La., by Avondale Shipyards (Hull No. 1188).
820' × 100' × 60', 26,456 gross tons.
Steam turbine, 32,000-shaft horsepower, 22.5 knots.
Cargo: 43 barges, 335 TEU containers.
Converted to full containership 1977 by Bethlehem Steel Co., San Francisco. 26,989 gross tons. Cargo: 1,856 TEU containers.
Ex-*Golden Bear,* Pacific Far East Lines. Acquired by APL 25 April 1979, renamed *President Grant.*

President Harding [I] (VC2-S-AP3)
Victory type, built 1945, Portland, Oreg., by Oregon Shipbuilding Corp.
455'3" × 62' × 38', 7,638 gross tons.
Steam turbine, 16½ knots.
Cargo: 483,300 cu. ft.; passengers: 4.
Ex-*Jackson Victory*. Renamed *President Harding* 10 March 1948.
Sold to Explorer Ships, Inc., 4 June 1962. Renamed *Smith Explorer* June 1962.
    Renamed *U.S. Explorer* 1965. Renamed *Oriental Comet* (Liberian flag) 1969.
    Renamed *Oriental Charger* 1972. Scrapped at Kaohsiung, Taiwan, 1976.

President Harding [II] (C2-S-AJ3)
C2 type, built 1944, Wilmington, N.C., by North Carolina Shipbuilding Co.
459'1" × 63' × 38', 8,189 gross tons.
Steam turbine, 15½ knots.
Cargo: 542,824 cu. ft.
Ex-*Vinton* (AKA 83); ex-*Gulf Shipper*, Gulf and South American Steamship
    Co., 1947. Purchased by APL 23 September 1964. Renamed *President
    Harding*. Sold to Pacific Far East Lines 29 September 1966. Renamed
    America Bear. Acquired by Columbia Steamship Co. 1969 and renamed
    Columbia Beaver. Scrapped at Kaohsiung, Taiwan, 1971–72.

President Harding [III] (C3)
See *President Van Buren* [III]

President Harding [IV] (C3)
See *President Taft* [II]

President Harrison [I] ("502")
502 type, built 1921, Camden, N.J., by New York Shipbuilding Corp.
522'8" × 62' × 42', 10,496 gross tons.
Reciprocating steam engines, 14 knots.
Cargo: 440,704 cu. ft.; passengers: 133.
Ex-*Wolverine State*. Renamed *President Harrison* 1922. Purchased by Dollar
    Steamship Lines from U.S. Shipping Board 1923. Transferred to APL
    1938. Captured by Japanese off Yangtze River 9 December 1941. Renamed
    Kakko Maru; renamed *Kachidoki Maru*. Sunk by U.S. submarine U.S.S.
    Pampanito 12 September 1944.

President Harrison [II] (C3-S-A2)
C3 type, built 1943, San Francisco, Calif., by Western Pipe and Steel Co.
492' × 69'6" × 42'6", 7,995 gross tons.
Steam turbine, 16½ knots
Cargo: 647,619 cu. ft.; passengers: 12.
Ex-*Sea Mink*; ex-U.S.S. *Callaway*.
Renamed *President Harrison* 1949, renamed *President Fillmore* [IV] 10 March
    1966. Sold to Waterman Steamship Co. 24 April 1968, renamed *Hurricane*.
    Scrapped at Kaohsiung, Taiwan, 1974.

President Harrison [III] C6-S-1qc)
Master Mariner type, built 1966, San Diego, Calif., by National Steel and
  Shipbuilding Co. (C4-S-1qa).
564' × 76' × 44'6", 10,412 gross tons.
Steam turbine, 20½ knots.
Cargo: 756,112 cu. ft.; passengers: 12.
Converted to containership by Todd Shipyards, Corp., Seattle, Wash., 1973.
  Lengthened to 668', 16,819 gross tons. Cargo: 838 TEU containers.
  Traded in to Maritime Administration 30 April 1979. Chartered back until
  1 May 1981. Converted by Maritime Administration to a crane ship at
  Manitowoc, Wisc., April 1984. Renamed *Keystone State,* T-ACS 1.

President Hayes [I] ("502")
502 type, built 1920, Camden, N.J., by New York Shipbuilding Corp.
522'8" × 62' × 42', 10,533 gross tons.
Reciprocating steam engines, 14 knots.
Cargo: 464,710 cu. ft.; passengers: 223.
Ex-*Creole State.* Renamed *President Hayes* 1922. Purchased by Dollar Steamship Lines from U.S. Shipping Board 1923. Transferred to APL 1938.
  Renamed *President Tyler* [I] 1940. Renamed *Howard A. McCurdy* March
  1945. Renamed *President Tyler* April 1947. Sold for scrapping March 1957.

President Hayes [II] (C3)
C3-P type, built 1941, Newport News, Va., by Newport News Shipbuilding
  and Drydock Co.
491'10 × 69'6" × 42'6", 9,255 gross tons.
Steam turbine, 16½ knots.
Cargo: 512,353 cu. ft; passengers: 96.
Renamed U.S.S. *President Hayes* (APA 20), 1941. Laid up in U.S. Navy
  reserve fleet June 1953. Returned by Navy to Maritime Administration 28
  October 1958 and laid up in merchant reserve fleet, Suisun Bay, Calif.
  Scrapped by Levin Metals, Richmond, Calif., May 1977.

President Hayes [III] (P2-S1-DN3)
V-2000 type, built 1951, Camden, N.J., by New York Shipbuilding Corp.
533'9" × 73' × 49', 14,000 gross tons, APL design.
Steam turbine, 19 knots.
Cargo: 570,000 cu. ft.; passengers: 228.
Acquired by U.S. Navy during construction. Completed to Navy specifica-
  tions and renamed U.S.S. *Upshur* (APA 198). Loaned to Maine Maritime
  Academy 1973; renamed *State of Maine.*

President Hayes [IV] (C4-S-lh)
Mariner type, built 1952, Newport News, Va., by Newport News Shipbuilding and Drydock Co.
563'7 ¾" × 76' × 44'6", 9,277 gross tons.
Steam turbine, 20 knots.

Cargo: 734,779 cu. ft.; passengers: 12.

Ex-*Old Dominion Mariner.* Renamed *President Hayes* 30 November 1955.

Sold to American Export Lines 10 September 1974 and renamed *Export Diplomat.* Transferred to Maritime Administration 1978 and renamed *Old Dominion Mariner.* In James River, Va., reserve fleet 1 December 1983.

President Hoover [I] (not an APL ship)

Built 1930, Newport News, Va., by Newport News Shipbuilding and Drydock Co.

654' 3" × 81' × 52', 21,936 gross tons.

Steam turbo-electric, 32,000-shaft horsepower, 20 knots.

Cargo: 608,850 cu. ft.; passengers: 845.

Built for Dollar Steamship Lines. Lost by grounding on Hoishoto Island, off S.E. coast of Formosa 10 December 1937. No lives lost.

President Hoover [II]

Built 1939, Quincy, Mass., by Bethlehem Steel Co., Shipbuilding Division.

493'6" × 64' × 46'9", 10,021 gross tons.

Steam turbine, 17 knots.

Cargo: 314,978 cu. ft.; passengers: 202.

Ex-*Panama* built for Panama Railroad Steamship Co. Renamed U.S.A.T.

James Parker 1941. Renamed *Panama* 1946. Renamed *President Hoover* January 1957. Sold to Chandris interests 3 December 1964. Renamed *Regina* 1965 (Greek flag). Transferred to Panamanian registry 1967. Renamed *Regina Prima* 1973. Laid up in Greece 1983.

President Hoover [III]

See *President Grant* [III]

President Hoover [IV] (C8-S-8le)

LASH type, built 1971, New Orleans, La., by Avondale Shipyards (Hull No. 1187).

820' × 100' × 60', 26,456 gross tons.

Steam turbine, 32,000-shaft horsepower, 22.5 knots.

Cargo: 43 barges, 335 TEU containers.

Converted to full containership 1978 by Bethlehem Steel Co., San Francisco. 26,989 gross tons. Cargo: 1,856 TEU containers.

Ex-*Thomas E. Cuffe*, Pacific Far East Lines. Acquired by APL and renamed *President Hoover* 25 April 1979.

President Jackson [I] ("535")

535 type, built 1921. Newport News, Va., by Newport News Shipbuilding and Drydock Co.

535' × 72' × 41', 14,124 gross tons.

Steam turbine, 17½ knots.

Cargo: 452,000 cu. ft.; passengers: 656.

Ex-*Silver State.* Renamed *President Jackson* [I] 1922. Renamed U.S.S. *Zeilin*

(APA 3) 1940. Renamed *President Jackson* 1946. Sold for scrapping 4 May 1948.

President Jackson [II] (C3)
C3-P type, built 1940, Newport News,. Va., by Newport News Shipbuilding and Drydock Co.
491'10" × 69'6" × 42'6", 9,255 gross tons.
Steam turbine, 16½ knots.
Cargo: 512,353 cu. ft.; passengers: 96.
Renamed U.S.S. *President Jackson* (APA 18) 1941. Renamed *President Jackson* [II] December 1958. Returned by U.S. Navy to Maritime Administration 1 December 1958 and laid up in reserve fleet, Suisun Bay, Calif. Sold to N. W. Kennedy (Canada) March 1973. Scrapped Kaohsiung, Taiwan, 1973.

President Jackson [III] (P2-SI-DN3)
V-2000 type, built 1952, Camden, N.J., by New York Shipbuilding Corp.
533'9" × 73' × 49', 14,000 gross tons. APL design.
Steam turbine, 19 knots.
Cargo: 570,000 cu. ft.; passengers: 228.
Acquired by U.S. Navy during construction. Completed to Navy specifications and renamed U.S.S. *Barrett* (AP 196). Loaned to New York State Maritime Academy 1973 and renamed *Empire State.*

President Jackson [IV] (C4-S-lh)
Mariner type, built 1953, Newport News, Va., by Newport News Shipbuilding and Drydock Co.
563' 7 ¾" × 76 ' × 44'6", 9,277 gross tons.
Steam turbine, 20 knots.
Cargo: 761,137 cu. ft.; passengers: 12.
Ex-*Volunteer Mariner.* Renamed *President Jackson* [IV] 11 October 1955.
Sold to Waterman Steamship Co. 15 July 1974 and renamed *Joseph Hewes.* Sold for scrapping July 1980.

President Jackson [V] (C5-S-75a)
C5 type, built 1968, Newport News, Va., by Newport News Shipbuilding and Drydock Co. (Hull No. 588).
605' × 82' × 46', 15,949 gross tons.
Steam turbine, 24,000-shaft horsepower, 20.8 knots.
Cargo: 1,082, 207 C.F. Bale, 332 TEU containers; passengers: 12.
Ex-*Indian Mail,* American Mail Line. Renamed *President Jackson* 5 September 1978.

President Jefferson [I] ("535")
535 type, built 1921, Camden, N.J., by New York Shipbuilding Corp.
535' × 72' × 41', 14,124 gross tons.
Steam turbine, 17½ knots.

Cargo: 452,000 cu. ft.; passengers: 867.

Ex-*Wenatchee*. Renamed *President Jefferson* [I] 1922.

Renamed U.S.S. *President Jefferson* [I] (APA 30) 1941. Renamed U.S.S. *Henry T. Allen* (APA 15) 1943, later designated AG 90. Renamed *President Jefferson* [I] February 1946. Sold for scrapping 26 March 1948.

President Jefferson [II] (C3-S-A4)
C3 type, built 1946, San Francisco, Calif., by Western Pipe and Steel Co.
491'7" × 69'6" × 42'6", 7,924 gross tons.
Steam turbine, 16½ knots.
Cargo: 548,981 cu. ft.; passengers: 12.
Ex-*Sea Oriole*. Renamed *President Jefferson* 23 August 1946. Sold to Ferndale Shipping Co. 20 February 1970. Renamed *Ferndale*. Scrapped at Kaohsiung, Taiwan, 1970.

President Jefferson [III] (C6-S-85b)
Pacesetter type, built 1973, Pascagoula, Miss., by Ingalls Shipbuilding Co. (Hull No. 1184).
669'2" × 90' × 53', 21,475 gross tons.
Steam turbine, 23 knots.
Cargo: 1,508 TEU containers.

President Johnson [I]
Built 1904, Camden, N.J., by New York Shipbuilding Corp.
615'8" × 65' × 51'3", 15,445 gross tons.
Reciprocating steam engines, 14½ knots.
Cargo: 577,816 cu. ft.; passengers: 252.
Ex-*Manchuria*. Renamed *President Johnson* 1930. Transferred from Dollar Steamship Lines to APL 1938. Sold 1946. Renamed *Santa Cruz* 1947. Broken up for scrap in Italy June 1952.

President Johnson [II] (C3-S-A2)
C3 type, built 1943, San Francisco, by Western Pipe and Steel Co.
492' × 69'6" × 42'6", 7,995 gross tons.
Steam turbine, 16½ knots.
Cargo: 647,619 cu. ft.; passengers: 12.
Ex-*Sea Carp*. Renamed U.S.S. *Clay* (APA 39) 1943. Renamed *President Johnson* [II] March 1949. Sold to Waterman Steamship Co. 24 April 1968. Renamed *La Salle*. Sold to Zui Feng Steel Co. and scrapped at Kaohsiung, Taiwan, 1974.

President Johnson [III] (C3-S-A4)
See *President McKinley* [II]

President Johnson [IV] (C6-S-69c)
See *President McKinley* [III]

President Johnson [V] (C6-S-85b)
Pacesetter type, built 1974, Pascagoula, Miss., by Ingalls Shipbuilding Co.
  (Hull No. 1187).
669'2" × 90' × 53', 21,475 gross tons.
Steam turbine, 23 knots.
Cargo: 1,580 TEU containers.

President Kennedy (C6-S-1xa)
C4-S-1s type, built 1964, San Diego, Calif., by National Steel and Shipbuild-
  ing Co. (Hull No. 335), C4-S-1sa.
563'7" × 76' × 44'9⅝", 12,440 gross tons.
Steam turbine, 19,250-shaft horsepower, 20 knots.
Cargo: 767,000 C.F. Bale; passengers: 12.
Ex-*Oregon Mail*, American Mail Line.
Converted to containership by Todd Shipyard, San Pedro, Calif., 1972.
  Lengthened to 668' 7¾", 16,542 gross tons, 22,000-shaft horsepower 20
  knots. Cargo: 1,124 TEU containers.
Transferred from American Mail Line to APL 1 October 1973. Renamed
  President Kennedy 24 September 1975.

President Lincoln [I] ("535")
535 type, built 1921, Camden, N.J., by New York Shipbuilding Corp.
535' × 72' × 41', 14,124 gross tons.
Steam turbine, 17½ knots.
Cargo: 480,600 cu. ft.; passengers: 834.
Ex-*Hoosier State*. Renamed *President Lincoln* 1922. Sold by U.S. Shipping
  Board to Dollar Steamship Lines 1925. Transferred to APL 1938. Sold 1940
  and renamed *Maria del Carmen*. Renamed *Cabo de Buena Esperanza*, 1940.
  Sold for breaking up 1958.

President Lincoln [II] (C4-S-1q)
Searacer type, built 1961, San Francisco, Calif., by Bethlehem Steel Co.
563'7¾" × 76' × 44'6", 13,223 gross tons.
Steam turbine, 20 knots.
Cargo: 721,656 cu. ft.; passengers: 12. Container capacity increased to 378
  TEU at Richmond, Calif., 1968; further expanded to 410 TEU at San
  Francisco, 1971.
Traded to Maritime Administration 30 April 1979. Renamed *Lincoln*.
  Laid up in reserve fleet, Suisun Bay, Calif., as of February 1983.

President Lincoln [III] (C9-M-132b)
C9 type, built 1982, New Orleans, La., by Avondale Shipyards.
860' × 106' × 66', 40,628 gross tons.
Sulzer 12-cyl. diesel, 43,200-brake horsepower, 23.9 knots.
Cargo: 2,590 TEU containers.

President Madison [I] ("535") (not an APL ship)
535 type, built 1921, Camden, N.J., by New York Shipbuilding Corp.
535' × 72' × 41', 14,124 gross tons.
Cargo: 452,000 cu. ft.; passengers: 852.
Ex-*Bay State*. Renamed *President Madison* 1922. Sold by U.S. Shipping Board
   to Admiral Oriental Mail Line 1926. Sunk at dock in Seattle March 1933.
   Raised and repaired but remained out of service for next six years. Sold
   to Philippines and renamed *President Quezon* 1939. Lost by grounding on
   Tanegashima Island, Japan, 16 January 1940.

President Madison [II] ("502")
See *President Garfield* [I]

President Madison [III] (C3-S-A4)
C3 type, built 1946, San Francisco, by Western Pipe and Steel Co.
491'7" × 69'6" × 42'6", 7,924 gross tons.
Steam turbine, 16½ knots.
Cargo: 548,981 cu. ft.; passengers: 12.
Ex-*Sea Starling*. Renamed *President Madison* June 1946.
Sold to Vintage Steamship Co. 7 August 1972. Renamed *Madison*. Scrapped
   at Kaohsiung, Taiwan, 1972–73.

President Madison [IV] (C6-3-85b)
Pacesetter type, built 1973, Pascagoula, Miss., by Ingalls Shipbuilding Co.
   (Hull No. 1185).
669'2" × 90' × 53', 21,475 gross tons.
Steam turbine, 23 knots.
Cargo: 1,508 TEU containers.

President McKinley [I] ("535")
535 type, built 1921, Camden, N.J., by New York Shipbuilding Corp.
535' × 72' × 41', 14,124 gross tons.
Steam turbine, speed 17½ knots.
Cargo: 452,000 cu. ft.; passengers: 835.
Ex-*Keystone State*. Renamed *President McKinley* 1922. Renamed U.S.S.
   J. Franklin Bell (APA 16). Renamed *President McKinley* [I] February 1947.
   Sold for scrapping 3 April 1948.

President McKinley [II] (C3-S-A4)
C3 type, built 1946, San Francisco, Calif., by Western Pipe and Steel Co.
491'7" × 69'6" × 42'6", 7,924 gross tons.
Cargo: 548,981 cu. ft.; passengers: 12.
Steam turbine, 16½ knots.
Ex-*Sea Phoebe*. Renamed *President McKinley* [II] July 1946. Renamed *President
   Johnson* [III] 11 April 1968. Sold to Pinedale Shipping Co. 16 December
   1969. Renamed *Pinedale*. Scrapped in Taiwan 1970.

President McKinley [III] (C6-S-69c)
Seamaster type, built 1968, Pascagoula, Miss., by Ingalls Shipbuilding
Corp. (C4-S-69a).
573'10^{15}⁄₁₆" × 82' × 45'6", 14,000 gross tons.
Steam turbine, 23 knots.
Cargo: 845,020 cu. ft.; passengers: 12.
Original intention was to name this ship *President Johnson* [IV]. During
construction decision was made to change to *President McKinley* [III].
Converted to containership by Todd Shipyard, San Pedro, Calif., 1972.
Lengthened to 664', 17,801 gross tons. Cargo: 1,094 TEU containers.

President Monroe [I] ("502")
502 type, built 1920, Camden, N.J., by New York Shipbuilding Corp.
522'8" × 62' × 42', 10,533 gross tons.
Reciprocating steam engines, 14 knots.
Cargo: 470,530 cu. ft.; passengers: 247.
Ex-*Panhandle State*. Renamed *President Monroe* 1922. Renamed *President
Buchanan* [I] 1940. Converted to a hospital ship and renamed *Emily H. M.
Weder* 1944. Renamed *President Buchanan* December 1946. Sold for scrap-
ping 21 March 1957.

President Monroe [II] (C3)
C3-P type, built 1940, Newport News, Va., by Newport News Shipbuilding
and Drydock Co.
491'10" × 69'6" × 42'6", 9,255 gross tons.
Steam turbine, 16½ knots.
Cargo: 512,353 cu. ft.; passengers: 96.
Renamed U.S.S. *President Monroe* 1943. Renamed *President Monroe* February
1946. Sold to White Star Shipping and Trading Corp. (Greek flag) 21
December 1965. Renamed *Marianna V.* Reportedly scrapped 1969.

President Monroe [III] (C6-S-1qc)
Master Mariner type, built 1966, San Diego, Calif., by National Steel and
Shipbuilding Co. (C4-S-1qa).
564' × 76' × 44'6", 10,412 gross tons.
Steam turbine, 20½ knots.
Cargo: 756,112 cu. ft.; passengers: 12.
Converted to containership by Todd Shipyards Corp., Seattle, 1972. Length-
ened to 668', 16,819 gross tons. Cargo: 838 TEU containers. Traded in to
Maritime Administration 30 April 1979. Chartered back until 29 January
1982. As of 31 October 1985, the ship was converted to a crane ship by
Continental Maritime, San Francisco, and renamed the *Gem State*, T-ACS
2.

President Monroe [IV] (C9-M-132b)
C9 type, built 1983, New Orleans, La., by Avondale Shipyards.

860' × 106' × 66', 40,628 gross tons.
Sulzer 12-cyl. diesel, 43,200-brake horsepower, 23.9 knots.
Cargo: 2,590 TEU containers.

President Pierce [I] ("535")
535 type, built 1921, Sparrows Point, Md., by Bethlehem Shipbuilding Co.
535' × 72' × 41', 14,124 gross tons.
Steam turbine, 17½ knots.
Cargo: 479,105 cu. ft.; passengers: 874.
Ex-*Hawkeye State.* Renamed *President Pierce* 26 June 1922. Sold by U.S.
    Shipping Board to Dollar Steamship Lines 1925. Transferred to APL 1938.
    Renamed *Hugh L. Scott* (U.S.A.T.) August 1941. Renamed U.S.S. *Hugh L.
    Scott* (AP 43) July 1942. Sunk by torpedo from German submarine U-130
    at Fedhala Roads, North Africa, 12 November 1942.

President Pierce [II] (C-3)
C3 type, built 1945, San Francisco, Calif., by Western Pipe and Steel Co.
491'7" × 69'6" × 42'6", 7,924 gross tons.
Steam turbine, 16½ knots.
Cargo: 548,981 cu. ft.; passengers: 12.
Ex-*Sea Jumper.* Renamed *President Pierce* 18 September 1945. Sold to Amber
    Jack Marine Corp. 14 December 1972. Renamed *Pierce.* Scrapped at Kaoh-
    siung, Taiwan, 1973.

President Pierce [III] (C6-S-85b)
Pacesetter type, built 1973, Pascagoula, Miss., by Ingalls Shipbuilding Co.
    (Hull No. 1186).
669'2" × 90' × 53', 21,475 gross tons.
Steam turbine, 23 knots.
Cargo: 1,508 TEU containers.

President Polk [I] ("502")
502 type, built 1921, Camden, N.J., by New York Shipbuilding Corp.
522'8" × 62' × 42', 10,496 gross tons.
Reciprocating steam engines, 14 knots.
Cargo: 439,680 cu. ft.; passengers: 128.
Ex-*Granite State.* Renamed *President Polk* 1922. Renamed *President Taylor* [I]
    1940. Grounded on coral reef, Canton Island, 14 February 1942, and
    subsequently destroyed by Japanese aircraft.

President Polk [II] (C3)
C3-P type, built 1941, Newport News, Va., by Newport News Shipbuilding
    and Drydock Co.
491'10" × 69'6" × 42'6", 9,256 gross tons.
Steam turbine, 16½ knots.
Cargo: 512,353 cu. ft.; passengers: 96.
Renamed U.S.S. *President Polk* 7 September 1943. Renamed *President Polk* 26

January 1946. Sold to Ganaderos del Mar, 15 July 1965. Renamed *Gaucho Martin Fierro*. Renamed *Minotauros* 1966. Scrapped at Kaohsiung, Taiwan, 1970.

President Polk [III] (C6-S-1qc)
Master Mariner type, built 1965, San Diego, Calif., by National Steel and Shipbuilding Co. (C4-S-1qa).
564' × 76' × 44'6", 10,412 gross tons.
Steam turbine, 20½ knots.
Cargo: 756,112 cu. ft.; passengers: 12.
Converted to containership by Todd Shipyards Corp., Seattle, 1972. Lengthened to 668', 16,819 gross tons. Cargo: 838 TEU containers. Traded to Maritime Administration 25 October 1982; chartered back until 8 November 1982. As of September 1984 in reserve fleet at Suisun Bay, Calif.

President Roosevelt [I] (P2-S2-R14)
P2 type, built 1944, Kearny, N.J., by Federal Shipbuilding and Drydock Co.
622'7" × 75'6" × 42'6", 18,298 gross tons.
Steam turbine, 20 knots.
Cargo: 218,167 cu. ft.; passengers: 456 first class.
Built as troop transport U.S.S. *General W. P. Richardson*. Renamed *La Guardia* 1949. Renamed *Leilani* 1956. Purchased by APL 1960. Renamed *President Roosevelt* 1961. Sold to Solon Navigation S.A. 10 April 1970. Renamed *Atlantis*. Sold to Ares Shipping Co. 1972. Renamed *Emerald Seas* (Panamanian flag).

President Roosevelt [II] (C6-S-1x)
C4 type, built 1961, San Pedro, Calif., by Todd Shipbuilding Co. (Hull No. 77) (C4-S-1s)
563'7" × 76' × 44'8", 12,436 gross tons.
Steam turbine 19,250-shaft horsepower, 20 knots.
Cargo: breakbulk; passengers: 12.
Ex-*Washington Mail*, American Mail Line. Converted to containership by Bethlehem Steel Co., San Francisco, 1971. Lengthened to 667'11", 16,518 gross tons. Shaft horsepower increased to 22,000, speed 20 knots. Cargo: 1,108 TEU containers. Renamed *President Roosevelt* 26 November 1975. Traded in to Maritime Administration 30 December 1982 and chartered back to APL. Trade-in canceled and vessel sold to Delta Lines 7 September 1983. Renamed *Santa Rosa*.

President Taft [I] ("535")
535 type, built 1921, Sparrows Point, Md., by Bethlehem Shipbuilding Corp.
535' × 72' × 41', 14,124 gross tons.
Steam turbine, 17½ knots.
Cargo: 479,105 cu. ft.; passengers: 846.
Ex-*Buckeye State*. Renamed *President Taft* 16 May 1922. Sold by U.S. Shipping

Board to Dollar Steamship Lines 1925. Transferred to APL 1938. Renamed (USAT) *Willard A. Holbrook* September 1941. Sold for scrapping 29 October 1957.

President Taft [II] (C3-S-A4)
C3 type, built 1945, San Francisco, Calif., by Western Pipe and Steel Co.
491'7" × 69'6" × 42'6", 7,924 gross tons.
Steam turbine, 16½ knots.
Cargo: 548,981 cu. ft.; passengers: 12.
Ex-*Sea Thrush*. Renamed *President Taft* from beginning of operation 20 July 1945. Renamed *President Harding* [IV] 28 February 1968. Sold to Bonito Maritime Corp. 26 January 1973. Renamed *Harding*. Scrapped in Taiwan 1973.

President Taft [III] (C6-S-69c)
Seamaster type, built 1967, Pascagoula, Miss., by Ingalls Shipbuilding Corp. (C4-S-69a).
573'10¹⁵⁄₁₆" × 82' × 45'6", 14,000 gross tons.
Steam turbine, 23 knots.
Cargo: 845,020 cu. ft.; passengers: 12.
Converted to containership by Todd Shipyards Corp., Seattle, 1972. Lengthened to 663', 17,803 gross tons.
Cargo: 1,094 TEU containers.

President Taylor [I] ("502")
See *President Polk* [I].

President Taylor [II] (C4-S-1a)
Mariner type, built 1954, Chester, Pa., by Sun Shipbuilding and Drydock Co.
563'7¾" × 76' × 44'6", 9,171 gross tons.
Steam turbine, 20 knots.
Cargo: 779,661 cu. ft.; passengers: 12.
Ex-*Hawkeye Mariner*. Renamed *President Taylor* [II] 8 February 1957. Sold to Farrell Lines 10 June 1974. Renamed *Austral Pilgrim*.

President Taylor [III] (C5-S-75a)
C5 type, built Newport News, Va., by Newport News Shipbuilding and Drydock Co. (Hull No. 589).
605' × 82' × 46', 15,949 gross tons.
Steam turbine, 24,000-shaft horsepower, 20.8 knots.
Cargo: 1,082,207 C.F. Bale; 332 TEU containers; passengers: 12.
Ex-*Korean Mail*, American Mail Line. Renamed *President Taylor* [III] 6 June 1978.

President Truman (C6-S-1x)
C4 type, built 1962, San Pedro, Calif., by Todd Shipyards Corp. (Hull No. 78) (C4-S-1s).

563'7" × 76' × 44'8", 12,436 gross tons.
Steam turbine, 19,250-shaft horsepower, 20 knots.
Cargo: breakbulk; passengers: 12.
Ex-*Japan Mail*, American Mail Line. Converted to containership by Bethlehem Steel Co., San Francisco, 1971. Lengthened to 667'11", 16,518 gross tons, shaft horsepower to 22,000, speed to 20 knots. Cargo: 954 TEU containers. Renamed *President Truman* 14 November 1975.

President Tyler [I] ("502")
See *President Hayes* [I]

President Tyler [II] (VC2-S-AP3)
Victory type, built 1944, Richmond, Calif., by Permanente Metals Corp.
455'3" × 62' × 38', 7,637 gross tons.
Steam turbine, 16½ knots.
Cargo: 483,309 cu. ft.; passengers: 4.
Ex-*Iraq Victory*. Renamed *President Tyler* [II] 13 February 1948. Traded in to Maritime Administration 28 February 1958. Operated on use agreement. Renamed *Iraq Victory* 9 September 1960. Redelivered to Maritime Administration 21 September 1960.

President Tyler [III] (C4-S-1q)
Searacer type, built 1961, San Francisco, Calif., by Bethlehem Steel Co.
563'7¾" × 76' × 44'6", 13,223 gross tons.
Steam turbine, 20 knots.
Cargo: 721,656 cu. ft.; passengers: 12. Container capacity expanded to 378 TEU at Richmond, Calif., 1968; further expanded to 410 TEU at San Francisco, 1971.
Traded in to Maritime Administration 30 April 1979. Renamed *Tyler*. In reserve fleet, Suisun Bay, Calif., December 1982.

President Tyler [IV] (C8-S-81e)
LASH type, built 1972, New Orleans, La., by Avondale Shipyards (Hull No. 1190).
820' × 100' × 60', 26,456 gross tons.
Steam turbine, 32,000-shaft horsepower, 22.5 knots.
Cargo: 43 barges, 335 TEU containers.
Converted to full containership 1978, at San Francisco by Bethlehem Steel Co. 26,989 gross tons. Cargo: 1,856 TEU containers. Ex-*Japan Bear*, Pacific Far East Lines. Acquired by APL 25 April 1979. Renamed *President Tyler* [IV].

President Van Buren [I] ("502")
502 type, built 1920, Camden, N.J., by New York Shipbuilding Corp.
522'8" × 62' × 42', 10,533 gross tons.
Reciprocating steam engines, 14 knots.
Cargo: 468,000 cu. ft.; passengers: 120.

Ex-*Old North State*. Renamed *President Van Buren* 1922. Purchased by Dollar Steamship Lines from U.S. Shipping Board 1923. Transferred from Dollar Steamship Lines to APL 1938. Renamed *President Fillmore* 1940. Converted to a hospital ship and renamed *Marigold* 1944. Renamed *President Fillmore* [II] 8 June 1946. Sold for scrapping 14 January 1948.

President Van Buren [II] (C3-P)
C3-P type, built 1941, Newport News, Va., by Newport News Shipbuilding and Drydock Co.
491'10" × 69'6" × 42'6", 9,260 gross tons.
Steam turbine, 16½ knots.
Cargo: 512,353 cu. ft.; passengers: 96.
Renamed U.S.S. *Thomas R. Stone* (APA 29). Badly damaged by torpedo in North African landing 7 November 1942. Towed to Algiers. Further damaged in air raid 24 November 1942. Salvage attempted unsuccessfully until spring 1944. Sold April 1944 for scrapping. Purchasers abandoned her, and she was destroyed by U.S. Government in July 1945.

President Van Buren [III] (C3-S-A2)
C3 type, built 1943, San Francisco, Calif., by Western Pipe and Steel Co.
492' × 69'6" × 42'6", 7,995 gross tons.
Steam turbine, 16½ knots.
Cargo: 647,619 cu. ft.; passengers: 12.
Ex-*Sea Angel*. Renamed U.S.S. *Bolivar* (APA 34) 1943. Renamed *President Van Buren* March 1949. Renamed *President Harding* [III] 8 October 1967. Sold to Pacific Far East Lines 25 March 1968. Renamed *Thailand Bear*. Acquired by Prudential Grace Line 1970. Renamed *Santa Monica*. Scrapped at Kaohsiung, Taiwan, February 1972.

President Van Buren [IV] (C6-S-69c)
Seamaster type, built 1967, Pascagoula, Miss., by Ingalls Shipbuilding Co. (C4-S-69a).
573'10¹⁵⁄₁₆" × 82' × 45'6", 14,000 gross tons.
23 knots.
Cargo: 845,020 cu. ft.; passengers: 12.
Converted to containership by Todd Shipyards Corp., Seattle, Wash., 1972. Lengthened to 663'. 17,803 gross tons.
Cargo: 1,094 TEU containers.

President Washington (C9-M-132b)
C9 type, built 1982, New Orleans, La., by Avondale Shipyards.
860' × 106' × 66', 40,628 gross tons.
Sulzer 12-cyl. diesel, 43,200-brake horsepower, 23.9 knots.
Cargo: 2,590 TEU containers.

President Wilson [I] ("535")
535 type, built 1921, Camden, N.J., by New York Shipbuilding Co.

535' × 72' × 41', 14,124 gross tons.
Steam turbine, 17½ knots.
Cargo: 478,100 cu. ft.; passengers: 488.
Ex-*Empire State*. Renamed *President Wilson* 23 June 1922. Sold by U.S. Shipping Board to Dollar Steamship Lines 1925. Transferred to APL 1938. Sold 1940 and renamed *Maria Pepa*. Renamed *Cabo de Hornos* 1940. Sold for scrap May 1959.

President Wilson [II] (P2-SE2-R3)
P2 type, built 1948, Alameda, Calif., by Bethlehem Shipbuilding Corp.
610' × 75'6" × 43'6", 15,437 gross tons.
Steam turbine, 20 knots.
Cargo: 193,984 cu. ft.; passengers: 330 first class, 220 economy class.
Sold to Oceanic Cruises Development (C.Y. Tung Group) 27 April 1973. Renamed *Oriental Empress* (Panamanian flag). After 8½ -year layup in Hong Kong, sold for scrap. Broken up in Taiwan 1984.

President Wilson [III] (C5-S-75a)
C5 type, built 1969, Newport News, Va., by Newport News Shipbuilding and Drydock Co. (Hull No. 590).
605' × 82' × 46', 15,949 gross tons.
Steam turbine, 24,000-shaft horsepower, 20.8 knots.
Cargo: 1,082,207 C.F. Bale, 332 TEU containers; passengers: 12.
Ex-*Hong Kong Mail*, American Mail Line. Renamed *President Wilson* 24 May 1978.

APPENDIX B
AMERICAN PRESIDENT LINES' SHIPS
BY CLASS AND/OR
DESIGN DESIGNATION

Class/Design	First Names	Class/Design Characteristics
502 (522)	*President Adams* *President Garfield* *President Hayes* *President Harrison* *President Monroe* *President Polk* *President Van Buren*	Approximately 10,500 gross tons 522'8" × 62' × 42' Reciprocating steam engines Built 1920/1921
535	*President Cleveland* **President Grant* *President Jackson* *President Jefferson* *President Lincoln* *President McKinley* **President Madison* *President Pierce* *President Taft* *President Wilson*	Approximately 15,500 gross tons 535' × 72' × 41' Steam turbines Built 1921
C2-S-AJ3	*President Harding* [II]	8,189 gross tons 459'1" × 63' × 38' Steam turbine Built 1944
C3-P	*President Adams* [II] *President Garfield* [II] *President Hayes* [II] *President Jackson* [II] *President Monroe* [II] *President Polk* [II] *President Van Buren* [II]	9,255–9,260 gross tons 491'10" × 69'6" × 42'6" Steam turbine Built 1940/1941
C3-S-A2	*President Harrison* [II] *President Johnson* [II] *President Van Buren* [III]	7,995 gross tons 492' × 69'6" × 42'6" Steam turbine Built 1943

C3-S-A4	President Grant [III] President Jefferson [II] President Madison [II] President McKinley [II] President Pierce [II] President Taft [II]	7,924 gross tons 491′7″ × 69′6″ × 42′6″ Steam turbine Built 1945/1946
V-2000 (P2-S1-DN3)	President Adams [III] President Hayes [III] President Jackson [III]	14,000 gross tons 533′9″ × 73′ × 49′ Steam turbine Built 1951/1952
Victory VC2-S-AP3	President Arthur [I] President Buchanan [II] President Fillmore [III] President Garfield [III] President Harding [I] President Tyler [II]	Approximately 7,650 gross tons 455′3″ × 62′ × 38′ Steam turbine Built 1944/1945
P2-SE2-R3	President Cleveland [II] President Wilson [II]	15,437 gross tons 610′ × 75′6″ × 43′6″ Steam turbine Built 1947/1948
P2-S2-R14	President Roosevelt [I]	18,298 gross tons 622′7″ × 75′6″ × 42′6″ Steam turbine Built 1944
Mariner C4-S-1h	President Adams [IV] President Coolidge [II] President Hayes [IV] President Jackson [IV]	9,271/9,277 gross tons 563′ 7¾″ × 76′ × 44′6″ Steam turbine Built 1952/1954
Mariner C4-S-1p	President Arthur [II] President Buchanan [III] President Garfield [IV] President Taylor [II]	9,171/9,177 gross tons 563′ 7¾″ × 76′ × 44′6″ Steam turbine Built 1952/1954
Searacer C4-S-1q	President Lincoln [II] President Tyler [III]	13,223 gross tons 563′ 7¾″ × 76′ × 44′6″ Steam turbine Built 1961
Master Mariner C4-S-1qa (C6-S-1qc)	President Harrison [III] President Monroe [III] President Polk [III]	564′ × 76′ × 44′6″ 10,412 gross tons Steam turbine Built 1965/1966
Seamaster C4-S-69a (C6-S-69c)	President Fillmore [V] President Grant [IV] President McKinley [III]	14,000 gross tons 573′10″ × 82′ × 45′6″ Steam turbine

	President Taft [III]	Built 1967/1968
	President Van Buren [IV]	
Pacesetter	*President Jefferson* [III]	21,475 gross tons
C6-S-85b	*President Johnson* [V]	669'2" × 90' × 53'
	President Madison [III]	Steam turbine
	President Pierce [III]	Built 1973/1974
C4-S-1s	*President Eisenhower* [I]	12,436 gross tons
(C6-S-1x)	*President Roosevelt* [II]	563'7" × 76' × 44'8"
	President Truman	Steam turbine
		Built 1961/1962
C4-S-1Sa	*President Kennedy*	12,440 gross tons
(C6-S1-Xa)		563'7" × 76' × 44' 9⅝"
		Steam turbine
		Built 1964
C5-S-75a	*President Adams* [V]	15,946/15,949 gross tons
	President Cleveland [III]	605' × 82' × 46'
	President Jackson [V]	Steam turbine
	President Taylor [III]	Built 1968/1969
	President Wilson [III]	
LASH	*President Grant* [V]	26,456 gross tons
(C8-S-81e)	*President Hoover* [III]	820' × 100' × 60'
	President Tyler [IV]	Steam turbine
		Built 1971/1972
C9-M-132b	*President Lincoln* [III]	40,628 gross tons
	President Monroe [IV]	860' × 106' × 66'
	President Washington	Diesel
		Built 1982/1983
C9-M-F148a	*President Eisenhower* [II]	36,859 gross tons
	President F. D. Roosevelt	853'9" × 105'8" × 62'4"
		Diesel
		Built 1980
Unclassified	*President Coolidge* [I]	21,936 gross tons
		654'3" × 81' × 52'
		Steam turbo electric
		Built 1931
	President Hoover [I]	Not an APL ship
	President Fillmore [I]	15,455 gross tons
	ex-*Mongolia*	615'8" × 65' × 51'3"
		Steam reciprocating
		Built 1904
	President Johnson [I]	15,445 gross tons
	ex-*Manchuria*	615'8" × 65' × 51'3"
		Steam reciprocating
		Built 1904

*Not an APL ship.

A NOTE ON SOURCES

Few histories of shipping lines have adequately covered operational, institutional, and management aspects of the companies they have dealt with. Those that have specialized in the maritime history of the West Coast are even more scarce. This work has attempted in some way to fill the gap, and as a result the author was faced at the outset with a difficult research problem. To be sure, anecdotal sources abound in maritime publications such as *The Guide*, *The Shipping Register*, *Marine Digest*, *Pacific Marine Review*, *Steamboat Bill*, *Railway and Marine News*. Specialized journals like *Sea History*, *California History*, the *Pacific Historical Review*, the *Pacific Northwest Quarterly*, *The Southern California Quarterly*, the *Oregon Historical Quarterly*, and *The Sea Chest: Journal of the Puget Sound Maritime Historical Society* have had occasional articles of significance to the maritime history of the West Coast. But for researching this book, the author's task would have been far more difficult had not he had at his disposal the invaluable work of John H. Kemble: *Genesis of the Pacific Mail Steamship Company* (San Francisco: California Historical Society, 1934); *The Panama Route, 1848–1869* (Berkeley and Los Angeles: University of California Press, 1943); "Sidewheelers across the Pacific," *The American Neptune* 2 (1942); and "The Big Four at Sea: The History of the Occidental and Oriental Steamship Company," *Huntington Library Quarterly* 3 (April 1940). These publications are the only scholarly sources for the early years of the Pacific Mail Steamship Company, one of American President Lines' forebears.

In addition Professor Kemble's unique library of Pacific Mail documents and western maritime history, the collection of a lifetime, was made available to the project. Similarly, Allan Yost of Santa Barbara gave unlimited access to his rich collection of American Mail Line documents. Both collections featured unbroken runs of annual reports, letters, newspaper clippings, and in the Yost collection, a typescript history of American Mail line written by A. R. Lintner, chief executive of the line for many years, and R. B. Bush, one of its senior financial officers. Due to the efforts of Professor Kemble, the records of the Pacific Mail Steamship Company are housed at the

Huntington Library in San Marino, California. He saved from destruction the records of the Pacific Steamship Company, which may now be consulted in the special collections of the Honnold Library, Claremont, California.

There are several printed sources that are particularly illuminating for the first voyages of the Pacific Mail steamers to California. They are: *The First Steamship Pioneers*, edited by a committee of the passengers (San Francisco: H. S. Crocker, 1874); *Festival in Celebration of the Twenty-Fifth Anniversary of the Arrival of the Steamer "California"* . . . (San Francisco: H. S. Crocker, 1874); *Re-Union of the Pioneer Panama Passengers on the Fourth of June, 1874, Twenty-Fifth Anniversary of the Arrival of the Steamship Panama at San Francisco* (San Francisco, 1874); "Journal of a Voyage from New York to Panama via Rio, Valparaiso, Callao & Peyta On Board the U.S. Mail Steam Ship California Commanded by Cleveland Forbes—A.D. 1848" and "Journal of a Voyage from San Francisco to Panama via Monterey, Santa Barbara, San Diego, Mazatlan, San Blas & Acapulco, 1849. Stemer [*sic*] California, C. Forbes, Master" in *California Gold Rush Voyages, 1848–1849: Three Original Narratives*, ed. John E. Pomfret (San Marino, Calif.: Huntington Library Publications, 1954); and Victor M. Berthold, *The Pioneer Steamer California, 1848–1849* (Boston and New York: Houghton Mifflin Co., 1932).

Notable collections particularly pertinent to this history are the Robert Dollar Papers at the Bancroft Library, University of California, Berkeley, California and the Dollar v. Land litigation papers at the California Historical Society. The Robert Dollar Papers, including Dollar's manuscript diary, are voluminous since they include also some of the private correspondence of R. Stanley Dollar, J. Harold Dollar, and Hugo M. Lorber, the principals in the various Dollar companies. Especially valuable are the confidential board minutes of the Dollar Steamship Company, the holding company for the Dollar enterprises and immediate predecessor of American President Lines. In these documents are recorded the uninhibited discussions of the officers and directors of the company. Thus management policy and agreements and disagreements are set forth in considerable detail. The Dollar v. Land papers, though they deal specifically with the trials whereby the Dollar interests sought to regain control of American President Lines after World War II, contain a wealth of retrospective material brought out in the testimony and through the various papers introduced as part of the record. American President

Companies' corporate files and archives in Oakland, California, contain the minutes of meetings of the various boards of directors of the line, its subsidiary companies and in part its predecessor companies; internal memoranda; and reports and other correspondence dealing with the line's activities. Company papers of former chief executives and senior officers, for instance, are a part of the archive, as are transcripts of the oral history tapes that the author recorded.

Supplementing these primary sources are Robert Dollar's *Memoirs*, 4 vols. (San Francisco: Privately printed, 1917–28), and his *One hundred thirty Years of Steam Navigation* (San Francisco: privately printed, 1931). Gregory C. O'Brien, "The Life of Robert Dollar," a Ph.D. dissertation (Claremont Graduate School, 1968), is also an important source, but must be supplemented with Robert Dollar's manuscript diary.

Throughout this work newspaper and periodical sources have been essential. The following are the more important ones that were consulted for relevant material within the dates indicated: *San Francisco Alta California* 1867–69; *Coast Seaman's Journal*, 1915–25; *Gangway*, 1946–52; *Los Angeles Examiner*, 1901–83; *Los Angeles Express*, 1910–12; *San Francisco Call*, 1901–10; *New York Herald*, 1848–66; *New York Times*, 1915–80; *Portland Oregonian*, 1921–29; *San Francisco Daily Commercial News*, 1909–18; *San Francisco Chronicle*, 1901–84; *San Francisco Examiner*, 1901–25; *Seattle Post-Intelligencer*, 1925–74; *Seattle Times*, 1969; *Seattle Star*, 1937–45; *Seattle Union Record*, 1922.

United States government documents are a primary source for anyone interested in maritime history. Two hearings by the Merchant Marine and Fisheries Committee of the House are especially pertinent. They are found in House Documents, *Committee Hearings*, vol. 2, 58th Cong., 3d sess., 1905, and in *Hearings to Develop an American Merchant Marine*, 74th Cong. 1st sess., 1935. Annual Reports of the United States Shipping Board from 1917 to 1937, the United States Emergency Fleet Corporation, 1917–21; the Federal Maritime Board, 1939–49; the Federal Maritime Commission, 1937 to the present, and the Federal Maritime Administration, 1950 to the present, are essential for any understanding of government policy and its impact on the shipping industry. Two special reports of the Maritime Commission are indispensable for the history of American President Lines. They are: *Financial Readjustments in Dollar Steamship Lines, Ltd.* (Washington, D.C., 1938); and *Reorganization of American President Lines, Ltd.* (Washington, D.C., 1939). Though both of these reports were issued to justify the government takeover of the Dollar Steamship Company, they nevertheless present a wealth of factual material that is most useful in describing and evaluating Dollar management from 1926–38. Two additional special reports of the War Shipping Administration give interesting details in a concise form on the role of the American merchant marine in World War II, "The United States Merchant Marine at War," 1944 and 1946 (Washington, D.C., 1946, 1947). For the immediate postwar period, government policy was set forth in United States Maritime Commission, "The Post-War Outlook for American Shipping, a Report Submitted by the Post-War Planning Committee," 15 June 1946.

From the purchase of American President Lines by APL Associates in 1952 to its merger into the Natomas Company in 1956 and the spinoff of American President Lines when Natomas was merged into Diamond Shamrock in 1984, the following primary printed sources were drawn upon extensively in writing the history: Chandler Ide et al., *Ralph Davies As We Knew Him* (San Francisco: Privately printed, 1976) and the annual reports of American President Lines, Ltd., 1938–84, American Mail Line, 1939–74, Natomas Company 1956–84, and Pacific Far East Line, 1959–69, APL Archives. But much of the more recent history of the line has been developed from some fifty oral history interviews with past and current executives or board members of American President Lines and Natomas Company. Like all oral histories, the testimony reflects the personal opinions and recollections of the individual respondents and must be used with care. The author's judgments on the data were as far as possible balanced by repeated cross-checking and balancing of opinions as the interviews progressed.

Secondary sources that were useful in this work are the following: C. Bradford Mitchell, *Touching the Adventures and Perils: A Semicentennial history* (New York, 1970); Giles T. Brown, *Ships That Sail No More* (Lexington, Ky.: University of Kentucky Press, 1966); Julius Grodinsky, *Jay Gould, His Business Career, 1867–1892* (Philadelphia: University of Pennsylvania Press, 1957); John Gunther, *Taken at the Flood, the Story of Albert Lasker* (New York: Harper, 1960); N. E. Harrison, "Dollar Steamship Company," *The Guide* (August–September 1969); Edwin P. Hoyt, *The Goulds, A Social History* (New York: Weybright and Talley, 1969); Kathryn C. Hulme, *Annie's Captain* (London: F. Muller, 1961); John H. Kemble and Lane C. Kendall, "The Years Between the Wars," in *America's Maritime Legacy*, ed. Robert A. Kilnarx (Boulder, Colo.: Westview Press, 1979); Walter A. Radius, *United States Shipping in Trans-Pacific Trade, 1922–1938* (Stanford, Calif.: Stanford University Press, 1944); Darrell Hevenor Smith and Paul V. Betters, *The United States Shipping Board: Its History, Activities and Organization* (Washington, D.C.: Brookings Institution, 1931); American Mail Line Staff, "History of American Mail Line 1850–1946," mimeograph, Allen Yost Coll.; and Paul M. Zeis, *American Shipping Policy* (Princeton: Princeton University Press, 1938).

INDEX

A. Rodger and Co., 54
Admiral Line (Pacific Steamship Co.),
    57, 63–64, 69, 72; bankruptcy of, 111–12
Admiral Oriental Line, 66–67, 69, 72, 75,
    78, 135, 138
Admiral Oriental Mail Line, 65, 70–71,
    75; acquires *President* vessels, 66, 74
Afrika Korps, 147
Agnes Dollar, 54
Alaska Coast Co., 62
Alaska Mail, 214
Alaska Pacific Steamship Co., 62
Alaskan Mail, 231
Alexander, H. F., 57, 60–62, 75; incorpo-
    rates Pacific Steamship Company, 63;
    enters trans-Pacific trade, 64; and Ad-
    miral Lines, 64–66, 72–73; acquires
    535s, 65–66; troubles with the Ship-
    ping Board, 67; and the Dollars, 67,
    69–73, 77–78; resigns as head of Ad-
    miral Line, 111
Alioto, Joseph, 250, 259
Allen, William Stephen, 217–18
Alley, Rayford W., 137
Allis-Chalmers Co., 275
Ambler, John, 136–39
America, 16, 30
America (United States Lines), 143
American Bureau of Shipping, 102
American Export Line, 88
American–Hawaiian Steamship Co., 41,
    99
American Independent Oil Co., 159, 171,
    178, 183–84, 198, 247
American International Corp., 41
American Mail, 210, 215
American Mail Line (AML), 10, 75, 84,
    95, 101–6, 108, 111, 115, 148, 150–55, 175,
    197, 223, 225, 230, 235–36, 245, 247–
    48, 251, 254, 266, 274; financial diffi-

culties of, 103; *President Madison* cap-
sizes, 105; operations terminated, 122–
23; reorganized, 134; conflict with Pacific Northwest Oriental, 133–39; capital from R. J. Reynolds, 138–39; A. R.
Lintner takes charge, 139–41; replacement program, 141–42; World War II
operations, 149–53; earnings, 153, 193;
postwar planning, 154–55; APL purchases controlling interest, 191; profit
potential, 192; construction program
in 1960s, 204–5, 214–16; Worth Fowler
takes over, 209; containership program, 241–42; Robert E. Benedict as
president, 234
American President Companies, Ltd.,
    10, 282
American President Lines, Ltd. (APL),
    7, 9, 81, 133, 165, 183, 190–96, 212, 216–
    21, 223–28, 230, 232, 242, 245, 247–51,
    257–83; name change 123, 128–29;
    William G. McAdoo, chairman, 123;
    Joseph Sheehan, president, 123, 143;
    new managerial policies, 130–31; and
    World War II, 132, 143, 146–48, 150–51;
    Henry F. Grady, president, 145; Pearl
    Harbor attack, 148; war losses, 148–50;
    profits, 153–54; George Killion, presi-
    dent, 166–67, 169, 171–72, 219–21; new
    construction, 160; postwar financial
    position, 169; Korean War, 174; APL
    Associates purchase, 179–80; replace-
    ment and construction program, 198–
    99, 205; passenger business, 201–3,
    234, 236–39; semi-containerships, 211;
    Raymond Ickes, president, 221, 223,
    234; LASH concept, 223–26; Worth
    Fowler, president, 234; maritime
    strike of 1972, 248; containership pro-
    gram, 241, 248–49; moves to Oakland,

PHOTOGRAPHS

John Niven is a native New Yorker who was brought up in Connecticut and has lived the past twenty-five years in Southern California. After graduating from college, he spent four years as a naval line officer, serving in both the European and the Pacific theaters of operations during World War II. He attended Columbia University, where he studied under Allan Nevins. From 1951 until 1960, he worked for the Electric Boat Company and then for General Dynamics Corporation in New York. While with General Dynamics he, along with Courtlandt Canby and Vernon Welsh, wrote the corporation's history, *Dynamic America*, a pioneer work in the use of graphics to illuminate the text.

John Niven is a professor of history at the Claremont Graduate School, specializing in nineteenth-century political and social history and biography. His most recent book is *Martin Van Buren: The Romantic Age of American Politics* (1983). He is also editor of the Salmon P. Chase papers, whose publication is being sponsored jointly by the National Historical Records and Publications Commission and the Claremont Graduate School.